Euromoney Encyclopedia of Debt Finance

Euromoney Encyclopedia of Debt Finance

Edited by
Tony Rhodes

Published by
Euromoney Institutional Investor Plc
Nestor House, Playhouse Yard
London EC4V 5EX
United Kingdom

Tel: +44 (0) 20 7779 8999 or USA +1 800 437 9997
Fax: +44 (0) 20 7779 8300
www.euromoneybooks.com
E-mail: hotline@euromoneyplc.com

ISBN 1 84374 269 1

This publication is designed to provide accurate and authoritative information with regard to the subject matter covered. In the preparation of this book, every effort has been made to offer the most current, correct and clearly expressed information possible. The materials presented in this publication are for informational purposes only. They reflect the subjective views of authors and contributors and do not necessarily represent current or past practices or beliefs of any organisation. In this publication, none of the contributors, their past or present employers, the editor or the publisher is engaged in rendering accounting, business, financial, investment, legal, tax or other professional advice or services whatsoever and is not liable for any losses, financial or otherwise, associated with adopting any ideas, approaches or frameworks contained in this book. If investment advice or other expert assistance is required, the individual services of a competent professional should be sought.

Typeset by Florence Production Ltd, Stoodleigh, Devon
Printed by TJ International, Padstow, Cornwall

Contents

Contents

Contents

viii

Foreword

Investors have moved from currency arbitrage plays to credit arbitrage plays (primarily due to the elimination of many European currencies as a result of the introduction of the euro) and the debt capital markets have met their needs. The range of secured and unsecured issues has blossomed with new products emerging regularly for investors hungry for assets. The sovereign sector has joined in with, for example, Italy's big securitisation projects; financial institutions have found ways to refinance the assets they source more efficiently and cost effectively through the increasing use of covered bonds; and companies have found a ready market for their funding needs, be they for general corporate purposes or for merger and acquisitions.

The last business has changed most in recent years. The use of private equity funds combined with debt has been the most powerful force for the restructuring of European companies (including, of course, the UK), as many company boards failed to see the opportunities for themselves. Almost no company is beyond the range of this combination and the constraint on capacity is only determined by the leverage multiples which banks are prepared to accept in the facilities they provide to fund the acquisition. The US$31.3bn acquisition by Kohlberg Kravis Roberts (KKR) of RJR Nabisco in 1989 has long held the record for the largest leveraged buyout of all time, but this is now likely to be eclipsed by the US$33bn buyout of Hospital Corp of America (HCA) by a consortium of buyout specialist firms, including KKR.

Bankers need to be constantly aware of the alternative instruments that can be used to meet a borrower's needs. These can be satisfied by short-term instruments such as commercial paper, long dated issues through the loan or bond markets or equity linked products such as bonds with equity warrants or convertibles. It is difficult for many bankers, except in the early periods of their training, to work in many of these product areas. The General Editor, Tony Rhodes, identified this difficulty and Euromoney Books was delighted to commission this new encyclopedia of debt instruments. As the reader will see, it brings together a detailed analysis of the core debt products with relevant case studies to illustrate their use. The individual contributors were all chosen from institutions which have strong market positions, thereby validating their descriptions and opinions for the reader.

The difficulty identified for bankers applies equally to the teams of treasury staff charged with raising the most cost-effective debt for their institutions. Rarely has the choice been so great. Trade-offs between tenor, security and currency all play their part and it is beholden on these treasury teams to be totally aware of the alternatives in the debt capital markets that are relevant to their situation. A company of investment-grade standing which becomes the target of a leveraged buyout will, if the takeover is successful, find its ratings change dramatically and the products/debt markets that can be accessed change equally radically.

Whereas for an investment-grade issuer, a long-term unsecured bond in most currencies is a real choice, the weaker ratings post-acquisition may limit the treasury to syndicated loans and high yield bonds.

Investors have evolved too and, perhaps, ultimately drive the search for new products. Many funds have been formed to take advantage of securitised products, be they mortgages, credit card receivables or loans. The rating agencies have a key role to play in this as they are able to guide the bankers in their structuring of products and provide the investor with a readily understandable nomenclature to assist in making investment choices. In many cases, the rating agencies determine the nature of the instrument, albeit indirectly, as they advise and respond to proposals from bankers. Understanding the rating process is an essential part of product innovation, just as being part of the rating process requires an in-depth knowledge of the debt capital markets.

I am a strong supporter of this encyclopedia – an invaluable source document for many bankers, investors, rating agency specialists and treasury teams.

Padraic Fallon
Chairman, Euromoney Institutional Investor PLC
September 2006, London

Preface

The debt capital markets have become increasingly sophisticated and integrated over recent years as borrowers, particularly corporate borrowers, have found investors willing to accept a broader range of credit risks and a greater variety of instruments. Whereas, in the past, non-bank financial institutions concentrated on the fixed-income market, they are now active buyers of loans, particularly high-yielding loans. Moreover, with the huge financial resources of the sponsors of leveraged buyouts and the liquidity available in the debt markets, it is fair to say that almost no company is outside the range of a takeover and the debt on its books subject to event risk. A company that is rated as an investment-grade credit can abruptly become sub-investment-grade and, as a consequence, will need to examine different alternatives for effective funding. As an investment-grade credit, a company may choose to rely on relationship banks for its loan facilities and bond issues for its core funding. As a sub-investment-grade credit, securitisation of assets and off-balance sheet financings may be more cost effective.

It is apparent, therefore, that individuals working in treasury departments of borrowers and the bankers providing them with ideas on how to raise funds most cost effectively need to have in-depth knowledge of the entire spectrum of debt products. This means having a comprehensive understanding of the short-term markets such as commercial paper, the medium-term highly flexible loan markets, the long-term US private placement market, the medium-term note (MTN) and bond markets, the securitisation markets, the covered bond markets (for financial institutions), the convertible market and ways to use *Sukuk* structures effectively. Each of these markets is described in the first part of this encyclopedia where an outline of each product is given, its uses for borrowers and investors specified and the current leaders in the field recorded by way of league tables. The risks of using these products are also evaluated thereby bringing the reader up-to-speed on the opportunities available from each market, permitting them to assess the relevance of the products for their situation.

In Part II of this encyclopedia, the reader is given examples of the use of these markets in practice. So how do corporates and financial institutions access the commercial paper market? How do you use the loan market for a leveraged acquisition? What does it take to access the US private placement market and how do you set up an MTN programme? How are projects financed and how can aircraft be financed? Can credit be enhanced and, if so, how? Can issues of hybrid debt be accounted for as equity? What is the capacity of the covered bond market for new issues? These questions are addressed for the reader and the application of the different markets for borrowers developed in detail. The range of markets and instruments covered means that this is a *must have* book for new entrants into the debt markets and will be a useful reference book for those who have previously specialised in one area and need to take a broader perspective.

The genesis for this encyclopedia came from discussions I had with Samir Assaf at HSBC in 2004 when I was writing the 4th edition of *Syndicated Lending – Practice and Documentation* (also published by Euromoney). We were discussing the increasing demands being placed on the front office where bankers had historically specialised in one area of the debt capital markets rather than the full range. The clients, borrowers, faced with demands for lowest-cost funding from their executive management boards, expected their bankers to be capable of discussing the full range of debt product alternatives relevant to their situation and credit standing. Bankers, being required to meet the needs of their clients in this way, have had to expand their knowledge base, an effort that can be supported by this comprehensive book on the debt capital markets.

Dr Elizabeth Gray, Managing Director and Sanjeevi Perera, Commissioning Editor, both at Euromoney, have worked with me to assemble the world class set of contributors that have provided the content for this book. A key criterion was to choose individuals from institutions whose position in their respective markets makes them de facto leaders in their field. They have shared their knowledge and experience for the benefit of the readers and it is for this reason that this book will be essential reading for all who wish to expand their knowledge of the debt capital markets.

Tony Rhodes
General Editor
June 2006

Author biographies

Silvio Angius

Silvio Angius is Managing Director in European Structured Finance at Lehman Brothers, where he is responsible for the origination and structuring of the firm's structured finance business for southern Europe. Before joining Lehman Brothers in 2001, Silvio held a similar position at UBS Warburg in London, and prior to that he was a Director in the structured finance group at rating agency Standard & Poor's for five years. Silvio is an experienced securitisation and structured finance professional, having worked in complex transactions involving a wide range of asset classes and jurisdictions. He has authored numerous articles on securitisation and participated in many conferences in Europe and the United States. Silvio holds a degree in economic studies at LUISS University in Rome and an MBA from Bocconi University in Milan.

David Bassett

David Bassett, Managing Director and Global Head of Loan Markets, joined The Royal Bank of Scotland in January 2004 and is responsible for the Loan Markets division, an integrated loan capital markets, syndicate and distribution platform with over 100 professionals in seven offices around the world. Prior to RBS, David was with Citigroup for more than 12 years, starting in New York and moving to London in 1997. In London, he was Managing Director and Head of European Loan Distribution, and prior to taking that position he was responsible for originating and structuring acquisition and telecom loan financings. In New York, David worked on a variety of leveraged and high-grade loan transactions. David also spent two years with Wharton Econometrics in Philadelphia as an analyst for forecasting and modelling US economic performance. David holds a BA in Economics from Williams College in Massachusetts and an MBA in Finance and International Business from the University of Michigan.

Moorad Choudhry

Moorad Choudhry is Head of Treasury at KBC Financial Products, the London-based derivatives and convertible bond trading arm of KBC Bank N.V., Brussels. He joined there from JPMorgan Chase Bank, where he was a vice president in Structured Finance Services sales and marketing. Prior to that he was a gilt-edged market maker and money markets trader at ABN Amro Hoare Govett Sterling Bonds Ltd. He began his City career at the London Stock Exchange in 1989. Dr Choudhry is also a Visiting Professor at the Department of Economics, London Metropolitan University, a Visiting Research Fellow at the ICMA Centre, University of Reading, a Senior Fellow at the Centre for Mathematical Trading and Finance, Cass Business School, and a Fellow of the Securities and Investment Institute.

Richard Cole

Richard Cole is Chief Executive of HSBC's Global Project and Export Finance Division. Richard is responsible for PEF's global activities including the management of over 200 staff across 15 international locations. Under his direction, HSBC has expanded its global project finance activities to be ranked in 2005 'Global Number 1 Adviser' by Dealogic and selected as 'Global Adviser of the Year' by Thomson PFI. Richard joined the HSBC Group in 1980 and has an MA from Cambridge University and is also an Associate of the Chartered Institute of Management Accountants.

Paul Eardley-Taylor

Paul Eardley-Taylor is a Director in HSBC's Project Finance Power & Utilities team. Paul joined HSBC in 1998 and has eight years' project finance experience. Notable transactions he has worked on include Financial Adviser to WEC on the Shuaibah and Shuqaiq IWPPs (Saudi Arabia, 2006), MLA on the Saltend IPP acquisition financing (UK, 2005), MLA on the Normanglade IV IPP portfolio financing (global, 2004), MLA on the Umm Al Nar IWPP (Abu Dhabi, 2003), and MLA on the Ras Laffan IWPP (Qatar, 2001). Paul is presently completing a MBA at Henley Management College, UK.

Andrew Ellis

Andrew Ellis works within the Investment Banking Division at Goldman Sachs where he is currently Head of Money Market Origination in Europe, a position he has held since 2004. He joined the firm in 1997 and spent the first part of his career in the Investment Management Division, where he was responsible for the establishment of Goldman Sachs' businesses in European sub-advisory/third-party distribution and cash management. A history graduate from the University of Durham in the UK, Andrew spent the early years of his banking career at Robert Fleming. This followed three years in Brussels as an adviser on European public policy.

Hussein Hassan

Hussein Hassan trained in both law and *shari'a*. He studied law in the UK first at the University of Lancaster and then at Oxford. He studied *shari'a* in Hadhramawt in South Yemen and in East Africa. Hussein has practised law specialising in commercial law. He has been a member of the Faculty of Law at Oxford University and a Fellow at the Oxford Centre for Islamic Studies teaching Islamic and Comparative Law. He has also been a consultant with a number of financial institutions and now works for Deutsche Bank as Vice President in the Islamic structuring team.

Jackie Ineke

Jackie Ineke is a Managing Director covering European banks at Morgan Stanley and is based in Zurich. Jackie is responsible for setting strategy for fixed income bank research, globally. She has been with Morgan Stanley since May 2000, joining from UBS Warburg, where she spent three years analysing the European banks sector. In 2006, the European Banks team was ranked first by *Institutional Investor* for the All-Europe Fixed Income Research Team (investment grade banks). Prior to these roles, Jackie worked at the Bank of England in the supervisory and foreign exchange divisions. Jackie holds an MSc from St Andrews University and an MES from College d'Europe, Belgium.

Harris Irfan

Harris Irfan is a Director in the Global Markets division of Deutsche Bank, with responsibility for Islamic structuring within the Emerging Markets team. He has over 12 years' experience in investment banking, spanning corporate and project finance origination and execution, and capital markets institutional sales and structuring. He transferred from Deutsche Bank's London office to Dubai in 2001, and is currently responsible for the creation of *shari'a* compliant investment products, including a number of unique capital markets instruments for multi-billion dollar projects and acquisitions. Prior to joining Deutsche Bank in 1998, he worked as a project financier at Hambros Bank Limited, and initially trained as a business modelling specialist at Andersen Consulting. He graduated with a Masters in Physics from Oxford University in 1993.

Heiko Langer

Heiko Langer is a Senior Analyst for Covered Bonds at BNP Paribas and has worked there since July 2005. Within the bank's London based credit research department he covers the full range of international covered bond markets. Before Heiko joined BNP Paribas, he worked for four years as an analyst for the covered bond and agency market at ABN AMRO in Frankfurt in 1996. Having graduated from the University of Cooperative Education in Karlsruhe in Germany with a diploma in Business Administration, Heiko joined L-Bank in 1994, where he worked in the international funding division in the field of investor relations and transaction management.

Rebecca Manuel

Rebecca Manuel is Managing Director, Head of European Loan Syndicate and has been with Royal Bank of Scotland since November 2004. Her team is responsible for providing loan pricing, structuring and underwriting advice, monitoring loan markets issuer and investor trends, as well as broader capital markets trends both in Europe and globally. Prior to RBS, Rebecca was with CIBC World Markets, where she was a Managing Director in the Loan Underwriting and Distribution group, with a primary focus on structured debt transactions, including telecommunications, media, and project finance. Prior to CIBC, Rebecca was with The Northern Trust Company in Chicago, responsible for corporate lending activities. Rebecca has a Bachelor of Arts degree in International Economic Relations from the University of Michigan, and an MBA in Finance and Marketing from the Kellogg School of Business, Northwestern University, Illinois.

Jean-François Mazaud

Jean-François Mazaud began his banking career at Banque Indosuez in 1990, where he worked in aircraft financing in Paris and in Tokyo until 1993. He joined Société Générale in 1993, as Vice President in ECM, where, amongst other things, he advised the French Treasury on its privatisation programme. In 1997, he was named Director and headed the bank's UK ECM group. In 1998, he became Managing Director and was given the task to develop

SG's equity-linked business. Jean-François became head of DCM corporate origination in September 2004 and currently heads a team of 25 corporate originators based in Paris, London, Madrid, Frankfurt and New York. His team currently ranks number 2 in Europe.

Andrew Menzies

Andrew Menzies has been with Société Générale's Debt Capital Markets Origination team for three years. Andrew became an Associate last July and is predominately focused on working for UK, Italian and Nordic clients. Andrew was integrally involved with the origination and execution of Eurobond benchmark transactions for Finmeccanica, Kingfisher and British American Tobacco and a large private placement for Telecom Italia. He has also worked in the US private placement market supporting the execution of such deals for European borrowers. Prior to joining Société Générale, Andrew graduated with a Masters in Economic and Political Geography from Edinburgh University.

Christine Miyagishima

Christine Miyagishima is an Associate covering European banks and insurance companies at Morgan Stanley and is based in London. In 2006, the European Banks team was ranked number 1 by *Institutional Investor* for the All-Europe Fixed Income Research Team (investment grade banks). Prior to this role, Christine worked at Lehman Brothers in the investment banking division for four years. Christine holds an MBA from UCLA Anderson and a BComm from Queen's University in Canada.

Cecilia Park

Cecilia Park is Executive Director at UBS Investment Bank, Transportation Asset-Backed Finance Group, and is responsible for origination, structuring and execution of transportation related asset-backed transactions. Cecilia was the primary banker responsible for the ACG Trust III securitisation completed in December 2005. She joined UBS in June 2005 from Morgan Stanley, where for several years she was a transportation structured finance banker, focusing on EETCs as well as aircraft securitisations, having led Iberbond 2004, Airplanes Pass Through Trust 2001 and AerCo 2000, among others. Cecilia received a BA from Columbia University and an MBA from the Wharton School of Business at the University of Pennsylvania.

Gerry Rawcliffe

Gerry Rawcliffe is a managing director in Fitch Ratings' financial institutions group. Gerry is responsible for developing the group's franchise with major European institutional investors and other capital markets participants. Gerry rejoined Fitch in September 2002 from Dresdner Kleinwort Wasserstein, where he was global head of investment grade credit research. He previously worked for Fitch's forerunner firm, IBCA, between 1993 and 1998, when he was responsible for covering German, UK and Middle Eastern banks. Gerry is a chartered accountant and has a BA and MA in German Studies from the Universities of Warwick and London.

Franck Robard

Franck Robard is Head of the Hybrid Capital Group of Société Générale. He runs a team specialised in structuring tax efficient hybrid capital for financial institutions and corporate issuers with a strong emphasis on raising regulatory and rating agency capital. Before joining SG in 2000, Franck was Head of Credit Research at Ixis CIB, where he originally started is career in 1994 as a credit research analyst. During his tenure at SG, he has structured and executed hybrid capital transactions for major European Groups totaling above €15bn in volume. Franck is based in Paris.

Zarrar Sehgal

Zarrar Sehgal is a partner in the Global Transportation Finance Group of Milbank, Tweed, Hadley & McCloy LLP. Mr Sehgal has experience in representing underwriters, lenders, lessors, and governmental agencies in a wide variety of aircraft finance transactions, including portfolio securitisations, leveraged leasing, EETC transactions, secured lending, structured financings and credit enhancements. Mr Sehgal received his J.D. from Georgetown University Law Center and his undergraduate degree from Boston University.

Sriram Soundararajan

Sriram Soundararajan is a member of the European ABS research team at Lehman Brothers. The team produces regular publications that cover a wide range of topics on the ABS markets and also provide market leading analytics such as the Lehman Brothers European ABS Index and European Mortgage Cashflow Calculator. Sriram joined the team in 2003 and covers several sectors including CMBS, treasury securitisations and SME CLOs. He holds an MBA from the Indian Institute of Management and prior to that worked as an engineer with Caterpillar India.

Michael Thilmany

Michael Thilmany is currently Managing Director focusing on cross-border transactions, previously having responsibility for this segment of the market at BZW, Merrill Lynch, and Lehman Brothers (latterly where he headed fixed income and mezzanine private placements). He is based in New York and has also worked in London and Frankfurt. He has 20 years of industry experience. Michael received his MBA from New York University and his BSFS from the School of Foreign Service, Georgetown University.

Part I

Core products

Chapter 1

Commercial paper and medium-term notes

Andrew Ellis
Goldman Sachs

Commercial paper

Introduction: what is it?

Commercial paper (CP) is a short-term debt security, predominantly issued by investment-grade issuers (that is to say, they have a minimum long-term rating of BBB–/Baa3). In the vast majority of instances, maturities are no greater than one year, and the shortest maturity is overnight.

There are two forms of the product, commonly known as unsecured CP and asset-backed CP (ABCP). With the unsecured product, an issuer will issue CP at a discount, for a fixed rate of interest and for a fixed tenor, usually via a dealer, and in return will receive cash. At the end of the tenor, the CP is redeemed at par – i.e. the CP matures and the issuer pays par cash (nominal plus pre-determined interest) to the dealer. In the event of issuer default before the CP matures, the holder of the CP (either the dealer or, more typically, an investor) is ranked at the same level as other senior unsecured creditors of the issucr.

The same cash flows occur with ABCP but the cash received by the issuer, which is typically an SPV (special purpose vehicle), is used to fund a pool of assets. In the unlikely event of issuer default (the SPV is structured in such a way so as to be bankruptcy-remote), these assets can be liquidated in order to redeem maturing ABCP.

There are two main markets – the US commercial paper (USCP) market and the Eurocommercial paper (ECP) market. The USCP market is currently around US$1.7tn in size (as at July 2006). All its issuance is in US dollars, and the predominant issuers in the market are asset-backed (over 50 per cent).

The ECP market is around US$603bn in size as at July 2006, and unsecured financial issuers predominate (approximately 50 per cent). Asset-backed issuers make up the next largest sector with a market share of 30 per cent. The ECP market is multi-currency (further details provided later in this chapter).

Many jurisdictions have their own domestic CP markets. These are small in comparison to the USCP and the ECP markets, the most notable one being the French CP market, known as the Billet de Trésorie (BT) market.

Exhibit 1.1

The growth of US money market instruments

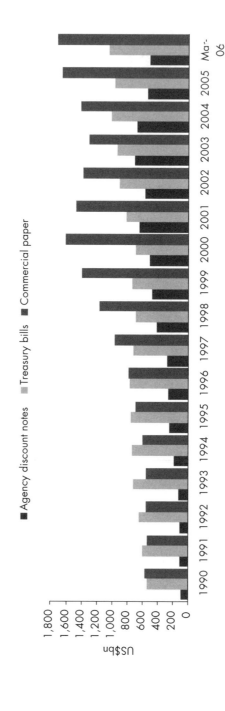

Source: Federal Reserve, Goldman Sachs, Bureau of the Public Debt.

Exhibit 1.2

The growth of the Eurocommercial paper market

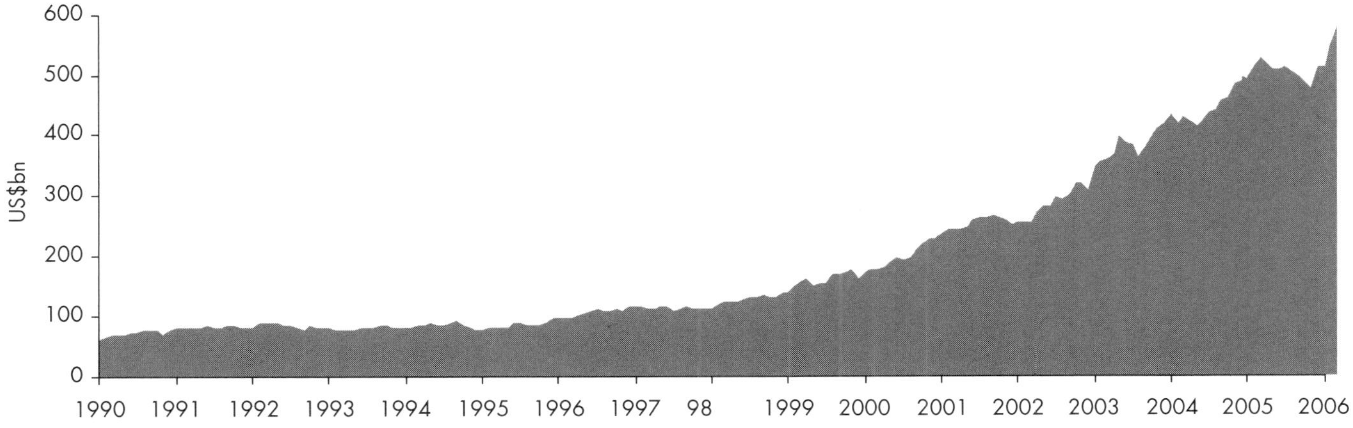

Source: Euroclear.

CP's relevance to issuers and investors

CP is a short-term cash management tool that is used to manage cash positions, whether long or short. Those who are short cash and need to borrow are CP issuers; those who are long cash and want to invest are investors.

In terms of issuer type, both the USCP and the ECP markets issue unsecured and asset-backed CP. In the USCP market the vast majority of issuance is done by financial institutions (this includes ABCP issuance). The remainder is comprised mostly of corporates (USCP is often used as a tool for acquisition funding or to ease dividend payments requirements).

For the ECP market, the trend over recent months shows that around 50 per cent of issuance is from financial institutions, around 30 per cent from asset-backed issuers, and around 10 per cent are corporates and sovereigns/supranationals apiece. The majority of growth in the ECP market has come from the asset-backed sector, which has increased from around US$5bn in 1996 to over US$160bn in 2006. It is also worth highlighting that, although the percentage of corporate issuance in the ECP market has decreased, in absolute terms it has remained roughly stable.

The majority of USCP investors are money market funds, also known as 2a-7 funds on account of a rule promulgated under the US Investment Company Act of 1940, Rule 2a-7. This rule stipulates that these funds cannot invest in a debt security with a tenor of longer than 397 days/13 months. Other investors of USCP include corporates, state and local municipalities, pension funds, insurance companies and banks.

ECP investors are comprised of corporates, financial institutions (including banks, building societies, insurance companies and brokers), fund managers, money market funds, private wealth individuals, securities lenders, sovereigns and supranationals.

Exhibit 1.3

Commercial paper outstandings by issuer type

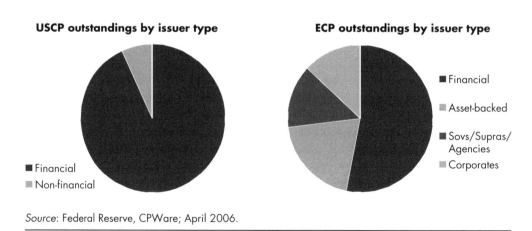

Source: Federal Reserve, CPWare; April 2006.

Exhibit 1.4

The evolution of the Eurocommercial paper market

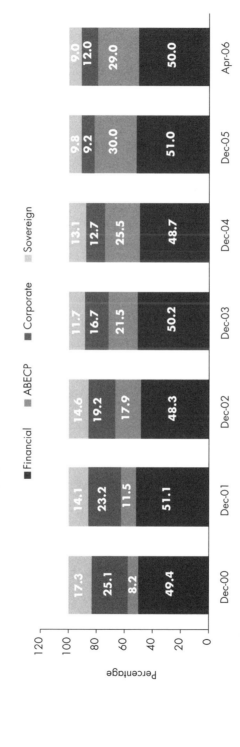

Source: CPWare, April 2006.

Issuers and investors are usually brought together by leading investment bank broker-dealers. Significant broker-dealers in the USCP market include Goldman Sachs, J. P. Morgan Chase, Lehman Brothers and Merrill Lynch; in the ECP market, the leading players are Citibank, Deutsche Bank, Goldman Sachs and Lehman Brothers.

Why use CP?

As previously stated, CP is a short-term cash management tool that is used to manage cash positions, whether long or short. Its uses are both strategic and opportunistic. As a strategic source of cash, CP has been successfully used, for example, when funding acquisitions, or if an issuer has wanted to raise its profile in the US domestic market. It can also be used opportunistically: issuers are able to use the product in credit arbitrage trades, thereby issuing debt at a certain fixed amount and using the funds raised to invest at a higher rate. The flexibility of the product has further been shown by the Homeland Investment Act, which has resulted in traditional borrowers (issuers) in the market becoming lenders (investors) through repatriation of cash.

There are further benefits to both issuers and investors. The market is huge and liquid (in aggregate over US$2.2tn outstanding as of April 2006), and the ECP market is multi-currency. Exhibit 1.5 shows the currency breakdown in the ECP market as at the end of April 2006. Since the introduction of the euro in 1999, euro issuance has become the largest portion of the market, although Sterling and the US dollar are also extremely liquid. In fact, there has been very little illiquidity in these three currencies – on the rare occasions we have seen illiquidity it has arisen due to uncertainty regarding central banks' interest rate policy. Other currencies play a lesser role in the ECP markets, primarily due

Exhibit 1.5

The currency breakdown of the ECP market (market outstandings US$573bn)

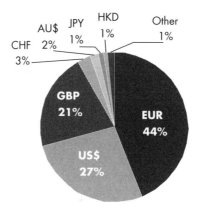

Source: Euroclear, 30 April 2006.

to the fact that for the vast majority of issuers, their funding needs are not generally in these currencies.

Maturities can be anything from one day to one year. Global issuers can take advantage of market dynamics to issue in either market depending on where the funding is more favourable. Nonetheless, it is worth remembering that issuer liquidity can dry up substantially if an issuer is downgraded to below an A2/P2 rating, also known as Tier 2, resulting in them no longer being able to rely on CP as a borrowing tool. Additionally, overall market liquidity can dry up, such as in times of interest rate uncertainty, or in the event of financial market disruption (such as 9/11 or blackouts).

Trading, pricing and distribution

CP is, in the main, a buy and hold security for investors – that is, they would be more likely to hold the instrument in their portfolios until it matures. Buybacks are a small feature of the market, and will occur not necessarily due to an investor's perception of the issuer's risk, but rather in order to change the maturity profile – i.e. a dealer will buy back paper that has one month to maturity in order to sell three-month paper. The secondary market is by no means extensive but it does exist. Pricing is largely a function of an issuer's credit rating and peer comparison. Prices are quoted as a spread to the relevant currency's London interbank offered rate (Libor). CP is usually bought from an issuer and distributed to an investor via an investment bank. Some issuers place directly with investors, rather than using a bank as an intermediary. Typically the investment bank will have a dedicated trading and sales team, whose responsibility it is to buy and place CP. Technology plays its part in facilitating the process, namely with electronic systems such as Bloomberg and TradeWeb.

Risks and mitigation

An issuer's credit quality is a significant consideration. To illustrate, for ECP specifically, approaching 90 per cent of issuers are rated A-1+/A-1/P-1 (short-term). The A-2/P-2 sector accounts for less than 3 per cent, and sub-Tier 2 less than 1 per cent.

As mentioned previously, the CP market is predominantly an investment-grade market, meaning issuers typically have a rating of a minimum BBB–/Baa3 (long-term). The most active and liquid part of the market is the Tier 1 sector; issuers need a long-term rating of minimum A3/A– to be able to participate in this segment. The necessary high rating of an issuer offers some protection to the investor and, accordingly, liquidity for an issuer can substantially diminish in the event of a downgrade.

When assigning short-term ratings to an unsecured CP issuer, the rating agencies require evidence of credit support. For corporate issuers they would typically require 100 per cent back-up in the form of revolving credit facilities. For financial institutions, who have greater access to funds, 100 per cent back-up is typically not required; instead, they require a swingline facility with another financial institution, showing that on any given day the issuer can meet its CP obligations to a certain degree (typically 10 per cent of its outstandings). This is particularly important for foreign issuers of USCP.

Exhibit 1.6

Commercial paper outstandings by rating

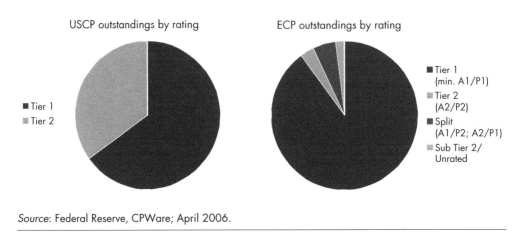

Source: Federal Reserve, CPWare; April 2006.

In many instances, unsecured CP issuers are additionally guaranteed by a higher-rated entity (typically the parent institution or a government), or are provided with a keep-well agreement (KWA) by such an entity. In these cases, subject to the terms and conditions of the guarantee/KWA, in circumstances where the issuer would have defaulted, the debt obligations become the responsibility of the parent/guarantor.

In a few, very rare cases, letters of credit are another form of issuer support. These, however, have become less cost-effective in recent years and have fallen out of favour.

If the parent/guarantor is unable to make good on outstanding CP, the holder of the CP is ranked *pari passu* with other senior unsecured creditors of the parent/guarantor.

Asset-backed issuers provide protection to their ABCP holders in the form of backstop liquidity (provided by one or more financial institutions) and the credit enhancement of the underlying pool of assets.

Documentation, disclosure and regulation

When an issuer prepares to enter the CP markets, various documents are required. These include authorising resolutions from the issuer's board (and guarantor's board, if applicable), dealer agreements, agency agreements (with the IPA), ratings confirmation letters and opinions from each counsel in issuing jurisdiction regarding authorisations, enforceability of agreements, notes and guarantees. In addition, a disclosure document will be produced by the issuer and its counsel, with dealer assistance.

There are various terms for the disclosure document. In the USCP market it is most commonly known as a private placement memorandum (PPM) or an offering circular (OC); in the ECP market it is usually referred to as an information memorandum (IM).

USCP is issued pursuant to one of two exemptions under the US Securities Act of 1933: exemptions under sections 3(a)(3) and 4(2). Depending under which of these two exemptions the CP is issued, the proceeds of cash raised, the maturity of the CP and the investor base, among other factors, are determined.

Programme documents and investor disclosure need to be updated in the event of a material change in the programme. Examples of changes can include an increase in authorised programme size, amendments to the dealer panel, ratings revisions, and a material development to the issuer's (or guarantor's) business which is of potential relevance to CP investors.

For both USCP and ECP, there are no reporting or listing requirements, as CP is considered an exempt (in the case of the US market) or unregulated (in the case of the European market) security.

Other issues

The CP market has proven to be a robust one as shown in July 2005. In the months leading up to the loss of the Landesbanks' state guarantee in Germany, there were fears for the liquidity and stability of the market. As it turned out, it was a non-event, causing barely a ripple in the market, and Landesbank issuers continue to be well supported by investors.

Other times when the resilience of the CP markets have been highlighted were during 9/11, the New York blackout (August 2003), and in times of corporate scandal and credit volatility.

We anticipate both the USCP and the ECP market will continue their steady upward trajectory, with issuers continuing to make use of the access they have to CP investors as a source of plentiful and cost-effective funding. This is not to say that threats to this analysis do not exist, and unforeseen external factors can always threaten to disrupt today's benign environment.

We see the main threats to the CP markets as being the following: regulatory, credit, interest rate and equity.

- *Regulatory risk*: with the advent of Basel II, the likely change in capital requirements for better-rated and better-capitalised banks may result in cheaper inter-bank funding than exists in the current environment.
- *Credit risk*: a series of high-profile downgrades or credit scandals could adversely affect CP investors' confidence, resulting in them preferring to place their money elsewhere.
- To a lesser extent, rising *interest rates* may impact on the overall CP markets, but as the cost of borrowing should increase across all maturity spectra, not just at the short-end, in theory issuers should continue to use the CP markets for their short-term funding needs.
- *Equity markets* will affect general consumer confidence, and would therefore only have an indirect impact on the CP markets.

Medium-term notes

What are they? – their relevance – why use them?

MTNs are debt obligations that are offered on a continuous basis via a debt issuance platform commonly known as an MTN programme. The feature that primarily distinguishes

Exhibit 1.7

Volume of MTNs issued by final maturity

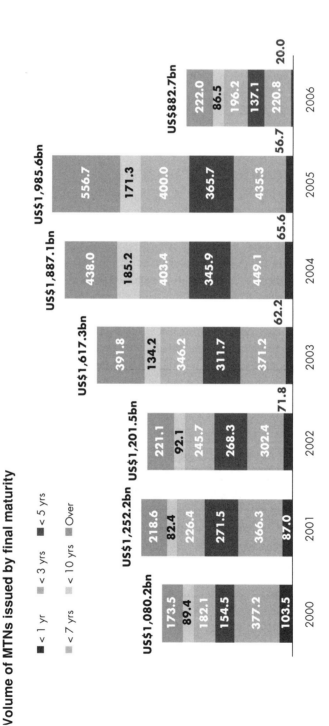

Source: Dealogic MTN Ware.

traditional debt issues from MTNs is that MTNs are offered through agents or dealers typically on a best efforts basis, rather than on a firm commitment (underwritten) basis as with public bond issuances. Since its establishment in the 1980s as a bridge between funding gaps of an issuer's short-term commercial paper and long-term borrowings in the bond markets, the MTN market has evolved to such an extent that the term 'medium' has become misleading. In fact, the MTN market can, today, be said to comprise all types of bond issuances between one-year and 30-year maturities.

MTNs differ from other products in the international capital markets in that an issuer can indicate funding rates or spreads to Libor every day for a range of maturities, structures and currencies that it wishes to issue. This means issuers can meet their funding privately without going through the rigorous process of public offerings and investors can structure their investments to match their needs.

MTN issuance off an MTN programme is divided into two general segments: non-syndicated and syndicated. The former is the classic private placement route whereby issuers' bonds are discreetly sold by a single dealer to a single investor. The latter is the traditional public offer of debt securities. The main difference between public and private is that on public deals there are many investors brought into the deal, whereas on private non-syndicated deals there tends to be one or, at best, a handful of investors. The use of the MTN programme has become especially important as issuers can use this platform both for the issuance of private non-syndicated deals as well as large public syndicated ones. Such a documentation platform, especially when it comes to public syndicated deals, offers considerable cost savings to an issuer over the execution of trades on a stand-alone basis. As a result, borrowers can issue debt virtually everywhere and access investors in any location via their MTN programme. A typical MTN programme will provide a number of options for the issuer, thus giving access to different investors in different regions, for example in Europe or in Asia. Issuers may also seek to sell to US investors by opting to include a Rule 144A option in their MTN programme which satisfies US requirements for primary resales to US Qualified Institutional Buyers, or may even go a step further by setting up a fully Securities and Exchange Commission (SEC) registered MTN programme, which meets all SEC disclosure requirements for placement into the United States.

In recent years, structured issuance by borrowers has increased considerably over plain vanilla MTNs. This is because structured MTNs can generate even lower costs of funding. The array of structures and products in this segment of the MTN market is becoming ever more complex. Today, MTNs can have their pay-off linked to a variety of components, including interest rates, equities, currencies, commodities and credit events.

Issuer profiles – investor profiles – leading players

Typical borrowers using the MTN market today include banks and other financial institutions, corporates, SPVs, sovereigns, municipalities, regions, agencies and emerging market issuers. All these borrowers have very different views on how best to utilise MTNs for themselves. For instance, the most frequent issuers in the MTN market tend to be the

Exhibit 1.8

Volume of issuance by currency

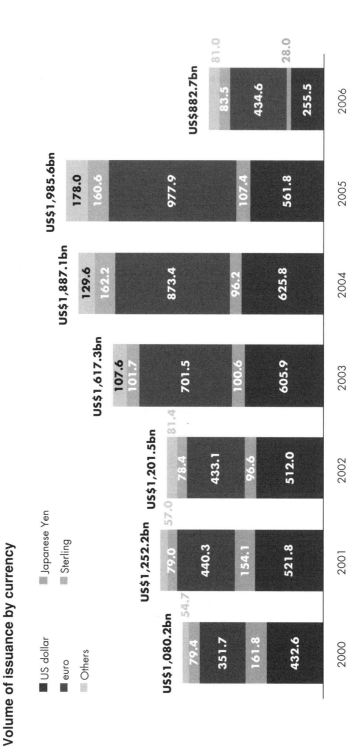

Source: Dealogic MTN Ware.

Exhibit 1.9

Volume by size of issuance

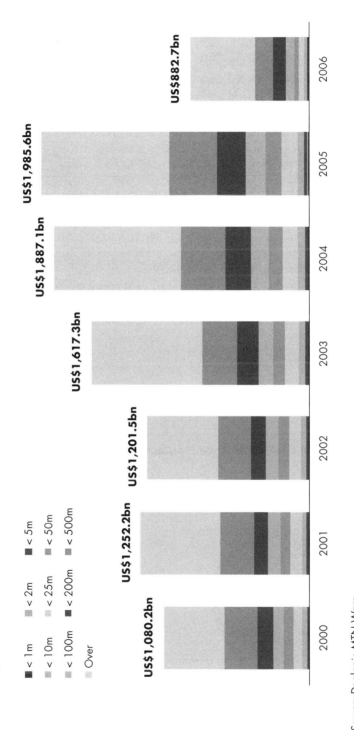

Source: Dealogic MTN Ware.

borrowers who are in constant need of cash to meet their daily liquidity needs. Typically these tend to be banks and other financial institutions, as well as numerous sovereign, supranational and agency borrowers. Such borrowers tend to be more opportunistic in nature, and are hence more likely to issue more structured MTNs to generate better funding costs for themselves, providing they have the means (systems, infrastructure, and so on) to value and price such structured trades. Corporates tend to be driven more by their specific funding requirements: as their needs for funds vary, they tend to issue more plain vanilla MTNs.

Traditionally, investor demand for credits in the MTN world has been concentrated on the debt of double-A and triple-A issuers, with a particular focus on sovereign and supranational borrowers. However, as investors have become more sophisticated, while their ability to categorise and quantify different risk profiles has improved, they have started to look further down the credit curve and, as a result, the array of MTN issuers available to them has expanded. The typical investor base today will still reflect specific investor appetite for holding a particular credit or structure. The typical MTN investor ranges from institutional investors such as banks, funds, and insurance companies, to retail investors who can purchase MTNs through their local bank branch.

With investors becoming more accustomed to MTNs, there has been greater acceptance of them by big pension funds and mutual funds. Many life insurance companies nowadays use MTNs as guarantees on some of their policies. Many investors are increasing their research of MTNs and, as a result, have become more comfortable with structured MTNs in their search for greater yield.

Exhibit 1.10

Goldman Sachs' EMTN issuance by issuer type and nationality

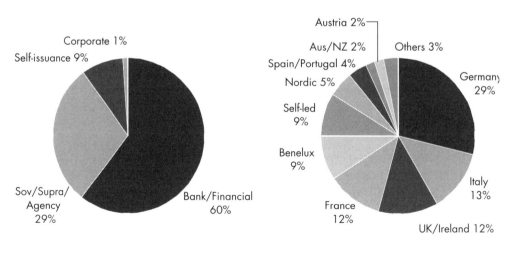

Source: Author's own.

Exhibit 1.11

Goldman Sachs' EMTN issuance by investor type and nationality

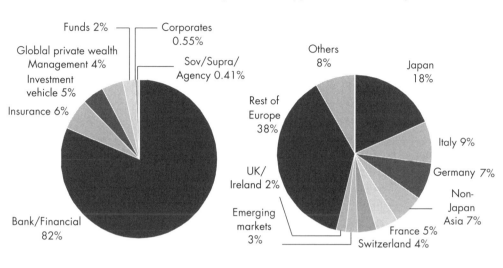

Source: Author's own.

Sample termsheet – secondary market, trading, investors – methodology for pricing – distribution methods

For MTNs, the secondary market plays an important role. A dealer on an MTN programme is obliged to provide liquidity for investors. While most MTNs, particularly those privately placed, are bought and held until maturity, most investors will require a secondary market commitment on such trades. On publicly syndicated MTNs, investors are accustomed to seeing good secondary market liquidity from dealers. This is because with a vast array of investors bought into a public deal, securing a bid/ask price through a dealer is not a problem. However, on privately placed MTNs a secondary market is not always to the advantage of investors and in some cases it works against them. For example, in a privately placed MTN trade, the structure utilised may have been tailored towards specific investor requirements, and it is not always certain that another investor would want to buy that same MTN if it was offered it. As a result, if an investor wants to get out of such a position, in most cases it is obliged to offer the MTN back to the dealer – which, due to illiquidity, may not always show an attractive bid/ask price to the investor.

Pricing a vanilla MTN is very different to that of a structured MTN, due to the different pay-off within the structured MTN. Even the pricing methodology is different. For vanilla MTNs, simply looking at swap rates for a fixed rate or Libor rates for a floating rate MTN is already a good enough means to determine pricing on such a trade, but on structured MTN trades it is not as simple. The crucial element in determining pricing on such trades is the swap that hedges the MTN. Many borrowers lack the ability to provide the payout of a structured MTN coupon to investors (in part due to the costs associated in developing such capabilities). As a result, an issuer will enter into a separate derivative swap transaction with the respective dealer on the structured MTN, whereby the issuer pays the dealer its funding on such a structure and, in turn, the dealer, through the swap, pays the issuer the structured coupons under the MTN, which it, in turn, passes on to the investor. The way a dealer prices up a derivative swap in the market for such a trade can result in it either winning or losing the structured MTN trade. Thus, the pricing methodologies and the way different dealers look at pricing certain MTNs, vary considerably.

The typical MTN distribution method that a dealer employs is through its own sales force, which may specialise in particular market segments – for example a particular geographic or regional focus, or strong retail networks via bank branches. However, most dealers attempt to be full-service providers across all market segments. What really makes the difference in winning an MTN trade is pricing. This is because the MTN market has evolved to such an extent that investors know exactly how they want to invest, dealers know exactly which borrowers can issue what form of MTN so that, when the two come together, the dealer who has the best price will win the trade.

Documentation, tax and accounting issues – listing requirements – reporting requirements

An MTN programme's documentation is the key to all MTN issuance. Programmes come in all shapes and sizes and can be altered to fit an issuer's changing needs. Programme documentation has become more standardised, but will still be governed by issuer objectives. For first time issuers, the amount of documentation work involved can be daunting, due to disclosure requirements and the need for regular updates. For example, if the programme provides for a wide range of currencies and types of notes, more detailed documentation will be needed. The same goes for an issuer who decides to list its securities on different stock exchanges requiring them to comply with the listing rules governing each exchange.

The cost of setting up a programme will vary, but will typically include ratings agency fees, auditor's comfort letters, dealers' and issuer's counsel, listing fees and financial printing fees. The trend for MTN programme documentation is towards standardisation of the legally significant elements – such as covenants, representations and warranties – while being flexible on the pricing features and the types of issues to be undertaken. The base prospectus or offering circular for a programme will also provide a description of the issuer and financial disclosure, as well as various other elements related to an issuer's MTN issuance, such as the number of dealers on the programme, selling restrictions, and so on.

Over time an MTN programme should generate considerable cost efficiencies when compared with issuing public bonds on a stand-alone basis. As a rule of thumb, if a borrower executes two or three trades off its MTN programme, it will be cheaper than executing the same two or three trades on a stand-alone basis. A typical MTN programme can take anything between six and eight weeks to establish and cost on average US$100,000, but this is very much dependent on the complexity of the programme.

Selling MTNs in the United States is more complex and can be more expensive to document. This is because the disclosure requirements and the due diligence procedures typically undertaken in relation to US distribution are more onerous. As a result, many non-US issuers stay away from the US market. There are two main avenues for accessing the US market. The first is to establish an SEC registered MTN programme (often referred to as a debt shelf) for which a registration statement is produced and filed with the SEC. The second is to rely on an exemption from registration under Rule 144A, under which securities may only be offered in the United States to qualified institutional buyers (QIBs). In connection with either avenue, dealers will typically require counsel to undertake detailed due diligence in connection with the disclosure in the prospectus and to deliver a disclosure or 10b-5, opinion which forms part of a dealer's (and issuer's) due diligence defence in the event that an investor investigates legal proceedings in respect of the MTNs.

The listing of an MTN programme is important. In order to obtain a listing, an issuer needs to meet the disclosure requirements set out in the listing rules of the stock exchange or listing authority, and thereafter to meet the ongoing filing, notification and disclosure obligations to maintain the listing. The usual listing exchanges for MTN programmes are London and Luxembourg. With the implementation of the EU Prospectus Directive in the summer of 2005, disclosure requirements have been harmonised across EU listing exchanges. Additionally, once an issuer's base prospectus has been approved by its 'home' listing authority, it can apply to have the programme passported into other EU jurisdictions in order to offer MTNs to the public there in compliance with the EU Prospectus Directive.

Pros and cons

Issuers who issue MTNs off an MTN programme will secure access to a wide variety of maturities and currencies. Additionally, a programme provides easier access to their paper for investors. Because of the continuous-offering process, the MTN market gives the investor immediate access to an almost unlimited array of fixed-income securities in widely varying maturities issued by a broad spectrum of issuers. The rapid growth of the MTN market has attracted the attention of a growing number of dealers, who have contributed to the expansion of the market in recent years and have as a result increased liquidity to this market segment.

However, setting up an MTN programme is not cheap and an issuer needs to be clear on what kind of programme it wants, how it is going to use it and how much it is prepared to commit to the process in terms of time, resources and investment. It typically costs substantially more to set up an MTN programme in terms of legal fees due to increased documentation requirements than to issue a prospectus for a stand-alone bond. If it is not likely to be used regularly, an MTN platform may not be a good idea for all issuers.

Chapter 2

The syndicated loan market

David Bassett
The Royal Bank of Scotland

Introduction

The only constant is change.

When Heraclitus coined this phrase nearly 2,500 years ago he could not have imagined that it would be so appropriate to commerce and the business world, especially regarding the speed with which such changes have reshaped the financial markets. Although only five years have passed since the last peak in the cycle, the global capital markets have experienced significant swings and record-setting performances (both positive and not-so-positive), and borrowers and investors are growing more and more sophisticated in their methods.

The syndicated loan market is no exception here: few of the records set in the loan markets during the previous cycle still stand today because the deals done in the past five years have been larger, more leveraged, longer in duration, lower-priced, in a wider range of markets and with more investors. As one would expect from a dynamic market, the list of changes is long – too long to be covered in this brief overview of syndicated loans. With this in mind, this chapter will focus on the situation in today's loan market – which regions are growing the fastest, what types of deals are getting done and, importantly, how the deal process works – and leave the more distant history more or less in the past.

Background

Before jumping into the themes in today's loan market, there are two key pieces of background information to discuss.

The first is definitional: what is a syndicated loan? In its simplest form, a syndicated loan is a credit facility in which two or more banks (the 'syndicate') agree to provide a loan to a borrower under a single loan document. This sounds very straightforward – at least two banks, one borrower, one document – but, as we shall see, the variations on this basic set-up are limitless due to the flexibility of the loan as a financial instrument. Because the loan market is a private market without formal requirements for standard documentation, public debt ratings, information disclosure or due diligence, it is possible to arrange syndicated loans in very short timeframes and for very large amounts for virtually any credit need that a borrower might have. The only constraints in the issuance of syndicated loans are the credit-worthiness of the borrower and the willingness of lenders to provide capital in a particular loan transaction. Thus, syndicated loans tend to be most effective in areas where other capital markets instruments might not be practical.

Exhibit 2.1

Global capital markets volumes 2005

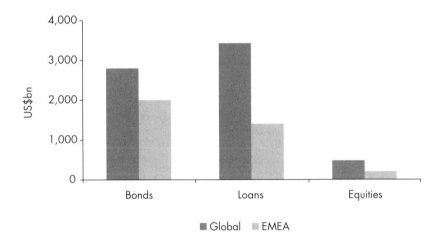

Source: Thomson Financial.

Exhibit 2.2

EMEA debt issuance by market segment 2005

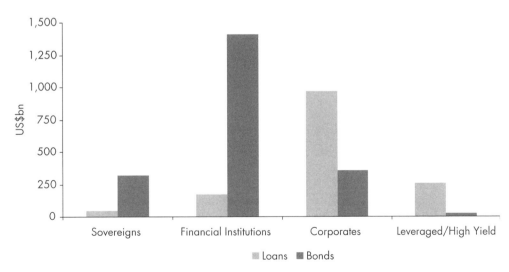

Source: Thomson Financial, RBS.

The second is contextual: how does the syndicated loan market compare to the broader capital markets in size and type of borrower? As indicated in Exhibit 2.1, the loan market is very large, comparable in size to the bond market globally and much larger than new issuance in the equity markets.

While the loan market and the bond market are similar in size, the types of borrowers are quite different. As shown in Exhibit 2.2, the loan market tends to be used more for corporate and leveraged issuance due to the more flexible nature of loans, while the bond market is favoured by financial institutions and sovereign borrowers for longer-term, more standardised issuance.

This situation is a natural result of the further development of the public capital markets for longer-term issuance: whereas in the past the only source of capital for all borrowers was banks, as new products have been developed the loan market has come to be used mainly in those areas where it makes the most sense; that is, for those client situations that require customised solutions rather than straightforward long-term funding.

Loan market overview

One of the most obvious changes in the loan market has been the tremendous growth in syndicated loan issuance globally. The increasing prevalence of syndicated loans can clearly be seen in Exhibit 2.3 which shows that on a global basis syndicated loan volumes have grown from US$1.2tn in 1995 to US$3.5tn ten years later; this represents annualised growth of approximately 11 per cent over that period, nearly three times the rate of general economic growth.

Exhibit 2.3

Global syndicated loan issuance

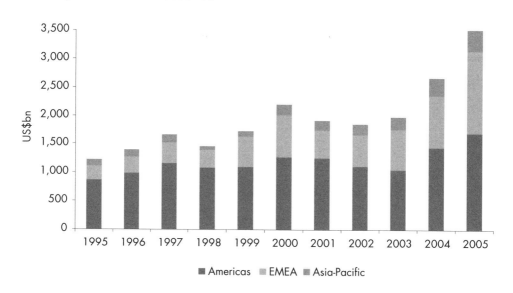

Source: Thomson Financial.

While each of EMEA (Europe, Middle East and Africa), the Americas and Asia-Pacific experienced growth over this period, the greatest area of growth was in the EMEA region. This is largely due to the increase in acquisition-related activity in Europe (partly as a result of the creation of the euro) and the trend of major corporates to rely less on bilateral funding and instead move into syndicated loans. This trend is also borne out by comparing syndicated loan issuance as a share of nominal regional GDP, as illustrated in Exhibit 2.4.

Exhibit 2.4
Syndicated loan issuance as a share of regional GDP

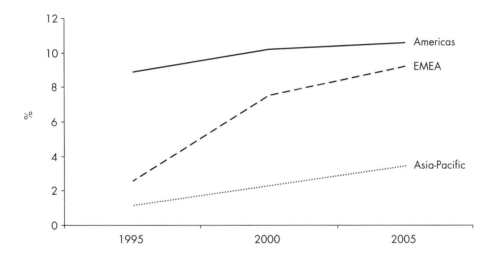

Source: IMF, Thomson Financial, RBS.

The United States, as the most mature capital market, retains the deepest penetration of syndicated loan issuance but has been the slowest-growing region (7 per cent per annum on average), while growth in the EMEA region has been much faster (19 per cent per annum) and has been linked to the rapid development of the capital markets in Europe. Asia-Pacific has also grown strongly (14 per cent per annum) but still lags the other regions in terms of total penetration, but one would expect that this gap will narrow substantially over the next five years.

Historically, the major regional loan markets developed relatively independently of one another, and structures or pricing in one market would not directly translate into similar deals in other markets. However, the loan market is becoming increasingly global as business itself becomes less linked to individual markets, cross-border acquisitions become commonplace, investors search for yield and assets on a global scale and as leading arrangers of syndicated loans move to a global model. This last point is especially important given that the capital demands of new transactions often surpass the ability of local investors to finance the deal themselves, thus requiring truly global banks to arrange these transactions in order to tap investor appetite in more distant regions. The leaders in arranging syndicated loans globally are illustrated in Exhibit 2.5.

23

Exhibit 2.5

Top bookrunners of global syndicated loans 2005

Bookrunner	Volume (US$bn)	Market Share (%)
J. P. Morgan	536.9	15.3
Citigroup	452.5	12.9
Bank of America	327.5	9.3
RBS	147.0	4.2
Barclays Capital	141.6	4.0

Source: Thomson Financial.

EMEA region

As noted above, the syndicated loan market in EMEA has experienced substantial growth and change, particularly among the Western European countries. Exhibit 2.6 illustrates the growth in loan volumes in certain large EMEA countries.

Exhibit 2.6

EMEA syndicated loan issuance – five largest markets

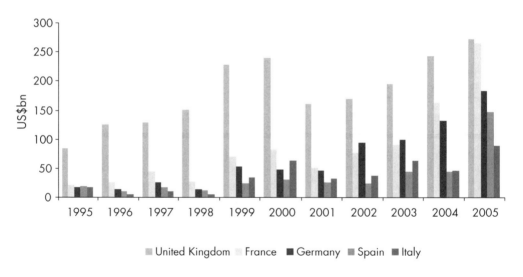

■ United Kingdom ▨ France ■ Germany ■ Spain ■ Italy

Source: Thomson Financial.

Across Western Europe, however, the composition of the larger markets has changed significantly over the past ten years. The UK, which historically had the most developed loan and capital markets, grew at a slower pace (14 per cent per annum on average) than the four largest continental markets (Germany, France, Italy and Spain) (25 per cent per annum altogether). Even within the continental markets there have been differentials in growth, with

France and Germany growing at a much faster pace (30 per cent and 27 per cent, respectively) than Spain and Italy (22 per cent and 17 per cent, respectively). Having said this, it is clear that there is still substantial room for additional growth in Germany (and in Italy) due to the relatively low penetration of syndicated loans in those countries as illustrated in Exhibit 2.7.

Exhibit 2.7

Syndicated loans as a share of national GDP

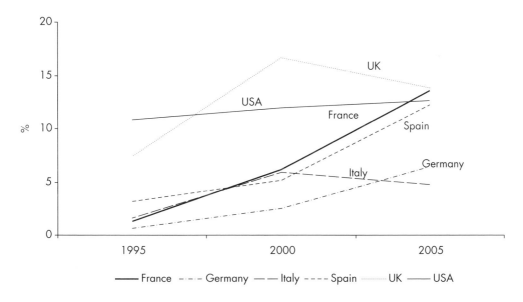

Source: IMF, Thomson Financial, RBS.

Using the United States as a benchmark for a 'mature' market in terms of penetration, it is clear that the UK, France and Spain have all achieved 'mature' status in the development of their syndicated loan markets, while there is still substantial room for further growth in Germany and Italy. With this in mind, it is not surprising that the leaders in arranging EMEA syndicated loans are largely drawn from the more mature markets as shown in Exhibit 2.8.

Exhibit 2.8

Top bookrunners of EMEA syndicated loans 2005

Bookrunner	Volume (US$bn)	Market Share (%)
Citigroup	149.2	10.4
RBS	127.8	8.9
BNP Paribas	115.4	8.0
Barclays Capital	106.5	7.4
Calyon	90.2	6.3

Source: Thomson Financial.

Syndicated loan segments

As mentioned before, syndicated loans are 'private' debt facilities and are not standardised or regulated like other capital markets instruments; furthermore, syndicated loans are sold on a 'wholesale' basis to sophisticated bank and fund investors and not to individual retail buyers. This combination offers borrowers tremendous flexibility and thus the loan may be adapted for a variety of purposes: mergers and acquisitions (M&A) financing and acquisition financing as the loans are confidential and can be executed quickly and in size; liquidity backstops as the loan facilities can remain undrawn; and highly structured transactions such as project or property financings. As noted previously, however, syndicated loans do not work as well for financial institution or sovereign borrowers which require long-term financing or for long-term capital where the tightly governed loan facilities are more restrictive in a permanent capital structure than long-term bonds.

Based on these uses, the syndicated loan market may be divided into three broad segments:

- *General corporate*: these deals are typically investment-grade or near investment-grade and are often positioned as 'relationship' transactions; vanilla backstop facilities, working capital lines and capex facilities would fall into this segment.
- *Acquisition finance*: these deals are event-driven transactions linked to M&A activity; leveraged buyout (LBO) financings, acquisition bridges and high-grade acquisition facilities would be in this segment.

Exhibit 2.9

EMEA syndicated loan market issuance

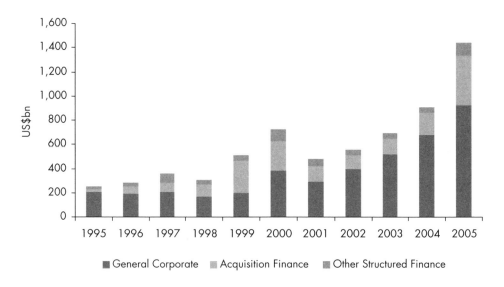

Source: Thomson Financial.

- *Other structured finance*: these transactions often involve structures that are unique to the particular funding requirement and are often linked to a particular underlying asset; project finance, property finance and aircraft finance would typically fit into this segment.

Exhibit 2.9 presents the composition of syndicated loans by use of proceeds in the European syndicated loan market since 1995.

As one might expect, the greatest year-on-year volatility in issuance has occurred in the acquisition finance segment, given that these deals are usually one-off transactions and are directly linked to M&A activity in the broader markets. General corporate issuance has increased substantially, largely due to continental European clients converting their bilateral backstop facilities into more flexible syndicated loans, often as the first step toward a more progressive capital structure. Other structured finance issuance has increased but at a slower pace than the other segments: these more tailored uses for syndicated loans do not lend themselves so easily to broader capital markets instruments and thus this segment is not positioned for explosive growth like acquisition facilities.

Each of these segments has distinct characteristics to be aware of.

General corporate

For an investment-grade borrower, the greatest flexibility will likely be achieved through a single revolving credit facility which can be used for a wide variety of purposes, although a borrower may prefer to spread its maturity profile in order to reduce any refinancing risk. Where liquidity available in the market might be limited (for instance, as a result of aggressive pricing or weakening market conditions), a facility structured to incorporate a term loan (to cover any long-term drawn amounts) and a revolving credit facility for the variable balance will often prove more attractive in the market.

In the investment-grade market, tenors range between 364 days and seven years, with the bulk of issuance in today's market occurring in the 5- and 7-year tenors. The 364-day facilities take advantage of a capital weighting benefit resulting from the implementation of the Basel capital adequacy directives which can be passed on to companies. This advantage is expected to be largely removed with the implementation of Basel II, expected in 2008/9. Seven-year facilities are usually only offered to the strongest names, though this varies by geography. For example, 7-year facilities currently are more common in Scandinavia and Germany than the UK. The longest facilities typically available to most investment-grade borrowers are therefore 5 years. However, a relatively recent addition to this is the '5 + 1 + 1 year' facility, consisting of a 5-year facility with an extension option which can be requested by the borrower at the end of the first and second years to extend the facility and 'renew' its tenor to 5 years from the date of the extension, thus creating the possibility of a 7-year end-to-end tenor for the transaction. This increase in tenor is an example of the strength of market liquidity shifting the balance of lending terms in favour of borrowers. Recent trends for vanilla corporate debt have been for facilities to incorporate fewer restrictions and lower pricing. A surge in growth in the M&A market has provided a partial counter to this with more structured deals and an 'acquisition premium' allowing lenders to be more selective about the transactions they consider.

Acquisition finance

This segment can be further divided into two parts: high-grade and cross-over acquisition loans; and leveraged acquisition loans.

High-grade acquisition loans are for borrowers with an investment-grade credit profile but are usually documented with stronger credit protections and higher pricing than standard investment-grade loans. These are often short-term bridges to capital markets issuance or to disposals, although in recent times some larger facilities have had a substantial element of 5- or even 7-year tranches to provide additional flexibility to the borrower, and margins on these deals can range from 20 to 75 basis points (bp). Cross-over acquisition loans are for investment-grade borrowers that become borderline investment-grade/non-investment-grade as a result of new acquisition debt. Bridge tranches can be more difficult for these types of borrowers because the credit profile is not strong enough to tap the high-grade bond market but is not weak enough to warrant the expense and restrictions of the high-yield bond market. Consequently, cross-over acquisition loans have stronger credit protections (for example, financial covenants), higher pricing (75 bp to 200 bp) and longer tenors than high-grade loans.

Leveraged loans apply to borrowers with non-investment-grade credit profiles and here the margins are typically 200 bp or more. These are typically LBOs and are considered more risky given the level of debt put onto the borrower versus the available cash flows, hence high loan pricing and a strong loan structure (including security and other restrictive documentation provisions) are required to attract investors into the syndicate. For leveraged companies, the European market has developed such that there is currently a typical LBO

Exhibit 2.10

Growth in European second lien and mezzanine facilities

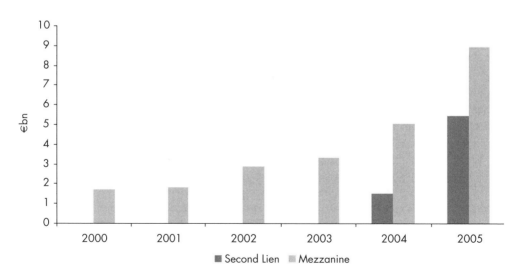

Source: Standard & Poor's LCD.

structure with regards to tenors and pricing: senior term loan facilities typically consist of Term Loans A, B and C which are characteristically 7-year amortising term loans, 8-year bullet term loans and 9-year bullet term loans, respectively, along with a 7-year revolving credit facility; margins on these tranches are typically 225 bp, 275 bp, 325 bp and 225 bp, respectively. Deals with lower pricing and shorter tenors have been launched into the market recently but usually these are only for the strongest of leveraged credits and where there is a considerable equity contribution from the financial sponsor. In order to provide solutions and flexibility to the financial sponsors to meet the demand for increased debt in LBO structures, the European market has seen a significant increase in second lien facilities and subordinated facilities such as private mezzanine facilities or public high-yield bonds (see Exhibit 2.10).

Other structured finance

Other structured finance covers a wide array of transactions that are tailored to a specific financing need, and often the loan market is the only market with the expertise or financial flexibility to provide the necessary capital. The three main areas of structured deals are project finance, property finance and aircraft finance.

Global project finance experienced a buoyant market in 2005 largely due to several large energy-linked deals that were executed last year. The popularity of the syndicated loan product in project finance can clearly be seen by the growth of project finance loans which rose from US$116bn to US$140bn in 2005. In particular the Middle East stands out, with volumes increasing by US$13bn to US$31bn. Given that 2004 was a record year for the Middle East, and indeed that 2003 was also a record at US$8bn, this represents extraordinary growth. Activity in Spain, on the back of a very active infrastructure financing sector, trebled to US$16bn in 2005. As a result, EMEA project finance volumes nearly doubled to US$94bn.

According to Project Finance International, 2006 is expected to be a year where project finance deals are done in other, perhaps slightly slower, countries in the Gulf Cooperation Council, plus other energy-rich but project finance-tougher places such as Yemen, Nigeria and Russia, to name a small selection. Another future trend in the project finance market is the use of the syndicated loan product to fund the initial project acquisition with a bond issuance take-out at a later date.

Property finance, which is often combined with a corporate syndicated loan transaction and can be referred to as 'opco/propco' financing, provides highly structured funding solutions for real estate owners, occupiers and investors with existing property portfolios and to support acquisitions. Such solutions can involve combinations of senior debt (secured or unsecured general corporate revolving credit facilities or senior secured term loans), bridge and M&A-related financing, mezzanine loans for both corporate and asset level financing, construction loans, and equity products in order to maximise and optimise the capital structure and the financial and tax position of the deal. In addition to syndicated real estate loans which typically range in size from US$50m to over US$2bn with tenors of up to five years, commercial mortgage backed securities ('CMBS') are also a key financing instrument in property financing (and are placed with securitisation investors).

Aircraft financing involves providing debt financing and leasing solutions to airlines worldwide. The leasing and financing market for the modern Airbus, Boeing and Regional Jet aircrafts involves over 100 airline customers in 36 countries. From a business perspective, the sale of aircraft assets enables flexibility to inject capital back into the business, incorporate lease-terms to fit fleet planning requirements, and avoids the time-consuming task of remarketing the aircraft. Consequently the sale and leaseback of new and existing aircraft is a central component in the suite of aircraft financing structures. Typical aircraft financing structures include: (i) senior secured loans on new and recently acquired aircraft, (ii) structured multi-tranche debt financing, (iii) debt into tax leases, (iv) finance leases, (v) European Export Credit Agency (ECA) and Export-Import Bank of the United States (Exim) financing and (vi), manufacturer pre-delivery payment financing (PDPs). The current trend in the aircraft financing sector is for club deals whereby the financing is syndicated to only a very limited number of investors; however, as the aircraft cycle is picking up again it is expected that the larger syndicated loans will return to the market.

Exhibit 2.11 illustrates some of the key differences among general corporate, acquisition finance and other structured finance loans.

Syndicated loan process

Regardless of the purpose of the syndicated loan, there are three main phases of the syndicated loan process that occur in nearly every transaction: the mandate phase; the syndication phase; and the post-closing phase. There are a number of variations on these three phases but, in general, understanding the basics here is essential to having the full picture on how the syndicated loan functions.

Mandate phase

The first stage of any syndicated loan transaction is the decision of a borrower to raise debt in the syndicated loan market.

A company or private equity house/financial sponsor (the 'borrower') recognises the need for debt facilities, resulting for example from the need for additional capital for an acquisition or from a need to refinance existing debt. Consequently, the borrower may request one or more banks in one or more products (e.g. syndicated loans, private placements, high-grade bonds) to provide indicative terms upon which they might be prepared to arrange a financing. This is known as a 'request-for-proposal' or 'RFP'. In leveraged transactions, the financial sponsors request banks to provide indicative financing support to their bid for a target company with the process usually occurring via a competitive auction process.

Over time, a bank will typically attempt to build up a strong relationship with potential clients and to present the financial products in which it has expertise in order to cement a position in the client's mind as a natural partner in any financing. This will include presenting senior bank personnel as well as product specialists who will aim to impress the borrower with their knowledge and market perspective. If there is no such prior relationship, banks may approach a prospective borrower without solicitation, marketing proposals for financial solutions to certain scenarios, for example the refinancing of existing debt or

Exhibit 2.11

Key differences between loan types

	General corporate	Acquisition finance: high-grade and crossover	Acquisition finance: leveraged	Other structured finance
Tenor	364 days to 7 years	364 days to 7 years; greater emphasis on short-term and amortising structures	7 to 9 years	3 to 30 + years
Size	Typically US$100m to US$3bn; could be up to US$20bn or more	Typically US$500m to US$5bn; could be US$30bn or more	Typically US$100m to US$2bn; could be US$15bn or more	Typically US$100m to US$2bn; could be US$5bn or more
Credit profile	Investment-grade, typically externally rated	Investment-grade and near investment-grade; may not be rated	Non-investment-grade; often not publicly rated	Investment-grade and near investment-grade; usually not publicly rated
Lenders	Typical lenders are banks	Typical lenders are banks	Typical lenders include investment funds in addition to banks	Typical lenders are banks, with some funds
Purpose	General corporate purposes, commercial paper backstop, standby undrawn facilities	Acquisition bridge to capital markets take-out, long-term acquisition financing, General corporate purposes	LBOs, MBOs, MBIs, Acquisition financings	Financing a particular project or asset (for example, infrastructure transactions, construction deals, property financings or aircraft transactions)
Facility types	Unsecured revolving credit facilities often including swing line provisions, term loans, LC facilities, Capex facilities	Unsecured (usually) bridge facilities (short-medium term), revolving credit facilities, term loans, LC facilities, Guarantee facilities	Secured revolving credit facilities, term loans, mezzanine facilities, second lien facilities, asset-backed financings, asset securitisation, receivables financing/financial engineering (derivatives)	Secured revolving credit facilities, term loans, standby facilities, VAT facilities, occasionally second lien or mezzanine tranches

Source: RBS.

the raising of new funds such as for an acquisition. The format and detail of such approaches will vary depending on the bank, its capabilities, and the relationship with the company.

Once the decision has been made to raise debt in the syndicated loan market, a bank or group of banks will be engaged by the borrower on an initially non-binding basis, during which period a number of key points in these initial proposals are agreed on in a 'Summary of Terms & Conditions' or 'termsheet'. Typically this will be agreed concurrently with a formal letter of engagement, or 'mandate letter' setting out the scope and responsibilities of both the borrower and arranging bank(s).

Of course, banks have to want to provide a loan in order to get to this stage and this requires them to obtain all necessary internal credit and distribution approvals. In any lending situation, the credit quality of the borrower is a key factor for banks in determining whether to provide a loan: can the borrower repay the facility and what are the risks involved? In a syndicated lending situation, there is the added dimension of distribution risk; the assessment of the attractiveness of the loan to other lenders is key as managing the underwriting risk is essential to the success of the syndicated loan process. When a prospective arranger is satisfied that the credit and distribution risks are manageable, then the bank is ready to accept a mandate for the financing.

Mandates are awarded for a variety of reasons, but most commonly they will be won on the following key criteria:

• strength of bank's relationship with the borrower;
• ability of the bank to provide, execute and distribute the debt facilities; and
• proposed pricing and structure of the facility.

For a borrower with a number of relationships with different banks, the pricing/structure of the facility is often the key differentiator. Any bank wishing to win the business of arranging a syndicated loan will, therefore, seek to offer competitive pricing and a flexible structure to the borrower. A balance must be maintained: economic return and credit protection for the participant banks vs. presenting a sufficiently attractive offer to the borrower to be of interest and competitive with rival offers. Setting the price too low or the structure too weak could result in a lack of investors willing to participate and the failure of the deal, while too high a price or too tight a structure could result in the loss of a potential mandate to competing banks. Correctly understanding and judging the size and position of the pricing and structure band within which participant investors are prepared to commit to the transaction is, therefore, critical to winning the business.

Prior to the preparation of the full loan documentation in the syndication phase, the key commercial terms are typically negotiated between the borrower and the lead bank. A termsheet typically includes, as a minimum, the basic structure (amount, type, tenor, any financial covenants (including covenant headroom levels), security, amortisation profile, pricing, permitted acquisition and disposal baskets/carve-outs) and basis of document preparation (which will often be either 'Loan Market Association (LMA) standard' or a previous facility). More detailed termsheets can specify general covenants, representations and events of default (usually as headings alone, but legal language can be expanded where necessary), as well as guarantors, conditions of prepayment, other restrictions imposed on the borrower such as dividend payment restriction, and may specify certain terms that will be included within the mandate letter, such as market flex (where the borrower agrees that the arrangers may change either structure or pricing in certain events in order to ensure successful syndication).

Included in the structuring discussions with the borrower will be whether the facility needs to be underwritten or whether it can be executed on a best efforts basis. Underwritten facilities, where arranging banks bear any risk of transaction failure for a fee, may be expected to be less aggressive than a corresponding best efforts facility. Therefore, a borrower looking to refinance a maturing working capital facility may, in a difficult market, welcome an underwritten facility to obtain certainty that the facility will be refinanced but, in more benign conditions, will likely opt for a more aggressive best efforts structure in order to benefit from improved pricing. Underwritten facilities are often required for acquisitions, either leveraged or investment-grade/corporate acquisition financing, both to provide surety of funding for certain jurisdictions and to maintain the confidentiality of the pre-announcement bid discussions.

Syndication phase

Once the mandate has been awarded, the process of preparing the loan documentation gets underway. If external counsel for the lenders has not been appointed in the previous phase then one will be at this stage to prepare the first draft documentation on the basis of the termsheet agreements.

Simultaneously, the arranging bank will seek to prepare to market the transaction through: (i) preparation of supporting marketing information (e.g. an information memorandum, a bank meeting presentation and, for leveraged transactions, the finalisation of financial, legal and tax due diligence reports by external advisers); (ii) preparation of an invitation letter to be sent to prospective lenders who may have been identified to be interested in participating in such a transaction; and (iii) direct announcements concerning the facility, if required, via the trade press or, in certain circumstances, to lenders directly (a process known as 'sounding out'). The scope and detail of the information released to the investor group is individual to each transaction with the level of detail dependent on prospective lenders' familiarity with the credit: detailed information will be required for a new entrant into the syndicated loan market and for particularly complex transactions, whereas less information is needed for a large, publicly listed company which has regularly tapped the syndicated loan market for refinancings. Prior to launch, market capacity and liquidity are key considerations: the greater the liquidity in the market, the more borrower-friendly terms can be achieved; and the more interested investors, the greater the potential liquidity available. This leads to a more complex interplay between a number of variables around the pricing, structure and number of lenders approached, and ultimately leads to a binary decision by any single lender to join the syndicate or not to.

The syndicated loan market consists of a finite number of investors, each with different attitudes towards risk/sector/geography/pricing, with individual relationship histories influencing investment decisions and amounts to be invested. This investor base has expanded considerably over recent years with the growth in institutional investors and the creation of the collateralised loan obligation (CLO) funds. Typically the institutional investors and CLO funds invest in the drawn non-amortising tranches in a leveraged capital structure with investments usually made in the Term Loans B and C and the second lien facilities. The growth and liquidity in this lender category can clearly be seen in Exhibit 2.12 which shows the significant growth in institutional lenders as a share of leveraged loan issuance.

The increase in institutional investor depth in the leveraged market has been one of the most critical changes to occur in the past ten years.

Typically, arrangers will prefer to approach more investors in order to minimise the risk of a failed syndication, while, conversely, borrowers often prefer smaller lender groups because they are easier to manage. This creates a tension that needs to be managed between the borrower and the arranger regarding the distribution of risk in the transaction: for best efforts deals, this distribution risk lies mainly with the borrower, but with underwritten facilities the risk lies with the underwriting arranger to make up any shortfall.

At an agreed time, the facility will be launched into the syndicated loan market by way of an invitation letter. The invitation letter will provide a minimum amount of information about the transaction: typically an introduction describing the borrower, the identity of the arranging bank(s), size of the transaction, requested participation amount and any associated fees and the transaction timetable. A confidentiality agreement is usually attached to the invitation letter, requiring investors to sign and return this in exchange for the full facility details (such as a termsheet) and any additional information released. Post this launch, the

Exhibit 2.12

Institutional lenders' share of the primary leveraged market

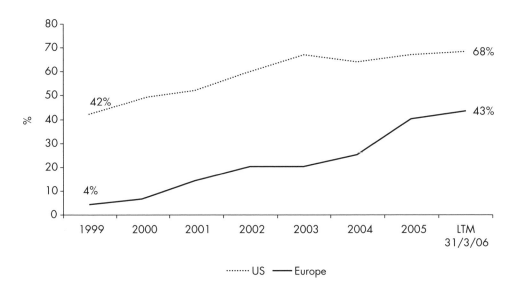

Source: Standard & Poor's LCD.

transaction will go through a syndication ('sales') process of typically three to four weeks, with a presentation by management to interested investors usually occurring in the week following launch to allow investors to become familiar with the borrower and transaction beforehand. This lender presentation is a useful way of enabling lenders and the borrower to meet with management of the borrower who present the future strategy for the borrower.

The sales process of a syndicated loan, also known as 'bookrunning', is the most visible role in a syndicated loan, requiring a detailed understanding of a facility as well as potential lenders. The syndication process is launched via the distribution of the invitation letters to the agreed investor invitee list and the provision of the information memorandum. Most syndicated loans involve the use of an electronic distribution system (for example, Intralinks) to allow investors secure access to any relevant information on a centralised basis.

The negotiation of the final loan documentation, based on the agreed termsheet from the mandate phase, can either occur prior to the syndication launch, as is typical in many leveraged transactions, or during the syndication process, as can be the case in investment-grade corporate transactions. Outside the normal legal and jurisdictional limitations there is an almost unlimited scope for variation among these documents and, as a result, a general framework has been developed over the years and standardised by the LMA. The LMA standard framework deals with a number of the necessary mechanical arrangements involved with the proper running of a syndicated loan, such as assignment and transfers, majority lender decisions, representations, information undertakings, interest payment mechanics, conditions precedent and notification and consultation of all parties. The standardisation of these 'boiler plate' terms frees up the parties to discuss more important commercial issues while minimising lengthy negotiation and expensive legal consultation.

At the end of this sales period, lenders will either commit to the facility (usually subject to individual satisfaction with the documentation) or decline. It is important to remember that lenders (either banks or institutional investors) in a syndicated loan do not necessarily contribute equal amounts to the deal as different commitment and title levels exist and each lender committing to the facility is acting on a several basis without responsibility for the other investors in the syndicate. Any individual disagreements with documentation are resolved between the borrower and prospective lenders and administrative details will be collected so that the facility can be prepared for signing. Lenders will sign into the facility via a number of different processes. The most common method of signing involves each lender signing individually and returning the signature pages to an arranging bank or lawyer, often by fax/scanned email. Once collected, the signatures are compiled into one document, and a conformed copy is sent around confirming that the process is completed. When the loan documentation is already signed, the committed lenders are funded into the transaction by way of the execution of transfer certificates.

Post-closing phase

This phase begins at the point of signing and lasts for the life of the facility. When a loan has been syndicated, lender allocations have been made and the lenders have been funded into the transaction (that is, they are now legal counterparties under the facilities), the syndicate is formed. From this point on, the agent has the key role coordinating all parties and monitoring the facilities, particularly in terms of financial reporting and covenant compliance. A key role for the agent is to distribute information to the syndicate so that all the syndicate members receive the same information and are able to monitor the performance of the credit themselves. An annual bank meeting is often arranged where the borrower's management report on financial performance to date and present the next year's budget to the syndicate. This enables the lenders to regularly meet with management and to raise any questions. Should any waiver or amendment of the loan agreement terms be required during the life of the facilities, the agent will coordinate this process. It is important to remember that the agent does not act on its own but, rather, always acts on the instructions of the lenders.

Once allocations have been made and announced, the loan then becomes 'free to trade' which means that lenders can trade the loan in the secondary loan market. As a result of the current liquidity in the loan market, it is becoming common for lenders who received a lower than desired allocation in primary syndication to come to the secondary loan market to increase their position in the deal. On the flip side of this, if lenders want to actively manage that position they can utilise the secondary loan market to sell some of their participation in the deal. The decision to buy and sell will obviously be driven by the price in the secondary loan market, and the agent will play a key role in maintaining the syndicate list and notifying the borrower of any changes in this list if trades have been executed. Trading has been important in the United States for some time now and has become more important in Europe in the past several years as institutional investors have become more pervasive in the market, as illustrated in Exhibit 2.13.

Exhibit 2.13

Global secondary loan market volumes

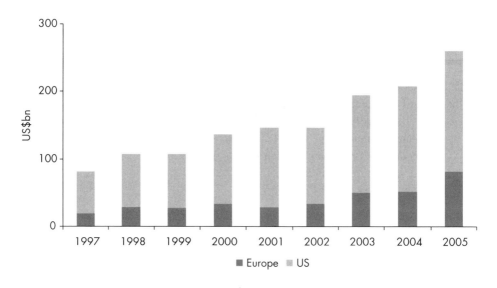

Source: LMA, Reuters.

Summary

The syndicated loan market is an integral part of the global capital markets and continues to evolve at a fast pace. One of the reasons for the rapid pace of change is the inherent flexibility of the loan product and its ability to complement other capital markets products in complex transactions. Further, the globalisation and increasingly interlinked nature of world markets has led to new uses for loans – both in terms of large acquisition financings as well as in structured special-purpose transactions – and has also led to the creation of global investors who are ready to deploy capital to geographic regions and industrial sectors with the most attractive opportunities. Consequently, successful arrangers of syndicated loans are using their global networks to reach these investors. Heraclitus' statement about constant change was correct, but whatever changes come in the near future we can be assured that the syndicated loan market will be able to adapt and add value for borrowers and lenders.

Chapter 3

US private placements

Michael Thilmany
HSBC

Introduction: what is a private placement?

Defined buyers

A private placement is the direct sale by an issuer, of its debt or equity securities, to a limited number of 'sophisticated' investors ('qualified investment buyers' (QIBs) or 'accredited investors' (AIs), as defined respectively). The investor base generally includes insurance companies, as well as pension funds, money managers, finance companies, and bank trust departments. Traditionally, private placements have been sold to investors for long-term investment purposes (that is, not for resale), and the secondary market has traditionally been inactive relative to the public markets. These securities are sold without registration under the United States Securities Act of 1933, as amended (the 'Securities Act') pursuant to the private placement exemption contained in Section 4(2) of the Securities Act. No resale of the notes may be made unless the notes are subsequently registered under the Securities Act or an exemption from the registration requirements of the Securities Act is available, such as that from the exemption provided by Rule 144A of the Securities Act relating to resales of the notes to QIBs.

Investors like the US private placement market because it has proven itself to be one of the safest asset classes for investors, particularly insurance companies, to buy investment grade fixed-income securities. Following the demise of Enron and other high-profile public issuers in the US public markets, executives at US insurance companies undertook strategic reviews of all their investments and learned that the performance of their private placement investments ranked among the best in their portfolios from a recovery and return perspective. Accordingly, these investors increased their allocations to the asset class following such reviews in 2002. Investors appreciate the ability to meet the issuer during the roadshow and certainly during investor due diligence, tailored documentation, which in senior note financings rank *pari passu* with bank debt and ongoing reporting and dialogue.

A growing market

The market for private placements has grown from US$16bn of total issuance in 1980 to almost US$839bn of outstanding issuance in 2005. Annual traditional private placement issuance reached US$45.7bn in 2003 as a result of historically low interest rates and other market factors we will further explore (see Exhibit 3.1). This expansion of the private placement market is attributed, in large part, to the introduction and growth of structured transactions including receivables securitisation and asset-backed securities as well as an increased volume of transactions by non-US issuers. Cross-border private placements have accounted for approximately half of all traditional issuance volume over the past three years.

Issuer appeal

The debt private placement market is available to issuers interested in raising from US$5m to over US$1bn principal amount. Issuers are attracted to the market for privately placed debt securities because it offers the following advantages:

- *Long-term, fixed-rate financing*. Although floating rate money is available, over 85 per cent of the total volume of privately placed debt is sold on a fixed-rate basis. By issuing fixed-rate securities, the issuer benefits from the knowledge that its cost of capital will remain constant until the maturity of the issue and, in the private market, these maturities can be significantly longer than maturities available in other markets – as long as 10, 20 or even 30 years.
- *No rating required*. Generally speaking, investors in the private market perform their own credit analysis and do not require issuers to obtain a credit rating. In certain circumstances a rating may be desirable in order to achieve optimal pricing and terms. If a rating is deemed necessary to ensure tighter pricing and terms, agents will assist the

Exhibit 3.1

Private placement volume

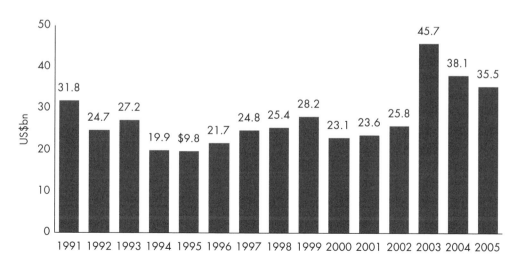

Source: Thomson Financial.

issuer in the preparation of materials and strategy with respect to the rating agencies. Such ratings are usually only required for structured notes, since the insurance industry regulator – the National Association of Insurance Commissioners or 'NAIC' – reserve the right to require one. For more information on the NAIC, please refer to the next section, Characteristics of a private placement issue – National Association of Insurance Commissioners.

- *Complex structures and 'story' credits*. The private market is especially attractive to issuers of 'story' paper where in-depth and sophisticated analysis is required to properly explain a credit. The private market allows the investor to hear a detailed description of a financing in a focused selling effort, rather than through a broadly disseminated document. As a result, the private market offers a source of capital that might not be available in other markets for complicated credits such as holding company structures, project financings, securitisations, asset-backed securities, leveraged buyouts, turnaround situations and leveraged leases.

- *Speed of execution*. Issuers have the ability to enter the market quickly since the private placement process does not involve Securities and Exchange Commission registration and generally includes a small number of investors. Interest rates are 'locked-in' as lenders commit to the financing and the documentation process follows. The entire process can be accomplished in eight to ten weeks for a typical first-time issuer and in as little as four weeks for well-known names or repeat issuers in the market. Since investors hope that issuers will issue more than once, documentation is increasingly drafted as master note agreements permitting future issuances.

- *Confidential market*. The private offering process can be tightly controlled. Information regarding the issuer is sent to a select group of sophisticated investors accustomed to treating offering information in confidence. While the majority of issues are executed on the basis of publicly available information, from time to time, offering materials do contain material, non-public information. By acceptance of offering materials, each prospective investor agrees to maintain the confidentiality of such information substantially in accordance with procedures adopted by such investor in good faith.

- *Flexibility of terms and structure*. Each private placement of debt securities is an individually negotiated, unique transaction. Maturity, amortisation, currency, issue amounts, economic compensation, covenants and other major terms can be negotiated to preserve management flexibility and to effectively pursue strategic business objectives and financial priorities. Such tailored solutions are unavailable in other bond markets, further enhancing the private placement market's value to issuers globally.

- *Expansion of investor base*. In the course of executing a private placement, an issuer's management can establish strong relationships with institutional lenders. These lenders develop an understanding of the issuer, follow the progress of the issuer and can become an important ongoing source of capital for the issuer in the future.

- *Documentation requirements*. Investors seem to develop long-term relationships with issuers. Each investor can invest anything from US$5m to US$150m. The majority of first-time private placement issuers are not well known to investors, so a good understanding of the issuer's businesses and financials is essential. Usually, only three offering documents need to be prepared: Private Placement Memorandum ('PPM'); Note Purchase

Agreement; and Investor Presentation. Depending on complexity and management's time availability, these usually take three or so weeks to prepare.

- *Transaction costs.* The expenses incurred in connection with a private placement of debt securities (legal, printing, miscellaneous, etc.) are typically significantly lower in total than those associated with a public offering. Credit analysts in the market are familiar with local generally accepted accounting principles (GAAP) practices and therefore do not require US GAAP reporting or reconciliation. Unlike the registered or 144A markets, auditor's comfort letters are also excluded. Similarly, opinions such as 10(b)5 letters are also not required. Documentation today is based on the Private Placement Enhancement Project's Model X, in the case of international issuers or guarantors (Forms No. 1 or 2), documentation resulting from industry-wide input. Such standardised documentation helps keep legal costs down as well.
- *Issue size.* Due to the relatively low level of expenses associated with private placements the private market can be more economical for smaller issues on an 'all-in' basis than other debt alternatives.
- *Timing flexibility.* In addition to being a relatively quick process, private placements offer the issuer significant flexibility with regard to both market entrance as well as the actual takedown of funds. The US private placement market is open year-round. Accordingly, depending on specific disclosure or other considerations, issuers can come to market at any time. Especially in this flat US dollar yield curve environment, investors in private placements can be quite accommodating to an issuer's funding needs, and structures incorporating delayed and/or multiple-stage takedowns are not uncommon. Investors are

Exhibit 3.2

Comparison of fixed income

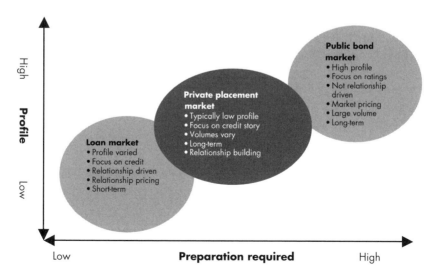

Source: HSBC.

willing to negotiate spreads over Treasury yields or actual coupon rates three, six or even 12 months in advance.

* *Minimal managerial distraction.* Issuer management teams are spared much of the time-consuming effort that is typically associated with a public offering of debt securities, as the lengthy Securities and Exchange Commission (SEC) registration process is avoided.

Characteristics of a private placement issue

Certain trends emerging in the recent private placement market environment have allowed for some generalisation of a typical issue. The following guidelines represent a summary of these characteristics.

Business

Issuers in the private market range from small private companies to well-known, publicly traded corporations across all industries, including companies in transportation, manufacturing, retailing, service, media and entertainment, natural resource, utility, banking and insurance industries, and many others. The unifying theme in the private market is that the issuer generally needs to provide an in-depth description to investors to be fully appreciated or does not want to get public credit ratings.

Geographic diversity

US insurance companies and pension funds have been investing abroad since the early 1970s. Historically, such investment activity took place in Canada and, to a lesser extent, Mexico, both of whom for regulatory purposes the NAIC classifies as 'domestic investments'. Investment in UK corporations is the largest and deepest among the geographies, having been one of the first markets outside of North America to attract strong interest from private buyers. This is the case since UK borrowers have used the US private placement market to fund or hedge US assets. Investors also became quickly comfortable with UK corporate legal jurisdiction, owing to well-established creditor rights. Accounting and business practices there also gained early praise. Since 2001, Australia, Ireland, Germany and other countries represented in Exhibit 3.3 have gained in investment popularity.

Structure

The private market will also accommodate various types of structures. The private market is capable of understanding complicated holding companies, special-purpose vehicles, private companies and foreign-based issuers (see Exhibit 3.4).

Credit profile

The majority of the transactions consummated in the private debt market are for companies with an A to BBB credit profile. While below-investment grade transactions had been rare in the early 1990s and common before that, a market for below-investment-grade issues has re-emerged. Companies with AA– or better credit qualifications and a relatively straight-forward 'story' have traditionally favoured the public market over the private market, where such issuers can often achieve lower coupon rates and less restrictive covenant packages.

The NAIC

The NAIC is an association of state insurance commissioners, formed to promote uniformity in the valuation of insurer investments. Every fixed-income investment held by an

---

Exhibit 3.3

2005 issuance by region

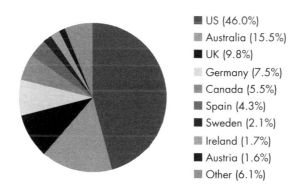

- US (46.0%)
- Australia (15.5%)
- UK (9.8%)
- Germany (7.5%)
- Canada (5.5%)
- Spain (4.3%)
- Sweden (2.1%)
- Ireland (1.7%)
- Austria (1.6%)
- Other (6.1%)

Source: Thompson Financial, HSBC.

Exhibit 3.4

Issuance by ranking

Holding companies	Very common
Operating subsidiaries	Very common
Special purpose subsidiaries	Very common
Sub Chapter S companies	Rare
Partnerships	Rare
Public companies	Very common
Private companies	Very common
US companies	Very common
Western European companies	Very common
Latin American and Asian companies	Very common

Source: HSBC

insurance company is assigned an NAIC rating. New issues without a formal credit rating are priced by investors based on their assessment of the NAIC rating. NAIC ratings are typically assigned after a deal is completed.

Types of securities

Investors in the private market prefer to purchase the senior debt securities of the issuer. Subordinated issues have been popular but have a higher coupon. The market does not always require that senior debt be secured, particularly if the issuer's bank debt is unsecured. In some cases, the market is receptive to private placements of convertible debt, as well as preferred and common stock.

Exhibit 3.5

2005 issuance by credit quality

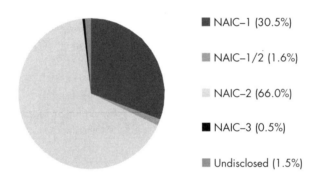

- NAIC–1 (30.5%)
- NAIC–1/2 (1.6%)
- NAIC–2 (66.0%)
- NAIC–3 (0.5%)
- Undisclosed (1.5%)

Source: Thompson Financial, HSBC.

Exhibit 3.6

Rating equivalent of NAIC designations

Designation	Rating equivalent	Reserve requirement (%)	
		Life	Property/Casualty/Health
NAIC-1	A− and above	0.4	0.3
NAIC-2	BBB− to BBB+	1.3	1.0
NAIC-3	BB− to BB+	4.6	2.0
NAIC-4	B− to B+	10.0	4.5
NAIC-5	CCC− to CCC+	23.0	10.0
NAIC-6	CC, C, D	30.0	30.0

Source: NAIC.

Exhibit 3.7

Issuance by type of security

Senior secured debt	Common
Senior unsecured debt	Most common
Special purpose subsidiaries	Common

Source: HSBC.

Issue size

Most debt private placements placed by the leading private placement agents are in the range of US$100m to US$250m principal amount. Most investment-grade issues below US$15m are typically handled by small boutiques that specialise in such smaller issues.

Maturity and amortisation

The majority of privately placed debt matures between five to 12 years. The market is, however, receptive to issues as short as two years and as long as 20 to 30 years in the case of some project financings, public utility issues and higher-rated issues. Amortisation is typically set to match the cash flows of the issuer and varies from transaction to transaction.

Interest rate

As mentioned earlier, over 85 per cent of debt private placements are structured on a fixed-rate basis. It is customary in the market to quote and price private debt issues in terms of a basis point (bp) spread above the yield on US Treasury securities with a comparable

Exhibit 3.8

2005 issuance by transaction size

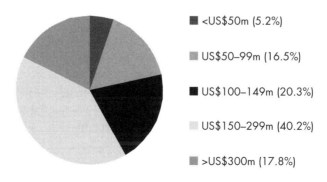

- <US$50m (5.2%)
- US$50–99m (16.5%)
- US$100–149m (20.3%)
- US$150–299m (40.2%)
- >US$300m (17.8%)

Source: Thompson Financial, HSBC.

Exhibit 3.9
2005 issuance by maturity

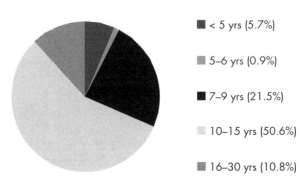

■ < 5 yrs (5.7%)

■ 5–6 yrs (0.9%)

■ 7–9 yrs (21.5%)

▓ 10–15 yrs (50.6%)

▓ 16–30 yrs (10.8%)

Source: Thompson Financial, HSBC.

average life. This spread varies with the credit quality of the issuer, the maturity of the issue, and the terms of the note agreement (covenants, all provisions, etc.).

Currency

US private placements are predominantly issued and funded in US dollars. However, non-US dollar financings can also be structured, with investors increasingly purchasing Sterling, Australian dollars, NZ dollars, euros and Japanese yen.

Callability and refundability

Since investors in the private market typically fund their investments with fixed-rate, fixed-term liabilities, they require protection against – or compensation for – optional prepayment of an issue. Investors are concerned about being prepaid in a lower interest rate environment. The private placement market permits prepayment by requiring the issuer to pay a Market Makewhole premium. The Market Makewhole is a provision designed to allow for prepayment by an issuer at any time, while ensuring that the investor is adequately compensated for the reinvestment risk resulting from such prepayment. This compensation takes the form of a premium over the face amount of notes prepaid and is calculated by discounting the remaining principal and interest payments of the notes by the current reinvestment rate. If the current reinvestment rate is less than the coupon on the notes a premium will result. Furthermore, the shorter the maturity the lower the premium.

Covenants

Covenant requirements vary from issuer to issuer and are negotiated with investors in each private placement transaction. Generally speaking, covenant restrictions in a private placement fall somewhere between the fairly 'loose' tests found in public offerings of debt securities and the relatively 'tight' tests typically associated with bank financings. Generally, issuers look to replicate the definitions and reporting requirements in their bank agreements.

Most senior bond transactions include both affirmative as well as negative covenants such as:

- compliance with laws, and so on;
- maintenance of properties;
- transactions with affiliates, and so on;
- line of business;
- asset sale and merger restrictions; or
- lien restrictions (negative pledge).

Typically, the private placement investors will seek to have the same or similar financial covenants as those of the issuer's commercial banks. Sometimes, ratios such as interest coverage or debt to earnings before interest, taxes, depreciation and amortisation (EBITDA) may be relaxed relative to prevailing levels, a concession to the tenor of the US private placement market.

For better quality senior debt issuers who provide no financial covenants to current banks, the market will often be satisfied with a most favoured lender provision. This provision has helped investors get comfortable with a lack of covenants while at the same time attracting it to the US private placement market issuers unaccustomed to providing covenants. Since the beginning of 2004, approximately US$8bn in volume representing about 30 separate issues carry most favoured lender provisions.

Private placement process

Transaction execution involves four phases with the agent guiding the issuer through each stage. The process itself is broadly consistent with other debt markets. However, issuers who have accessed both public and private markets have noted the US private placement market's transparency. Since the transaction is a direct offering to investors – as opposed to a sale to an underwriter who re-offers the securities – issuers get a much clearer perspective on investors.

The market for private placements

Growth of cross-border transactions

As the European private placement market develops, cross-border placements of private paper have become an increasingly important part of the market. In the first half of 2003, traditional cross-border issuance exceeded domestic US issuance for the first time.

Although dollar issues of private debt constitute the largest portion of placements, as issuers become more sophisticated and awareness of the private placement market spreads, companies are expressing an increased interest in Sterling, Australian and NZ dollars, euro

Exhibit 3.10

Typical transaction execution timetable

Transaction preparation	Marketing	Circling	Closing
▸ Prepare a detailed Information Memorandum ▸ Develop a detailed term sheet and Note Purchase Agreement with pre-appointed lenders' counsel and/or issuer's counsel ▸ Prepare an investor presentation ▸ Agent writes all marketing documents in draft to minimise the company's work load	▸ Information Memorandum sent to selected investors ▸ Initial marketing effort followed up by: - Management conducts direct meetings and /or conference call(s) with investors - Agents actively market the credit, answering investor questions, promoting credit strengths and giving price guidance	▸ Investors submit bids (amount, spread to treasuries and tranche, if applicable) ▸ The issuer, under guidance from the agent, decides on bond allocation for investors ▸ Transaction priced and coupon set	▸ Investor due diligence (site visit and meeting with management) ▸ Documentation finalised and financing closed

Offering process lasts between 7 and 9 weeks (although the process can be expedited)

Source: HSBC.

and Japanese yen denominated placements. Issuers benefit from receiving funding in their currency of preference and not having to incur swap costs. However, dollar denominated funding will remain dominant while there is the existence of dollar arbitrage opportunities and a relatively undeveloped European investor base.

Institutional investors

The market is comprised of a network of institutional investors including insurance companies, large pension funds, money managers and finance companies. Each major investor generally has a dedicated group of professionals to evaluate and purchase privately placed securities. This core investor base comprises approximately 50 to 60 insurance companies, 25 pension funds and money managers, and a handful of finance companies.

Strong pent-up demand

Despite consolidation in the US insurance market, volume capacity has grown, thereby at least keeping pace with issuance growth. Over the past few years, investment grade fixed-income issuance – both domestic and internal – has been met with ample supply of funds. Although the market has seen a few billion-dollar transactions, most are more modestly sized (see Exhibit 3.8). Issues are usually oversubscribed, with investors quite often severely cut back during bond allocation.

Exhibit 3.11
US and UK investor base

Non-dollar investors

Allied Irish Bank
AXA
ECM
Gartmore
Henderson Investors
Hermes
Legal & General
Morley FM
Prudential M&G
Standard Life

US investors

West and Northwest
Beneficial Life
GE Financial Assurance (GEFA)
Great West Life Assurance Co
Safeco Asset Management

New England and Canada
Cigna Corp
Hartford Life Insurance
John Hancock Mutual Life
D. L. Babson
Phoenix
Sun Life of Canada

Midwest
40/86 Advisors
Advantus
Aegon USA Investment Mgmt
Allstate Insurance Co
American United Life
AmerUs
Asset Allocation
Modern Woodmen of America
Mutual of Omaha Insur. Co
Nationwide Insurance Co
Northwestern Mutual Life Ins
Ohio Casualty Insurance Co
Ohio National
PPM America Inc
Principal Mutual
St Paul Companies Inc.
StateFarm Life Insurance
Stein Roe & Farnham
Thrivent

New York, New Jersey and Pennsylvania
Alliance Assurance Inc
Allianz
Delaware Lincoln Investments
Guardian Life Insurance Co
Metropolitan Life Insurance Co
New York Life Insurance
Penn Mutual Insurance Co

(Continued)

49

Exhibit 3.11 (*continued*)

> Prudential Insurance
> Swiss Reinsurance
> Teachers (TIAA)
>
> *California*
> Pacific Life Insurance Co
>
> *Southwest*
> AIG
> Pan American Life
> USAA
>
> *Middle Atlantic/Southeast*
> ING Investment Management Co
> Protective Life Insurance Company
> UNUM Provident

Source: HSBC.

Summary analysis

Exhibit 3.12 compares and contrasts fixed-income issuers' various financing options.

Exhibit 3.12

Comparison of alternative debt markets

	US Investment Grade	High Yield Public	'Public Style' Rule 144A Private	Traditional US Private Placement	Bank Market
Typical borrower credit quality	AAA to BBB–	BB+ to CCC	AA to B	A+ to BB+	AA to B
Credit rating requirement investor Base	Broad	Mutual funds and insurance companies	Both public and private buyers	Predominantly insurance companies	Banks
SEC registration	Yes	Yes	No	No	No
Required disclosure	Extensive	Extensive	Extensive	Limited to investors	Limited to investors
Interest rate	Fixed	Fixed	Fixed	Fixed or floating	Floating
Typical amortization	Bullet	Bullet	Bullet	Bullet/amortisation	Amortisation
Profile					
Typical maturity	Up to 30 years	Up to 20 years	Up to 30 years	Up to 30 years	Up to 7 years
Covenants	Non-financial[1]	Varies	Non-financial	Typically less restrictive than bank covenants	Generally restrictive
Timing	12 weeks	12 weeks	10 weeks	8 to 10 weeks	6 to 8 weeks
Prepayment	Yes (make-whole or predetermined call premiums)	Yes (following non-call period)	Unusual	Yes (make-whole or predetermined call premiums)	Yes (no premium)

[1] Non-financial covenants include negative pledge, merger restriction and, if applicable, sale-leaseback.

Source: HSBC.

Annex 1

Engagement letters

Once upon time, mandates in the US private placement market were sealed with a handshake. However, over the past several years, engagement letters have become both standard and consistent across the market. As bankers move from one institution to another (and lawyers from one law firm to another), these contracts are virtually indistinguishable from among the various agents.

These negotiated letters of engagement codify the following commercial and legal matters between issuer and agent(s):

1 *Exclusive engagement of the agent(s)*: the formal and exclusive engagement of the private placement agents on a best efforts basis, for a defined period of time, setting out the various services the agent(s) will provide. The issuer is directed to represent it will not offer substantially similar securities during the period of engagement for obvious commercial as well as US securities law reasons.

2 *Indemnification*: private placements are direct sales of securities by issuers to investors. Consequently, in the place of an underwriting agreement, engagement letters provide the various indemnifications each of the signing parties require in order to undertake the financing.

3 *Fees and expenses*: this section describes specifically what the issuer will (or will not) pay for and when it will pay.

4 *Disclosure*: this section describes the scope of the information contained in the offering materials. Issuers represent and warrant that the disclosure they provide in their offering materials essentially comports with Rule 10b-5 of the Securities Exchange Act of 1934, namely, that the offering materials are materially true in all respects and there is no information of material value missing.

5 *Termination and survival*: often called a 'tail', this section describes each signatory's ability to terminate the engagement. Usually engagements are cancellable within 30 days by either party. However, in the event that the issuer subsequently realises the financing with investors introduced to it by the prior agent, within a pre-specified period of time (typically six months to one year), the original agent(s) are owed a placement fee.

7 *Confidentiality*: the agent(s) agree(s) to use all non public information provided by the issuer confidentially and with the sole purpose of providing services agreed in the engagement letter.

8 *Governing law and submission to jurisdiction*: the vast majority of private placements are financed under State of New York law, so letters of engagement conform to the same.

Annex 2

Summary of principal terms and conditions

Issue: Senior Notes (the 'Notes').

Issuer: XYZ Inc. (the 'Issuer').

Final Maturity: Series A: 10 year bullet ($[ ] million due _____ 2016).

Series B: 15 year bullet ($[ ] million due _____ 2021).

Interest Rate on Each Series: Series A: [ ]%, representing a spread of _____ basis points over the relevant US Treasury Note yield at the time of commitment.

Series B: [ ]%, representing a spread of _____ basis points over the relevant US Treasury Note yield at the time of commitment.

Interest will be payable semiannually in arrears, on a bond-equivalent yield basis, assuming 12 30 day months per annum.

Use of Proceeds: To refinance existing bank indebtedness.

Ranking: The Notes shall rank *pari passu* with the Issuer's other senior unsecured Borrowings.

Optional Prepayment: The Notes are prepayable at any time in whole or pro rata in part. In the event of prepayment, the Company will pay an amount equal to par plus accrued interest plus a Make-Whole Premium of Treasurys plus 50bp.

Optional Tax Prepayment: If a change in tax law requires the Issuer to make additional tax gross-up payments on any Notes, it will have the right to prepay the affected Notes at an amount equal to par plus accrued interest plus a Modified Make-Whole Premium of Treasurys plus 100 bp.

Financial Covenants:

Total Borrowings to EBITDA The Company will not at any time permit Total Borrowings to exceed [ ]% of EBITDA.

Interest Coverage Ratio The Company will not at any time permit EBITDA to be less than [ ]% of all Interest Charges.

Priority Indebtedness The Company will not at any time permit Priority Indebtedness to exceed [ ]% of Consolidated Tangible Net Worth.

Other Covenants: Other covenants include merger and sale of assets; transactions with affiliates; maintenance of business; provision of financial statements and certificates; and so on.

Representations and Warranties: Customary representations and warranties.

Events of Default: Customary events of default.

Expenses: The Company and the Issuer shall reimburse lenders' reasonable expenses whether or not the transaction closes.

Lenders' Special Counsel: [ ].

Governing Law: State of New York.

Chapter 4

The bond markets

Focus on senior bonds, EMTNs, hybrids and high yield

Jean-François Mazaud and Andrew Menzies
Société Générale

Introduction to bonds

A bond is a debt instrument, which is a promise to repay an obligation, usually at par, on a specified maturity date. Specific features of a bond typically include the name of the borrower, a maturity date, an interest rate and the nominal value. During the life of a bond the borrower will typically make periodic interest payments of a set percentage of the par/nominal value (with the exception of a zero-coupon bond). If the borrower fails to make a specified payment, and defaults, it will be liable and bondholders may take legal action in order to recover the funds owed (principal and accrued interest). There are many different types of bonds, including senior bonds, EMTNs, hybrids and high-yield bonds.

Relevance of bonds

Sovereign issuers and agencies use the debt capital markets predominately to finance budget deficits. Financial institutions (FI) and corporates access the debt capital markets to raise finances for short-, medium- and long-term requirements and projects. FI and corporate issuers can raise both secured and unsecured debt (with the former type of borrowing backed by assets of the issuer).

Activity levels of debt issuance over the period 2000 to the end of July 2006 by major currency are shown in Exhibit 4.1, all in US dollar equivalent for ease of comparision. The US dollar market is by far the largest segment at US$3.6tn but the euro denominated market is the fastest growing market over this period (16 per cent per annum compound growth) leaving the sterling and yen markets as important but nevertheless niche markets.

Types of bonds

Much like with equity there are various levels of priority of debt. These levels can be broadly divided into senior secured, senior unsecured, senior subordinated and subordinated. The highest level, 'senior secured', is backed by various assets. Should the borrower default on the nominal or any interest payment, the investor can lay claim to their proportion of the underlying asset.

Exhibit 4.1

Value of debt issuance between 2000–2006

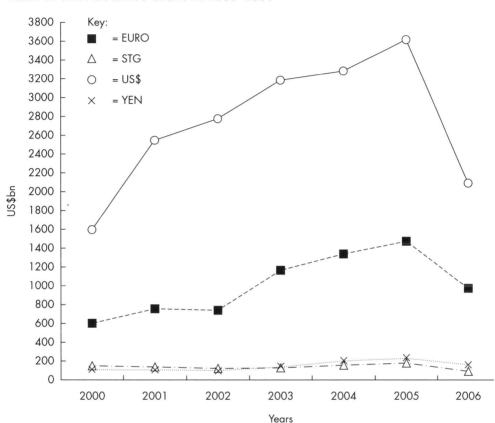

Key:
■ = EURO
△ = STG
○ = US$
× = YEN

Source: Author's own.

Below this level is the most common tier of debt issued, senior unsecured debt. There is no specified collateral against which the debt is backed but this debt is senior to subordinated forms of debt. Senior bonds and EMTNs make up the vast majority of this tier.

Junior to this tier are various forms of subordinated debt. Hybrid debt is within this tier. Hybrid capital is raised by issuing an instrument that is neither pure debt nor pure equity – the instrument has features of both debt and equity, such as preference shares or deeply subordinated debt. Given these hybrids carry equity features they rank subordinate to senior debt.

A high-yield bond is one that is rated 'sub-investment grade' by independent rating agencies. It is therefore deemed to be a riskier asset for an investor to hold since it is believed that the probability of default is greater on this instrument than that of a high grade or investment grade bond. Although the term is not used so often in today's marketplace, high-yield bonds are also known as 'junk bonds'.

Profiles of issuers

Issuers or borrowers can be divided into three broad categories. These are sovereigns and supranationals, financial institutions and corporates. The following entities make up these categories. An example of each entity has been provided in brackets:

- supranationals (EIB);
- sovereign governments (Republic of France);
- government agencies (KfW);
- regional authorities (Region of Lazio);
- banks (Société Générale);
- insurance companies (Allianz);
- other financial institutions (Nationwide Building Society); and
- corporates (Telecom Italia).

Profiles of investors

Investors buying bonds, risk or credit can also be divided into various entities. An example of each entity has been provided in brackets:

- central banks (Norges Bank);
- asset managers (Fidelity);
- money market funds (short-term funds within the large asset managers – CAAM);
- pension funds (AMF Pension);
- insurance companies (Generali);
- hedge funds (Bluebay);
- banks (Société Générale);
- corporates (Treasury departments); and
- wealthy individuals.

Leading players – league tables of banks leading bond issues

Although some banks try to compete on all products on a global basis, the majority of banks specialise in different jurisdictions on specific products. This strategy allows them to compete at a very high level within their chosen market. For example, Société Générale has focused on the euro capital markets as one of its three core areas. Within this market Société Générale aims to be the best provider of each and every product on which it has decided to focus. In the league tables shown in Exhibit 4.2, which are provided courtesy of the two most respected financial magazines in Europe and focus solely on the euro-denominated bond market, Société Générale has managed to obtain a high ranking in every area. As can be seen, Société Générale is a top arranger of bonds from corporates, sovereigns and supranationals, and also those from financial institutions.

Exhibit 4.2a

All international euro-denominated bonds

Rank	Managing bank or group	Total €m	Share (%)	No issues
1	Deutsche Bank AG	89,754	7.8	326
2	Citigroup	76,704	6.6	284
3	BNP Paribas SA	73,447	6.4	275
4	Barclays Capital	69,759	6.0	229
5	SG CIB	68,455	5.9	192
6	ABN AMRO	65,319	5.7	193
7	JP Morgan	63,329	5.5	237
8	HSBC Holdings PLC	46,034	4.0	165
9	Dresdner Kleinwort Wasserstein	41,682	3.6	157
10	Morgan Stanley	41,155	3.6	154
	Total	1,154,397	100.0	2,651

Source: IFR – 1 January to 31 December 2005.

Exhibit 4.2b

All bonds in euros

Rank	Managing bank or group	Total €m	Share (%)	No issues
1	Deutsche Bank	88,709	8.0	528
2	Citigroup	75,368	6.8	331
3	Barclays Capital	69,205	6.3	351
4	BNP Paribas	67,353	6.1	286
5	SG CIB	61,516	5.6	239
6	ABN AMRO	61,336	5.6	240
7	JP Morgan	60,784	5.5	325
8	UniCredit Banca Mobiliare	46,215	4.2	179
9	HSBC	44,745	4.1	179
10	Morgan Stanley	40,396	3.7	201
	Total	1,102,408	100.0	3,487

Source: EuroWeek – 1 January to 31 December 2005.

Exhibit 4.2c

Global securitisation in euros

Rank	Managing bank or group	Total €m	Share (%)	No issues
1	SG CIB	16,357	8.8	27
2	Deutsche Bank AG	15,682	8.5	30
3	ABN AMRO	14,042	7.6	22
4	BNP Paribas SA	11,676	6.3	18
5	Barclays Capital	11,645	6.3	24
6	JP Morgan	11,343	6.1	23
7	Citigroup	11,238	6.1	22
8	Calyon	9,050	4.9	25
9	Morgan Stanley	8,346	4.5	9
10	Merrill Lynch & Co Inc	8,316	4.5	13
	Total	185,024	100.0	207

Source: IFR –1 January to 31 December 2005.

Exhibit 4.2d

Global securitisation in euros

Rank	Managing bank or group	Total €m	Share (%)	No issues
1	ABN AMRO	18,345	8.8	81
2	SG CIB	15,989	7.7	82
3	Barclays Capital	15,592	7.5	84
4	Deutsche Bank	14,142	6.8	88
5	JP Morgan	13,449	6.5	111
6	BNP Paribas	12,715	6.1	61
7	Calyon	11,027	5.3	76
8	HVB	10,976	5.3	37
9	Citigroup	10,799	5.2	72
10	Morgan Stanley	9,292	4.4	27
	Total	209,077	100.0	776

Source: EuroWeek – 1 January to 31 December 2005.

Exhibit 4.2e

All international euro-denominated bonds for financial institutions (exclu. CB)

Rank	Managing bank or group	Total €m	Share (%)	No issues
1	Citigroup	31,536	8.9	115
2	BNP Paribas SA	21,333	6.0	95
3	Deutsche Bank AG	20,534	5.8	93
4	SG CIB	20,357	5.7	59
5	JP Morgan	16,533	4.6	69
6	Lehman Brothers	16,388	4.6	70
7	Barclays Capital	16,270	4.6	57
8	HSBC Holdings PLC	16,196	4.5	44
9	Calyon	15,877	4.5	61
10	Royal Bank of Scotland Group	15,324	4.3	97
	Total	356,138	100.0	1,028

Source: IFR – 1 January to 31 December 2005.

Exhibit 4.2f

All international euro-denominated bonds for financial institutions

Rank	Managing bank or group	Total €m	Share (%)	No issues
1	Citigroup	44,327	8.0	176
2	Deutsche Bank	35,497	6.4	248
3	Barclays Capital	35,062	6.3	180
4	SG CIB	31,453	5.7	91
5	BNP Paribas	27,625	5.0	118
6	JP Morgan	27,548	5.0	129
7	ABN AMRO	24,581	4.4	87
8	Dresdner Kleinwort Wasserstein	24,429	4.4	100
9	HSBC	22,973	4.2	81
10	UBM	22,135	4.0	82
	Total	553,729	100.0	1,869

Source: EuroWeek – 1 January to 31 December 2005.

Exhibit 4.2g

All international euro-denominated corporate bonds

Rank	Managing bank or group	Total €m	Share (%)	No issues
1	Deutsche Bank AG	14,469	12.3	61
2	BNP Paribas SA	10,510	9.0	59
3	Citigroup	9,922	8.5	49
4	SG CIB	8,566	7.3	45
5	JP Morgan	8,491	7.2	42
6	ABN AMRO	7,268	6.2	36
7	HSBC Holdings PLC	6,895	5.9	42
8	Credit Suisse First Boston	4,602	3.9	20
9	Royal Bank of Scotland Group	4,095	3.5	22
10	Barclays Capital	3,936	3.4	23
	Total	117,232	100.0	328

Source: IFR – 1 January to 31 December 2005.

Exhibit 4.2h

All international euro-denominated corporate bonds

Rank	Managing bank or group	Total €m	Share (%)	No issues
1	Deutsche Bank	14,694	12.5	72
2	BNP Paribas	10,147	8.6	59
3	Citigroup	9,927	8.4	55
4	JP Morgan	9,248	7.8	49
5	SG CIB	8,335	7.1	45
6	HSBC	7,170	6.1	42
7	ABN AMRO	5,889	5.0	31
8	Credit Suisse First Boston	5,535	4.7	26
9	Barclays	4,737	4.0	36
10	Royal Bank of Scotland	4,617	3.9	31
	Total	118,161	100.0	370

Source: EuroWeek – 1 January to 31 December 2005.

Exhibit 4.2i

All supranational issues – euro denominated

Rank	Managing bank or group	Total €m	Share (%)	No issues
1	Unicredito Italiano	3,147	15.2	9
2	Morgan Stanley	2,593	12.5	20
3	HSBC Holdings PLC	1,878	9.1	7
4	BNP Paribas SA	1,800	8.7	6
5	Credit Suisse First Boston	1,448	7.0	3
6	Barclays Capital	1,440	7.0	4
7	SG CIB	1,322	6.4	3
8	Deutsche Bank AG	1,311	6.3	12
9	JP Morgan	1,247	6.0	1
10	Lehman Brothers	726	3.5	8
	Total	20,680	100.0	86

Source: IFR – 1 January to 31 December 2005.

Exhibit 4.2j

All agency issues – euro denominated

Rank	Managing bank or group	Total €m	Share (%)	No issues
1	Deutsche Bank AG	15,252	12.4	32
2	SG CIB	10,473	8.5	26
3	BNP Paribas SA	9,772	7.9	29
4	JP Morgan	9,243	7.5	26
5	Citigroup	8,228	6.7	29
6	Barclays Capital	7,066	5.7	33
7	Morgan Stanley	6,352	5.1	14
8	Credit Suisse First Boston	5,752	4.7	16
9	Dresdner Kleinwort Wasserstein	5,446	4.4	16
10	Lehman Brothers	4,860	3.9	11
	Total	123,437	100.0	309

Source: IFR – 1 January to 31 December 2005.

Why use the bond markets? Common reasons for bond issuance

Financing of budget deficits

Many sovereign governments and agencies are unable to balance their public sector finances. In years of surplus, cash can be invested, saved or spent on projects, but in years of deficit, finance is required to meet the shortfall. Given that governments are unable to raise equity, the majority of their financing is done through the sale of bonds. In the UK, in 2006, 60–70 per cent of the national debt is financed through bonds and the remainder from National Savings, Treasury Bills (bonds with less than 1-year maturity) and short-term borrowing from the Bank of England.

Acquisition financing

Acquisitions can be funded through either cash or equity. Should a predator not have adequate cash reserves on its balance sheet, debt can be raised to fund the balance. In certain cases, acquisitions can be purely financed through new debt. In the context of a leveraged buyout (LBO), the private equity company leverages up the acquired company in order to finance the acquisition. Acquisition finance bonds, naturally, are closely correlated to periods of high volumes of mergers and acquisitions (M&A) activity. For example, in 2006, the number of corporate euro-denominated bonds issued in relation to an acquisition is expected to rise to in excess of 30 per cent compared to only 8 per cent in 2005. It should be noted that there is often a lag time between the acquisition and the bond issuance. In the interim banks often fund the acquisition through loan facilities called 'bridges'. These loans are usually refinanced through the bond markets since the banks do not wish to take such large exposure to single companies for a significant time period.

Project financing

Bonds can be launched in order to raise large sums of capital to make initial investments. Bond financing can raise the cash required to build new infrastructure such as a pipeline, mobile telephone network or electricity grid. Once the project has been completed, the cash flows resulting from the investment can be used to pay down the debt raised.

Capital raising

Many bonds are issued to raise finance for what is commonly known as general corporate purposes. The capital raised in such an issue can be used as the corporate wishes, such as to finance a pension deficit, finance an acquisition, raise money for internal investments or even pay equity dividends.

Increasing reserves

Borrowers may wish to strengthen the cash portion of their balance sheets. This can provide them with increased firepower when it comes to any future financing. Raising the money ahead of the project can be beneficial since it does not constrain the company in any manner and also investors will not hold the borrower ransom when they look to buy into the issue. In the context of an acquisition there can be a shift in the balance of power from issuer to investor as the investor knows that it is essential for the company to raise the capital and the issue cannot be delayed. Thus, with the extra bargaining power, investors can demand an increased premium.

Refinancing maturing debt

Should the borrower not have available cash reserves to pay down an existing bond which is maturing, it may wish to issue another bond with similar terms.

Taking advantage of low interest rates

Sustained periods of low interest rates create windows where issuers can opportunistically raise cheaper debt capital. Such an environment can lead to issuers pre-financing. However, given that issuers will have to pay for the carry of the capital in the period they would not normally be holding the debt on the balance sheet, issuers have to calculate whether the pre-financing is actually cheaper with the additional cost of carry than if they funded when actually required. Furthermore, interest rates could move even lower and so pre-financing decisions must be taken with caution. During late 2003 many corporate issuers pre-financed 2004 requirements, eventually leading to a 40 per cent reduction in investment-grade corporate Eurobond supply in 2004. In 2005, supply was down again a further 10 per cent. Year to date (YTD) supply in 2006 stands at €54bn, already 60 per cent of the total for 2005.

Pros and cons of using the bond markets

EMTN programmes

To understand the dynamics of the bond markets, it is important to explain the role of an EMTN programme. An EMTN programme is set up with banks prior to any issuance. They provide the general standardised documentation that would need to be provided in any bond issue. At the back of the programme would be the 'Final Terms' where the specifics on various bond issues can be entered. By having the programme in place prior to the issuance, much of the documentation process can be avoided near the issue date, thus rapidly speeding up the total time required to issue a bond. EMTN programmes are often set up for frequent issuers, that is, those that know they are likely to issue a number of bonds in a set period of time. However, there are significant upfront legal costs in creating a programme and, therefore, unless the borrower intends to issue frequently, it may not be cost-efficient to set up a programme. Should the borrower wish to issue a bond without a programme this is known as a Stand-Alone issue.

Senior bonds

The main advantage for the borrower of issuing plain-vanilla senior debt is that it is possible to raise large volumes of cash in a short space of time. For investors, they are able to take large exposure in certain credits within the primary market and gain substantial positions on their favoured credits.

In the secondary market, given the majority of bonds carry similar terms, conditions and legal documentation, investors can quickly trade in and out of positions. Furthermore, large issues support liquidity due to the increased volume of paper in the market and the larger number of investors that hold the paper. The main disadvantage to both the issuer and borrower is that the bond has to follow a particular form and thus cannot necessarily be structured to support specific requirements. These can be launched off an EMTN programme or executed on a Stand-Alone basis.

EMTNs

Such instruments can be almost the reverse of senior bonds. Their main advantage is that they can be tailored to meet the requirements of both the borrower and the investor. EMTNs are often sold on a reverse-enquiry basis where investors inform the borrower of what structure they are seeking to invest in. These structured and reverse-enquiry EMTNs can be sold in a more controlled market and would rarely be traded away into hands that are unfavourable to the borrower. Having said this, although many EMTNs are structured, many are also 'plain-vanilla' in format. These bonds can be sold into the market in a very short timeframe due to their simple nature. All EMTNs must be launched off an EMTN programme.

Hybrids

Hybrid debt is typically issued to achieve strategic objectives such as raising capital in acquisition financing, funding an under-funded pension fund, capital structure management or managing regulatory or rating agency capital. A borrower of hybrid capital enjoys the benefits provided by debt and equity in a non-dilutive and tax efficient manner. Hybrid capital benefits from the following features of deeply subordinated debt:

- coupons which are tax efficient despite the equity content;
- no dilution of earnings per share;
- no dilution of shareholders' existing voting rights; and
- instrument with a fixed charge.

Hybrid capital benefits from the following features of equity:

- rating agencies assign the benefit of equity content;
- improved leverage;
- if preferred, equity accounting can be gained; and
- equals equity when considering bank or private placement financial covenants.

High-yield

Such bonds provide capital for borrowers from a broad variety of industries and sectors. Initially, medium-sized companies with limited access to capital tapped the sub-investment-grade market. By the late 1980s, sub-investment-grade bonds became the financing tool of choice for LBOs, and in the 1990s, a permanent asset class and an indispensable source of capital for growing companies.

The main benefits of high-yield bonds are:

- they provide a market to companies where they can locate long-term capital;
- increased flexibility and fewer restrictions than bank debt;
- cheaper financing than equity or mezzanine financing;
- they can enhance a profile facilitating access to the capital markets or even lay the ground for an initial public offering (IPO); and
- they can provide investors with higher-yielding assets. This is particularly helpful during times that are characterised by low interest rates when investors struggle to locate assets that can match their yield requirements.

The main disadvantages of high-yields bonds include:

- they are expensive to finance in terms of interest payments and issuing costs;
- the non-callability of bonds for standard periods;
- amendments and the processes involved can be difficult;
- the burdens of current coupon payments are not alleviated by ratings upgrades resulting from strong business performance;
- public reporting requirements; and
- for investors such companies are more likely to default, thus potentially leaving investors with heavy losses.

Documentation, tax and accounting issues

Accounting, documentation and rating issues can generally be viewed from an international perspective. However, tax issues have to be treated on a local domestic basis given different countries have different tax treatments for different securities. This is an especially complex problem for an evolving market such as hybrid capital. The new International Financial Reporting Standards (IFRS) have provided common ground for the treatment of bonds from an accounting point of view and the international nature of the rating agencies makes the treatment similar regardless of jurisdiction. This is similar for documentation purposes. Increased legislation from international law and rule-making institutions such as the EU is leading to common and accepted ground for most issues.

Documentation

Before launching a bond the borrower should decide whether it expects to become a regular issuer within the market. If the bond is likely to be a one-off then the borrower should move ahead with what is known as a Stand-Alone issue. If the borrower believes they will access the market on a regular basis it would make sense to set up what is known as an EMTN programme. Although setting up an EMTN programme does cost money and takes time, it is beneficial in the long run (regarding both time and money) so long as the borrower returns to the bond market on a fairly regular basis.

Below we have highlighted the main documents required for a bond issue, for both a Stand-Alone issue and for an issue launched off an EMTN programme.

Standard documentation for a Stand-Alone issue includes an invitation telex, a subscription agreement, a fiscal agency agreement, the prospectus (offering circular) and some closing documents:

- *Invitation telex*: prepared by the bookrunners (lead managers). This contains a summary of the terms and conditions of the bonds and a brief description of the issuer.
- *Subscription agreement*: prepared by the issuer and the bookrunners. This contains the conditions of the subscription of the bonds.
- *Fiscal agency agreement*: agreed between the issuer and the fiscal and paying agent. The latter is the agent of the issuer during the life of the bonds towards the bondholders as regards, in particular, to the payments.
- *Prospectus*: contains the terms and conditions of the bonds and the information about the issuer.
- *Closing documents*: to be agreed by, and delivered to, the bookrunners. A certificate of no material adverse change of the issuer, legal opinions from the legal advisers to the issuer and from the legal advisers to the bookrunners, comfort letters from the auditors of the issuer.
- *Temporary and permanent global bond*: representing the bonds to be signed by the issuer and delivered to the fiscal agent on or before the closing date.

The documentation required for an issue off an EMTN programme would be identical with the exception of the Prospectus. In this scenario the Prospectus would be split into two documents, the EMTN programme (offering circular or prospectus) and the Final Terms (pricing supplement).

The EMTN programme (prospectus) is set up with banks prior to issuance. They provide the general standardised documentation that would need to be provided in bond issue. At the back of the programme would be the 'Final Terms' where the specifics on various bond issues can be entered. This format can save significant amounts of time to frequent issuers and allows them to launch and price new issues in a short timeframe. This lowers execution risk since the timeframe in which the bond issue is subject to external market conditions (that is between announcement and closing) is reduced.

Tax issues

As stated, tax issues, unlike accounting and rating issues, have to be treated on a local basis since different states have different treatments for bonds. There are no commonly accepted international tax rules. In general, however, bond coupons are tax deductible, that is generally quoted gross of income tax or withholding tax. This is one of the main advantages of such a bond versus a share dividend.

To highlight the difficulties of tax treatment, the development of the corporate hybrid market will be illustrated. As previously discussed one of the main features of the hybrid market is that of the equity content of the instrument. Therefore, at what point the coupon stops being a coupon and starts being a dividend can be a contentious point. In some jurisdictions, tax law contains several provisions that challenge the tax deduction on interest paid on debt with 'excessive' equity characteristics. Accordingly, the hybrid instrument needs to be structured in a way that ensures tax relief.

Accounting issues

As a general rule, bonds are accounted for as debt instruments. However, IAS 32 of the IFRS should be viewed to understand the reasons for treatment and the anomalies.

A financial instrument is an equity instrument only if both of the following criteria are met:

- there is no obligation to deliver cash or another financial asset or to exchange financial assets or financial liability under conditions that are potentially unfavourable to the issuer; and
- the issuer will exchange a fixed amount of cash or another financial asset for a fixed number of its own equity instruments.

Thus, an equity accounted debt instrument should have the following features or treatment:

- perpetual instrument – interest paid in perpetuity;
- redeemable non-cumulative preference shares – holder has right to require redemption;
- irredeemable cumulative preference shares – holder has right to receive dividends;
- compound instrument = part equity and part debt, for example, convertible debt; and
- split accounting required.

As such, the majority of bonds are treated as debt instruments, with the exception of some hybrid capital. Recent high-profile benchmark sized corporate bonds that have been granted equity treatment from an accounting perspective include Thomson, Sudzucker, Dong, Porsche and Vinci. High-profile corporate hybrids that have not been granted an equity treatment from an accounting perspective include Henkel and Bayer. The prime reason for this is these two issuers had 99-year non-call ten and 100-year non-call ten maturity structures (respectively). Each of the previous issues had perpetual non-call ten year structures (with the exception of Dong, 1000NC10). The maturity extension to perpetual from 99 or 100 years means the equity content is such that they can be accounted for as equity under IAS 32. It should be noted that if a hybrid instrument is classified as equity for balance sheet purposes, any coupon paid will be accounted for as deduction of equity (treated as dividend).

Sample termsheet

It is important for both investors and issuers to know how to determine the price of a bond because it will indicate the yield. Bonds can be priced at a premium, discount or at par. When you calculate the price of a bond, you are calculating the maximum price an investor would want to pay for the bond, given the bond's coupon rate in comparison to the average rate most investors are currently receiving in the bond market. Required yield or required rate of return is the interest rate that a security needs to offer in order to encourage investors to purchase it.

Fundamentally, however, the price of a bond is the sum of the present values of all expected coupon payments plus the present value of the par value at maturity.

In practice, a simple termsheet is used to underline the main features of the new bond in order to show how much the borrower has to pay to investors that are buying its bonds. Below we have provided three termsheets (see Exhibits 4.3, 4.4 and 4.5). It is important to note that all such data that have been provided are for the sake of example rather than to provide indicative terms for any specific borrower.

Termsheet – EMTN

In this case the termsheet could be identical to that of the FRN except the issue size would be smaller than a benchmark. Although the above termsheet indicates a FRN there are no restrictions and depending on requirements a fixed-rate note is just as likely.

Termsheet – hybrid bond

In this case a classic perpetual non-call ten structure has been outlined. However, as with the others there are no restrictions and the structure is flexible to accommodate a borrower's requirements.

Exhibit 4.3

Termsheet – senior fixed-rate bond

Tenor	5-year	7-year	10-year	15-year
Issuer rating	Relevant rating	Relevant rating	Relevant rating	Relevant rating
Issue size	Benchmark	Benchmark	Benchmark	Benchmark
Type	Fixed	Fixed	Fixed	Fixed
Maturity	Mon-09-May-11	Thu-09-May-13	Mon-09-May-16	Mon-10-May-21
Re-offer spread vs mid swap*	+35.0 bp/+40.0 bp	+45.0 bp/+50.0 bp	+60.0 bp/+65.0 bp	+85.0 bp/+90.0 bp
Mid swap rate	3.858%	3.996%	4.160%	4.332%
Government reference	OBL 3 1/2 04/08/11	DBR 4 1/2 01/04/13	DBR 3 1/2 01/04/16	FRTR3 3/4 04/25/21
Reference yield	3.682%	3.813%	3.937%	4.139%
Re-offer spread vs reference*	+52.6 bp/+57.6 bp	+63.3 bp/+68.3 bp	+82.3 bp/+87.3 bp	+104.3 bp/+109.3 bp
Coupon	4.250%	4.375%	4.750%	5.125%

*Euro-denominated corporate bonds are typically priced versus the European swap curve. For the benefit of additional information the relevant price versus the equivalent government bond is also provided (in Europe this would be the German Bund or French OAT). However elsewhere, such as in the Sterling market or US Dollar market, bonds are typically priced directly versus the relevant UK Gilt or US Treasury.

Source: Author's own.

Exhibit 4.4

Termsheet – senior floating rate note (FRN)

Tenor	2-years	3-years
Issuer rating	Relevant rating	Relevant rating
Issue size	Benchmark	Benchmark
Note type	Floating rate note	Floating rate note
Coupon frequency	Quarterly	Quarterly
Announcement date	01-May-2006	01-May-2006
Payment date	08-May-2006	08-May-2006
Maturity date	09-May-2008	09-May-2009
Re-offer spread	+30.0 bp/+35.0 bp	+40.0 bp/+45.0 bp
Issue/Fixed reoffer price	100.000%	100.000%
Index	3-month Euribor	3-month Euribor
Index yield	2.783%	2.783%

Source: Author's own.

Exhibit 4.5

Termsheet – hybrid bond

Tenor	Perpetual Non Call 10-year
Issuer rating	Relevant Rating
Type	Hybrid
Issue rating*	Two notches below senior rating*
Issue size	Benchmark
Maturity	Perpetual
Re-offer spread	+350.0 bp/+375.0 bp
Reference rate: mid-swap 10y	3.832%
Coupon	7.250%
Reoffer rate	7.33% − 7.58%
Announcement date	02-May-06
Settlement date	09-May-06
First call option	19-May-16
Step up	1.000%

*Indicates a typical subordination of corporate hybrids. The rating will depend on how subordinate to the senior rating the instrument ranks.

Source: Author's own.

Secondary market, trading and investors

Much like in the primary market, certain banks will specialise in chosen markets so as to optimise their ability to advise upon and execute deals for their clients. Banks will stream-line their research, sales and traders in a way that fosters the focus on a market. For example Société Générale, a bank that is focused on the euro capital markets, has developed an inte-grated debt platform where the research, sales and trading teams are focused on the euro-denominated market. At the bank a research team of 30 professionals analyses the credit of all types of borrowers which issue euro-denominated debt products. Although the research team is completely independent, their analysis and recommendations can be leveraged upon by a team of around 153 sales professionals who are based locally throughout Europe. Then, once sales has agreed upon a transaction with a client, they can go through one of the 16 traders which each focus on various products and execute the deal in an extremely short timeframe. In a rapidly moving and evolving market, the key to being a successful bank and, ultimately, profitable is speed of execution.

Secondary market

Much like with equity, bonds are traded in a secondary market in order to reflect differing views of relative value. By having customised trading platforms, investors can gain access to liquidity and thus ease their ability to enter and exit positions at short notice.

In order to create a common marketplace where bonds can be traded with ease, various indices have been established. Within the euro-denominated market, all bonds that are looking to be traded, will attempt to qualify for the iBoxx index. In order to gain qualification for such an index, the bonds must meet certain minimum criteria. For the sake of ease not all will be listed here, but maturity (all bonds must have a minimum remaining time to matu-rity of at least one year at the re-balancing date) and size (corporates must be a minimum of €500m) are common examples.

Certain investors are not allowed to invest in bonds unless they are included within the various indices. Thus, the importance of being included within the indices is underlined should the issuer wish the bond to trade in the secondary market.

The secondary market for hybrids is rapidly growing as the liquidity deepens with ever more instruments issued. However, given the relative nascence of the market and the small number of bonds it contains, liquidity is still light. Having said this there is a substantial amount of trading in the bonds that do exist because, given their high beta nature (expo-sure to volatility), the relative value of the instruments can swing quite dramatically.

In general there is no secondary market for MTNs. Their nature of being small and mostly privately placed means there is little knowledge and/or interest for bonds in the secondary market. Primary market investors tend to be buy-to-hold in nature and are not looking to profit from a swing in the relative value.

Trading

Most trading on the euro-denominated bond market is conducted over the counter (OTC) via the telephone rather than on domestic exchanges. Once a deal is struck, it is reported to TRAX before it is processed for settlement. Trade reporting must occur within 30 minutes of the transaction. TRAX is the system operated by ISMA (International Securities Markets Association) and is able to offer trade reporting, confirmations and operational risk management. It is not a settlement system.

Settlement of Eurobonds occurs through the two clearing houses, Euroclear and Clearstream and usually secondary trades settle T+3. Counterparties to the trade must have an access to an account at one of their houses. Given the international nature of the euro-denominated market and different public holidays, all parties involved will agree settlement details at the time of dealing.

Euro-denominated bond prices are quoted as clean prices, which are adjusted for accrued interest to convert them into settlement prices. The accrued interest calculation is generally actual/actual, although some Eurobonds use the actual/360 convention.

Investors

An excellent distribution among investors during the primary market is a key requirement for a successful bond issue. It is important to sell new bonds to the correct balance of buy-to-hold investors and trading accounts. A large amount of buy-to-hold accounts should be located in order to ensure stability of the bond's price in the secondary market and, at the same time, it is important to have some accounts looking to trade the paper in the 'book' so as to ensure liquidity in the secondary market. Therefore, it is import to mandate banks with an expert knowledge of the relevant investor base when selling bonds in the primary market. This is essential to secondary market performance.

Methodology for pricing

Credit quality

The pricing of a bond is primarily a function of the credit quality of a borrower. If an investor is looking to buy bonds from a borrower that is poorly rated and, accordingly, has a higher probability of default, they will require a higher yield to compensate for this risk. Thus, highly rated AAA government bonds are priced to yield far less than a high-yield or junk bond. Typically sovereign issuers carry the highest ratings, followed by financial institutions and then corporates.

Within the corporate market there are many sectors that would need to be considered. The sector within which the company operates is extremely important. For example, utilities tend to have extremely stable and predictable cash flows given their customers mostly pay bills on a monthly basis. On the other hand, a large DIY company may suffer from economic cyclicality since people are only likely to spend significant sums of money on big ticket items when they have large amounts of cash. Tobacco, pharmaceutical and chemical companies have all been in the press in recent years over litigation fears. A substantial court settlement against a company could have a considerable impact on the borrower's cash flows.

Exhibit 4.6

Worldwide bond markets

US

The largest investor base in the world

A highly developed public and private market

Investors almost exclusively USD focused

US domestic private market is typified by 5–10yr fixed rate amortising deals

The domestic public market usually sees 7–30yr fixed rate bullet transactions

ABS transactions constitute a growing portion of the US market with appetite seen for all asset classes in fixed and floating format

Major investor types:

   Banks — short-end, floating, senior investors

   Fund Managers – short to intermediate, fixed and floating, senior and subordinated investors

   Insurance – long term fixed buyers, buyers of yield so prefer sub debt investors

Also a growing hedge fund, Arbitrage vehicle and CDO investor universe. These investors have a preference for floating rate paper

Europe

Large and diverse investor base with significant institutional and retail interest

Largely EUR focused though there is significant GBP (in UK) and USD interest

Large institutional investor base in the UK, France and Germany dominated by insurance, banks and mutual funds

Significant retail investor bases in Benelux, Italy and Switzerland

Retail investors favour high quality secure names in shorter maturities (< 5yrs)

Institutional investors have a longer duration appetite to match liabilities and tend to look at more diverse issuers

Withholding tax is a major issue to investors buying transactions from Spain and Italy

Italian investors require passporting in order to buy non-Italian issues

Asia

Investor base dominated by branches of European banks

Increase in responsibility for regional product

Major focus on Asia/Pacific originated product

Major product types: Corporate, Wrapped, ABS, RMBS

Corporate/Wrapped interest out to 10yrs

RMBS/ABS interest < 3yrs

Increasing interest in subordinated RMBS product

Centralising of global portfolio purchasing for product originated in this region

Australia

Large and diverse investor base, mostly Banks and Asset Managers

Asset Managers are extremely active in corporate securities

Banks are extremely active in ABS/RMBS & 20% risk weighted assets

Asset Managers prefer shorter maturities (< 3.0 WAL) to put into their cash funds

Almost all product, both ABS and RMBS is issued in AUD

Periodical interest in fixed rate tranches

Strong appetite for the subordinated tranches of RMBS

Superannuation funds growth has seen a consistent demand for securities

Source: Author's own.

Interest rates

The level of interest rates will significantly affect the price of a bond. Bonds will need to offer increased yield versus the base level of interest rates. If this is not the case investors will place their money in the bank and receive more interest (yield) at a reduced risk.

Other factors

Other than understanding the credit quality (cash flows, cyclicality, leverage and so on), there are many other factors that need to be considered when pricing a bond. Maturity is a major consideration. Longer-dated bonds must offer increased yields versus shorter-dated ones since the chances of the investor receiving their nominal back many years in the future are greatly reduced. The nationality of a borrower can have an impact. For example, should a corporate from an emerging market wish to access the euro-denominated bond market, it is likely they would need to pay an upfront premium in order to entice investors into the deal. Although the nationality will be embedded within the credit risk, investors will differentiate from certain jurisdictions (they may have concerns over political risk). The size of the bond can influence the pricing. Should the deal be of benchmark size then the universe of investors that can invest in the bonds can grow substantially and, therefore, it may be possible to shave off a few basis points (bp).

Structural subordination will have a major influence on the pricing. Should the bond rank junior to other outstanding debt, investors will expect extra yield. A strong marketing campaign with clear explanations of the borrower's intentions for the capital and future corporate strategy may also assure bond investors about the credit quality. Roadshows (discussed later in this chapter) where investors are properly treated can save a few bp.

Distribution methods

Different borrowers have different strategies for issuing debt securities.

Sovereign issuers

Government bonds are typically sold through agencies that manage bond issuance on behalf of the government. In the UK, government gilts are issued by the Debt Management Office (DMO). Sovereign bonds are usually sold through auctions. Investment banks are only used to run a book system when the sovereign is looking to access an area of the market where they have previously not issued. Often this includes the first tranche of longer-dated bonds and inflation-linked bonds. For additional tranches the government agency tends to manage the sale.

The typical method used to sell the bonds is an 'auction'. Auctions usually happen on set dates that have been pre-arranged in a calendar. This way the market can understand the sovereign's borrowing requirements, plans and intentions for the coming year. Bids at auctions can be either on a 'competitive' or 'non-competitive' basis.

Competitive bids must be for a certain amount at a certain price. There is usually a minimum amount and then multiple amounts for which a bid can be placed. Competitive bids are then ranked in descending order of price and bonds are sold to the most competitive bids. Under this method the very same bonds can be sold at different prices. Non-competitive bids can also be placed in certain auctions. The price which is then determined is often derived by calculating the weighted average price at which all the competitive bids have been accepted. Bids can be rejected.

The success of an auction can be determined by looking at the 'tail' as well as the number of orders amassed during the auction. The 'tail' is the delta between the average price paid for a bond and the lowest price paid that was accepted for a bond.

Financial institutions and corporates

Non-sovereign borrowers tend to use one of two methods for selling bonds to investors. These include 'private placements' and 'book-building'.

'Private placements' usually occur for smaller bond issues. Under this scenario, the borrower and the investor can, together, 'tailor' the structure of the bond and thus it can be adapted to suit needs. In a private placement the bonds will typically be placed with a small number of investors (anywhere between one and 20, although the lower end of the range is more common). They can be sold to both institutional and retail investors. The main advantages to the borrower include:

- they do not have to embark upon extensive marketing exercises to sell the bonds;
- the bonds can be easily sold without a public rating; and
- the processes are faster since all the counterparties are already known.

Therefore, privately placed bonds are useful when an issuer is likely to access the market on a frequent basis for smaller amounts of money (prior knowledge of timing of bond sales is not required). Also documentation will be lighter, largely because the majority of privately placed bonds can be sold off the EMTN programme (EMTNs). Often these bonds are sold on a reverse-enquiry basis, that is, an investor can inform a borrower, usually via a bank, that they would be interested in buying a certain structure of paper from a certain issuer.

'Book-building', the same method that is used during an equity issue (IPO or Rights issue) is the common method utilised for the sale of public bonds by financial institutions and corporates. When a corporate decides to raise money in such a manner, it will mandate the deal to a syndicate of banks. These banks will leverage upon their relationships with investors to locate the optimal placement for the bonds. For a benchmark sized issue (in the euro-denominated market that is one with a minimum size of €500m), between three and four banks are commonly mandated to act as bookrunners on the deal. Often, co-managers, who tend to have no placement or allocation, can be mandated to allow the borrower to reward relationship banks.

Once the borrower has announced their intentions for the sale of the bond it will set indicative terms for the issue. These are likely to include price guidance and a rough size as well as provide a rough indication of the borrower's intentions with regards to the timing of launch. The books will be opened and investors will place orders through banks into the book. Banks will try to ensure that the book size accelerates and will release relevant announcements to support the momentum of the transaction.

'Pot' systems are becoming commonplace for transactions that utilise the book-building process. Under a 'pot' system the orders placed into the book are credited to all the bookrunners working on the transaction and, thus, the bookrunners should work seamlessly together for the success of the transaction rather than compete with each other for individual orders. This book-building process carries the following advantages:

- it is fully transparent;
- it enables momentum to be gathered thus allowing for substantial and progressive tightening of the spread during the process;
- it allows for the size, duration and funding cost to be optimised;
- it supports significant diversification of the placement during the allocation process.

As the book develops, the bookrunners will release updated information to the market regarding the size, timing of issue and any refinements to the price guidance. Once the bookrunners believe that the necessary numbers of orders have been garnered for the optimal deal, the book will be closed and the allocation process begins. The banks will try to ensure that the majority of the bonds are sold to high-quality accounts, typically those who buy to hold the paper rather than sell it in the market for a quick profit. Having said this, it is necessary to have a certain amount of liquidity in the secondary market. Thus, it would be inadvisable to allocate no bonds to hedge funds and bank trading desks. If there was unlikely to be any secondary market liquidity, especially on a benchmark transaction, many buy-to-hold investors may not put in orders in the first place.

Investor roadshows

Prior to public bond issues, whether for a sovereign, financial institution or corporate, the borrower's credit is often marketed to investors via a 'roadshow' (much like with equity issues). At the roadshow not only can investors learn about the borrower, their business and its credit, but the borrower can also gain an understanding of what sort of bond price and maturity might be popular with the investor community. A roadshow would typically involve one-on-one meetings with selected high-profile investors, group presentations and a conference call. This type of marketing campaign will maximise the breadth of demand and helps to ensure the most favourable pricing. This kind of marketing is essential to first-time issuers (inaugural), and not so necessary for regular issuers, although post a major credit event such as an acquisition it would be advisable.

Tapping

It should be noted that all borrowers can tap outstanding issues much like a rights issue. Yet again the borrower can choose to do this via a 'private placement' or through 'book-building'. Tapping is common when there is significant residual demand for previous bonds that have been placed and the borrower requires extra finance. By tapping an outstanding issue capital can be raised in a far cheaper and quicker manner than if the borrower was to launch a new bond altogether. It is essential that there is significant residual demand in the market for a bond in order to tap an issue because otherwise current bondholders may be disappointed because the new paper will supply the residual demand in the market rather than increase the relative value of their paper.

Listing requirements

The primary purpose of listing the bond on an exchange is to ensure its liquidity in the market. Should a bond not be listed, many investors will not be able to buy and sell into the instrument due to investment regulations and company policies. Thus, in order to guarantee liquid trading of the bond it is imperative to list the bond on an exchange.

As with tax law, different jurisdictions have different requirements depending on the laws and regulations that govern financial activity in that region. However, with the integration of the international financial, economic and political community, common ground is now being established in areas such as the EU, through requirements such as the Transparency and Prospectus Directives.

It is commonly accepted that the listing requirements in New York are more onerous than on the major exchanges elsewhere. Within Europe the majority of euro-denominated and Sterling bonds are listed on the London, Frankfurt and Luxembourg stock exchanges. The disclosure requirements on these exchanges are fairly similar since they are all within the EU.

A borrower may wish to list on an exchange where the disclosure requirements are more relaxed. However, when considering the listing it is necessary to also understand the requirements of investors. There is a chance that some will not be permitted to buy bonds that are listed off the major exchanges. In addition, investors may become suspicious as to why the borrower chose to list on an exchange where the information requirements are less stringent. This may have implications when it comes to pricing, or may even result in the borrower being unable to find any investors with which to place the bonds.

Chapter 5

Securitisation
Core concepts

Sriram Soundararajan and Silvio Angius
Lehman Brothers

Introduction

> *Securitization is the creation and issuance of debt securities, or bonds,*
> *whose payments of principal and interest derive from cash flows gener-*
> *ated by separate pools of assets.*[1]

> *Securitisation is a method of funding receivables of any kind and involves*
> *producing bearer asset-backed securities which can be freely traded and*
> *are secured on the portfolio of receivables.*[2]

There are several ways in which securitisation can be defined, but as the definitions above illustrate, the basic concept is fairly straightforward. It is a form of secured funding in which a specific pool of assets is funded by issuing bonds whose cash flows and credit perfor- mance are directly and almost solely dependent on the performance of the assets. While different forms of secured funding have been around for many years, securitisation as a capital market asset class was born in the 1970s in the United States. Since then the market has grown and expanded globally and is estimated to issue $2 trillion new bonds each year. Clearly, securitisation has now established itself as a significant part of the global fixed- income market and is likely to grow and develop even further. In this chapter we will try to get an understanding of the basic concepts behind securitisation, who does it and why, how it is structured and how the risks and returns are measured.

A brief history of securitisation

It would be difficult to pinpoint the exact time when the basic concept of securitisation originated in the financial markets. The idea to lend money that will be paid back from a dedicated pool of assets was used even as far back as the twelfth century by merchant bankers in parts of Europe.[3] However, securitisation in modern capital markets was born in the 1970s when the government mortgage agencies in the United States (Freddie Mac, Fannie Mae and Ginnie Mae) started to issue pass-through mortgage backed certificates to investors. These certificates mainly transferred the risk of the timing of cash flows from the fixed-rate mortgages onto the capital markets while the agencies retained the credit risk or the risk of the borrowers of the mortgages defaulting on their payments. By the early 1980s the private sector started using the technique to fund mortgages that would not qualify for an agency pool. The market rapidly evolved and other assets including auto loans, credit card receivables, aircraft leases and so on were being securitised. Today, the US market issues more than a trillion dollars of securitised bonds each year, of which agency mortgages constitute the most significant share.

The concept did not travel across the Atlantic until the early 1990s and for nearly a decade the market remained fairly niche and small, mainly confined to a few transactions in the UK. By the late 1990s the market started growing in earnest and the introduction of the euro further helped the growth into Europe. The market has truly come of age in Europe in the current decade, growing at an average annual rate of 25 per cent over the past five years from 2000. Today the market issues about €350bn a year and has close to a trillion euros of bonds outstanding. The UK remains the dominant player accounting for 40 per cent of issuance and among the assets, mortgages again dominate. From about 2003, securitisation has been expanding fairly rapidly into other regions as well, including Asia, the Middle East and eastern Europe.

Investment banks now concentrate significant resources in structuring and distributing securitisations. In fact, some investment banks have also moved into the business of generating assets such as sub-prime mortgages with a view to securitising them. Exhibit 5.1 gives the leading investment banks involved in the global securitisation markets.

Exhibit 5.1

Bookrunners of worldwide structured-finance deals in 2005

	2005			2004		
	Issuance (US$m)	No. of deals	Market share (%)	Issuance (US$m)	No. of deals	Market share (%)
Lehman Brothers	176,521.2	263	8.5	124,166.9	229	8.4
Bear Stearns	146,867.7	269	7.0	124,267.3	237	8.4
Royal Bank of Scotland (Greenwich)	146,813.3	237	7.0	110,515.6	216	7.4
Credit Suisse	144,462.6	243	6.9	118,346.0	233	8.0
Deutsche Bank	141,942.5	261	6.8	91,124.8	213	6.1
Citigroup	141,876.6	235	6.8	114,168.6	225	7.7
Morgan Stanley	134,888.2	175	6.5	90,600.3	179	6.1
Merrill Lynch	127,755.6	186	6.1	78,613.0	145	5.3
Banc of America	118,308.0	200	5.7	102,273.0	183	6.9
J. P. Morgan Chase	117,941.3	180	5.6	80,015.9	153	5.4

Note: Includes ABS (asset-backed securities), MBS (mortgage-backed securities), CMBS (commercial mortgage-backed securities) and CDOs (collateralised debt obligations).

Source: Asset-Backed Alert.

Exhibit 5.2a Global securitisation volumes (2005)

Securitisation issuance volumes

Exhibit 5.2b Securitisation volumes in Europe

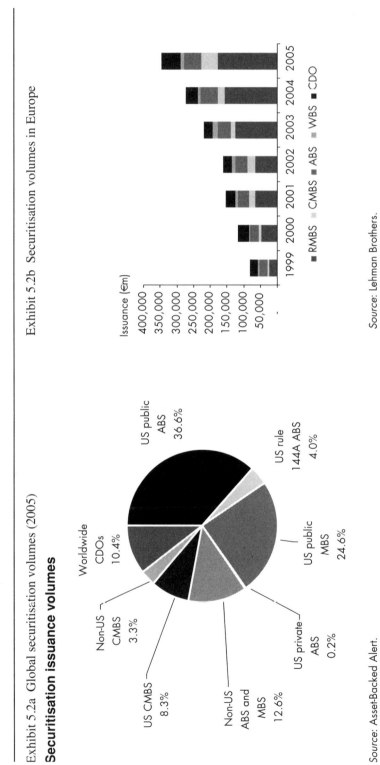

Issuance (€m)

Worldwide
CDOs
10.4%

US public
ABS
36.6%

US rule
144A ABS
4.0%

US public
MBS
24.6%

US private
ABS
0.2%

Non-US
ABS and
MBS
12.6%

US CMBS
8.3%

Non-US
CMBS
3.3%

400,000
350,000
300,000
250,000
200,000
150,000
100,000
50,000
-

1999 2000 2001 2002 2003 2004 2005

■ RMBS ■ CMBS ■ ABS ■ WBS ■ CDO

Source: Asset-Backed Alert.

Source: Lehman Brothers.

What can be securitised?

There have been a plethora of assets that have been securitised. Practically any asset that produces a predictable stream of cash flows can be securitised. The market started with mortgages and even today residential mortgages form the largest part of the securitised asset classes. RMBS (residential mortgage-backed securities) and CMBS (commercial mortgage-backed securities) form the largest two sectors in the securitisation markets. Other assets that have proven popular in the securitisation market include credit card receivables, auto loans, leases and corporate loans. The actual list of assets that have been securitised include several more esoteric assets including insurance contracts, pubs, government tax claims, utility bills and so on (see Exhibit 5.3).

The basic concept and structure

A securitisation typically involves the sale of assets by the originator to a special purpose vehicle (SPV) which issues bonds to fund the purchase of these assets. The bonds are then paid interest and principal from the cash flows that the assets generate and carry the risks of the asset performance. An SPV is a bankruptcy-remote company whose sole purpose is to purchase the assets and issue the bonds under the securitisation. It helps isolate the assets from the rest of the originator's balance sheet and insulates the bonds from any risks other than those directly related to the assets. The originator usually retains some functions, mainly that of servicing the assets, and gets paid a fee for the same. Exhibit 5.4 shows a typical structure of a securitisation.

Exhibit 5.3

List of some of the assets that have been securitised

Aircraft leases	Manufactured housing loans
Auto leases	Medical equipment
Auto loans	Motorcycle loans
Boat loans	Railcars
Catastrophe loans	Recreational vehicle loans
CDOs	Rental cars
Consumer lines of credit	Royalties (for example, music)
Credit cards	Small business loans
Dealer floorplans	Student loans
Defaulted credit cards	Sub-prime autos
Equipment leases	Tax liens
Emerging market receivables	Trade receivables
Excess spread	Trucks
Export receivables	Utility bills
Franchise loans	Whisky/champagne stock
Health care receivables	

Source: Author's own.

Exhibit 5.4

Typical securitisation set-up

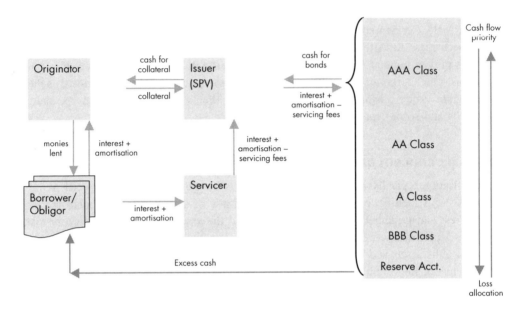

Source: Lehman Brothers.

The SPV can issue several kinds of bonds depending on the exact structure of the deal. Often bonds are tranched into different levels of credit: that is, bonds carry different levels of exposure to the risk of losses from the assets. The most junior bonds in the structure carry the greatest exposure to losses and are the riskiest. The bonds that are above this in the transaction structure carry lower risk since they will not be affected till the junior bond gets completely written off due to losses. Apart from bond subordination, other external enhancements can be provided to improve the credit quality of the bonds. The bonds are rated by the credit rating agency based on the quality of the securitised assets and the structural protections that are provided. Often, since the risks are purely those of a well diversified pool of assets, a significant portion of the bonds can be tranched to have the least risk and are rated triple-A by the rating agencies. Apart from credit tranching bonds can be designed according to other aspects. For instance, bonds can be tranched to have the same credit but different maturities, or tranched to receive only certain cash flows such as principal, interest or prepayment cash flows. In fact, one of the key benefits of a securitisation is the ability to design bonds with specific risks characteristics.

There are other features associated with securitisations, including hedging mechanisms to remove some or all of the interest rate and currency risks that exist between the assets and the liabilities (the bonds). There are also other participants in the transaction including a trustee and administrator who oversee the cash flows in the transaction and ensure that the transaction documentation is followed. They do not have any managerial control on the assets or liabilities but can only carry out the instructions in the deal documents. While this is an advantage that a securitisation structure provides, by removing management uncertainties, to some extent this is also a disadvantage, since there is less that one can do to improve asset performance in case of a worsening in performance. Also, there are often more legal risks surrounding securitisations due to the significance of the documentation and its execution.

Structuring a securitisation – the nuts and bolts

The basic securitisation structure is summarised in Exhibit 5.4 and, as mentioned earlier, the transaction structure at the issuer SPV level helps design the type of bonds that are issued. The most common type of structures in Europe include:

- *Stand-alone pass-through structures*. Stand-alone deals usually have one pool of assets supporting one series of bonds, with the bonds being paid off as and when the assets pay down. In a purely pass-through structure, all cash flows received from the assets are passed onto the liabilities in a certain priority.
- *Stand-alone revolving pool structures*. These are similar to the above structure, except in this case the principal cash flows that come from the assets are used to purchase new assets instead of being passed onto the bonds. During the revolving period, the asset balance is maintained at the same level by purchasing new assets. At the end of the revolving period the transaction is either terminated or it switches to a pass-through structure. The main advantages of revolving pools are that it helps reduce prepayment risk on the bonds and it also gives the originator funding over a longer term.
- *Master trust structures*. This is a more sophisticated form of transaction structure that was first created in the United States for the credit card market. In this structure a common revolving pool of assets is used to support different series of bonds issued at different points in time. The bonds can be designed to have different amortisation profiles and cash flows are revolved (to purchase new assets), accumulated (to meet an expected bond amortisation) or passed through as required. Such structures are more expensive to set up initially but offer originators much greater flexibility in the types of bonds that can be issued. Investors also benefit from the increased liquidity of the bonds from master trust, which comes from the fact that all the bonds from the trust are backed by the same pool of assets.

The transaction structure helps channel the risks from the assets to liabilities and it does this through the use of several features. There are several such characteristics of a transaction structure that enable such liability risk and maturity tailoring, and we highlight a few of the key ones below.

- *Cash flow waterfall*. This is the sequence of how cash should be distributed to the various participants in the transaction and to the bonds. Transaction can either have separate waterfalls for interest cash flows and principal cash flows or use a single combined water-fall. The normal priority of payments is interest cash flows first, from the most senior bond to the junior bonds followed by principal cash flows again from the senior to the subordinate bonds. The waterfall can also separate different sources of cash flows and tie them to different bonds. For instance, in some UK RMBS deals all prepayment penal-ties that are collected from borrowers are collected separately and paid to a single tranche.

- *Credit enhancement and loss allocation mechanisms.* There are various ways in which losses are absorbed and allocated in a deal. The first layer of protection is the 'excess spread' which is effectively the excess interest cash flows in the deal left after paying all the dues to the bonds. If the excess spread proves insufficient, losses would then be absorbed by a 'reserve fund' that is in place at the bottom of the transaction. This is just a cash reserve put in place by the originator to absorb losses ahead of it reaching the bonds, and once the reserve fund has been depleted any losses would result in a write down of the bonds starting from the most junior. Normally there are mechanisms such as deficiency or loss ledgers to keep a track of losses so that any gains or cash flows that occur in the future can be used to write down the level of recorded losses. This 'bottom-up' approach to loss allocation is what gives a transaction a senior-subordinate structure.

- *Revolving or lock-out periods.* Structures can incorporate revolving periods during which principal payments received from the assets are used to purchase further assets or can have lock-out periods when principal is just accumulated without being passed onto the bonds. Such features help reduce the prepayment risk on the bonds and also help control the average life[4] or maturity of the bond.

- *Optional redemption calls.* Another feature that helps originators control the average life of the bonds and the transaction is the redemption option. Many originators retain the option to redeem the remaining bonds from a certain point in time. This could either be from a specific date or from when the asset balance has reduced to a certain level. The maturity of the bond is often computed assuming that this option will be exercised, thereby limiting its life. Otherwise, bonds would be outstanding as long as the assets are outstanding, which is normally several more years away.

- *Liquidity facilities, reserves and hedges.* The bonds in a securitisation are often sheltered from most risks apart from those arising from the credit quality of the assets themselves. To this extent transaction structures often have interest rate and currency swaps to elim-inate risks arising from differences in the asset and liability characteristics. Also, transactions sometimes feature liquidity facilities, which ensure that temporary cash flow disruptions are not transferred from the assets to the liabilities.

The choice of the type of structure to be used and the features it should incorporate depend on a variety of factors including the level of risk that needs to be transferred, the type of assets and the risks they carry, the originator's funding and asset-generation strate-gies and, most importantly, on what type of liabilities are in demand from investors. As the market has grown, structures have become more sophisticated in order to cater to the different demands of the investors and issuers and this evolution is expected to continue over time.

The issuer's perspective – why securitise?

There are several reasons why originators choose securitisation as a funding tool. All originators take advantage of securitisation as an additional source of funding that offers them exposure to a different and diverse investor base as compared to the typical equity and debt markets. Securitisation also tends to be a relatively cheap source of funding and helps originators better manage their risk. Each type of originator usually finds a different aspect of securitisation advantageous.

Corporates usually find the cost of funding of a securitisation as the main advantage. For many regular asset classes such as auto loans and credit card receivables, a significant portion of the bonds issued through a securitisation are triple-A rated and hence the overall interest costs of the bonds tend to be quite low. The corporates themselves are often rated well below the triple-A level, making it more expensive for them to issue straight corporate debt. For instance, General Motors and Ford are two fairly frequent issuers of securitisations. In 2005, both these firms had their ratings downgraded to well below investment grade and their corporate debt cost them anywhere between 300 basis points (bp) to 500 bp of spread over the London interbank offered rate (Libor). In comparison, a securitisation of their auto loans completed in the same period would have cost them just around 30 bp over Libor. Thus, funding costs tend to be a significant factor for lower-rated corporates and financial firms, as well as for some lower-rated banks.

For banks, especially those with higher ratings, one of the main reasons to securitise is the ability to free up regulatory capital by transferring the risk associated with the assets. Banks are expected to have some risk-based regulatory capital held against the assets that they hold on balance sheet. This is mainly to protect the depositors from deterioration in the bank's asset quality. In a securitisation, since the assets and the risks associated with them are transferred to the capital markets, the banks can reduce their regulatory capital suitably. This, however, is a simplification. In most securitisations, the originating bank retains a significant portion of the risk by retaining the first loss or equity portion of the transaction. Despite this, a securitisation was considered as a complete transfer of risk under many earlier and some current regulatory regimes. This gave rise to the concept of 'regulatory capital arbitrage' where the bank can reduce the regulatory capital required without a commensurate reduction in risk. More recently, the regulatory regime is in the process of being changed under the new 'Basel II' regulation. Under the new regime such an arbitrage will go away to some extent since it would recognise and punish any retained risk exposure. Despite this, the basic idea of risk transfer would still be a compelling reason for banks to choose securitisation as a funding tool. With the change in the regulatory regime, banks are now using securitisation to maximise the use of economic capital. In other words, banks are now using securitisation to better manage their risks and transfer those for which they get adequately compensated in the capital markets.

Securitisation also offers smaller firms an efficient means of increasing leverage. In many areas, securitisation has helped firms build up a relatively reasonable sized business with a small amount of capital. Such firms typically use securitisation as a means of funding their assets and retain a small portion of equity. In the UK, for instance, many sub-prime mortgage lenders use securitisation as their primary source of funding and use the tool to grow the business through leveraging a small amount of capital.

Another area where both banks and corporates can feel the benefit of securitisation is in asset and liability management. For instance, a bank that funds their mortgage lending by issuing corporate bonds will be faced with the risks associated with the different interest and repayment profiles of the mortgages and the debt. In a securitisation, the cash flows from the assets can be directly transferred to the bonds or can be repackaged in several ways and then passed onto the bonds. This obviously helps the originator better manage their asset and liability positions.

In Europe, a significant portion of issuance to date has come from the large commercial banks (see Exhibit 5.5). However, other players also actively participate in this market including corporates, financial firms such as leasing companies and even the European governments.

The investor's perspective – why buy asset-backed bonds?

There are a variety of reasons as to why investors are attracted to asset-backed bonds. The main advantage with the securitised markets is that it allows investors to choose the level of risk that they would like to take. Any transaction can be structured to offer bonds that carry different levels of risk or ratings. With most granular consumer asset classes transactions carry a significant portion of triple-A rated bonds. The market thus offers investors a fairly safe asset class: away from the government bond markets, the asset-backed market is one place where investors can get a significant volume of triple-A rated bonds. It also offers investors direct access to consumer risk through assets such as residential mortgages,

---

Exhibit 5.5

Originators of securitisations in 2005 (total volume issued – 347m)

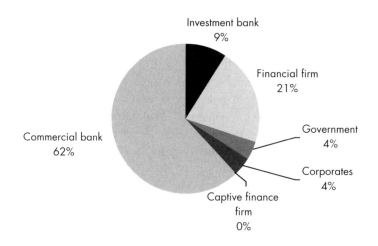

Source: Lehman Brothers.

---

credit card receivables and auto loans and other forms of risk that are otherwise not easily accessed, such as commercial property, small and medium enterprise risk, and so on. Last but not least, securitisations are free from corporate governance and management issues, the often unpredictable part of corporate bond exposure. The risks in securitisations are thus directly related to the assets and are both measurable and predictable.

In Europe the asset-backed markets consist largely of floating rate bonds. The market was, and is still, seen by banks looking to invest cash in safe assets, as a more valuable alternative to commercial paper and bank floating rate paper. Banks are thus the most significant part of the investor base for securitised products in Europe. This remains true at the triple-A part of the market even today. In the riskier part of the market, that is, for bonds rated single-A or triple-B, banks were again dominant in the early years. However, when the corporate markets went into a downturn in the early part of the decade, many asset managers and even CDOs started to notice the relative value in switching into asset-backed bonds. In recent years, they have started to form a more significant part of the investor base for the lower rated bonds (see Exhibit 5.6). In a further extension of this trend, as most high-risk asset classes across the world, including emerging markets and high-yield bonds, are yielding very little, many hedge funds and leveraged investors have started to participate in the sub-investment-grade part of the securitisation market. In fact, there has never been a better time over the past several years for originators to dispose of their risk in the capital markets. However, with the increase in the investor base, the difference in the pricing of asset-backed bonds and other fixed-income securities has started to compress. Thus while in earlier years asset-backed bonds clearly offered significantly better value than other markets, more recently the relative value of the sector, while still positive, has decreased (see Exhibit 5.8).

With the Basel II regulation coming into play, the regulatory capital that a bank investor would have to hold against an asset-backed bond would be much lower than other assets including corporate bonds. For instance, an investor buying a triple-A rated mortgage-backed bond would have to hold only 0.56 per cent of regulatory capital against it, whereas with a corporate bond the requirement would be as high as 8 per cent. This advantage would see the participation of banks in the market go up as the regulation is slowly implemented.

Risks and returns – pricing an asset-backed bond

Similar to many other securities in the bond market, asset-backed bonds carry the following risks:

- credit risk – the risk of the assets not performing or defaulting on payments;
- liquidity – the risk of being able to convert the bond to cash when needed; and
- mark-to-market risk – the risk of the price of the bond fluctuating over its life.

In addition, asset-backed bonds also carry the following risks:

- prepayment risk – the risks surrounding the timing of principal cash flows; and
- extension/contraction risk – the risk of the transaction or the bond terminating earlier or later than anticipated.

Exhibit 5.6

Distribution of the investor base for securitisations in Europe

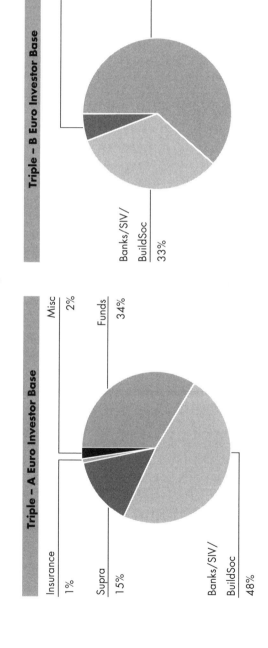

Triple – A Euro Investor Base

Misc
2%

Funds
34%

Insurance
1%

Supra
15%

Banks/SIV/
BuildSoc
48%

Triple – B Euro Investor Base

Supra
6%

Funds
61%

Banks/SIV/
BuildSoc
33%

Source: Lehman Brothers.

Exhibit 5.7

List of the largest investors in the global securitisation markets in 2005

Investor	Amount (US$bn)
HBOS Treasury Services	54.0
ING Investment Management	50
Citigroup	45
J. P. Morgan Chase	41.9
Merrill Lynch	35.5
Bear Stearns	30.5
Fannie Mae	26.9
Aegon	25
Freddie Mac	21.7
Dresdner Kleinwort	20
Gordian Knot	19.2
HSBC	18

Source: Asset-Backed Alert.

The first three are risks common to most asset classes. The credit risk of the bond is captured through its rating, where available. Despite this, credit risk and even the liquidity and market risks are usually factored into the bond's price based on what the market perceives is the expected magnitude of each of those risks. Exhibit 5.8 shows the indicative discount margin (margin over the Libor rate) that investors would like to receive for some asset-backed bonds. As we can see, the margin is higher for lower-rated bonds since the credit risk is expected to be higher for such bonds. However, even within a rating category the margin varies significantly across the bonds based on the risk of the assets backing them. Investors perceive differences in the underlying risk even within a rating category and trade the bonds accordingly. Furthermore, the liquidity of many parts of the asset-backed markets in Europe is still perceived to be lower than the corporate markets and, consequently, such bonds require slightly more margin to compensate investors.

Apart from these risks, asset-backed bonds also carry prepayment risk or the risk around the actual timing of principal cash flows. All assets have a schedule for the repayment of principal that is normally known at the time of securitisation. However, many assets, such as residential mortgages or corporate loans, can be prepaid ahead of the agreed schedule. Such prepayments need to be handled by the transaction structure. In many cases transaction structures just simply pass through all cash flows onto the bonds, making the bonds sensitive to prepayments. In other words, if, as and when the assets are prepaid, the principal is used to pay down the bonds. When the bond pays a fixed coupon, prepayments introduce reinvestment risk. To explain this further – the price or the yield earned on a bond normally incorporates a schedule of principal payments and an assumption that principal received will be reinvested at prevailing rates. Thus, if principal is received earlier or later than scheduled, it will influence the returns on reinvestment depending on the interest rates at that time of the prepayment. This, in turn, influences the yield earned on the bond.

Exhibit 5.8

Spreads in European securitisation markets

a. Bond spreads by rating category

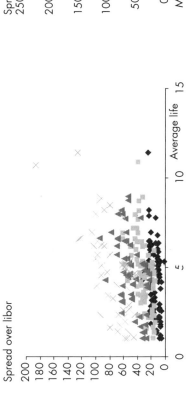

b. ABS and Corporate spreads in Europe

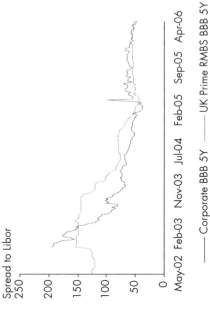

Source: Lehman Brothers.

It is prepayment risk that makes pricing of asset-backed bonds different from other securities. This is further complicated in situations where the level of prepayments is related to the level of interest rates as is the case in the US market. Thus, if interest rates move down, borrowers are likely to prepay their mortgage and take out a new, cheaper one. Thus, as rates move down, prepayments increase and bondholders would receive more principal which they would only be able to reinvest at a lower rate. For instance, an upward movement of interest rates depresses the price of a bond both due to the rate effect and the prepayment effect. This is termed as 'negative convexity'.

There are several ways in which the prepayment risk is incorporated into the bond pricing. In the US mortgage markets, where prepayment risk is significant and linked to the level of interest rates, the pricing of bonds is more involved. Typically there are prepayment models that predict how prepayments change with changes in interest rates. Such models are used to generate several scenarios of rates and prepayments in order to determine the price of the prepayment risk in the bond. The spread over the treasury curve that equates the price of the bond to that obtained by the above scenario analysis is called the 'option adjusted spread'.

Another simple way to price in prepayments would be to assume a likely level of prepayments, determine the cash flows under that scenario and discount those cash flows at an appropriate yield to price the bond. An alternative would be to do the same under a few different prepayment rate assumptions and then compute a price based on the cash flows and prices calculated in each scenario. Such methods are adequate for, and are used in, areas where the prepayment risk is low. This is especially true of the European asset-backed markets where bonds are mostly floating rate. Thus, prepayments have little impact on the bond pricing since there is very little reinvestment risk with a floating rate bond, that is, if principal is paid back earlier, investors would reinvest it at prevailing rates, which is what they would be earning on the floating rate bond if the prepayment did not occur. Thus in Europe, such scenario-based pricing is the most commonly used.

Secondary markets and liquidity

The amount of trading in the secondary markets is often related to the size of the primary market, the transparency and understanding of the risks and also on how often the estimate of these risks changes. Even within the ABS market, this rule holds true. For instance, the secondary market for securitised products is fairly large in the United States, which is the largest market for securitisations. Within the United States, the agency mortgage-backed bond market has always been the most liquid due both to its size and to its link with the interest rate markets. More recently, the liquidity and volatility of bonds backed by sub-prime mortgages has also grown substantially. Again, this has been due both to the growth in the size of the primary market and, more recently, to speculation about house prices in the US markets and its perceived impact on the sub-prime mortgage market. Other parts of the US market differ in size and liquidity but, there, with several banks operating large trading desks for securitised products, the size of the secondary market for most asset classes remains significant.

The secondary market for asset-backed bonds in Europe has been growing steadily over the past few years. The nature of the investor base, especially in the initial years of the

European market has meant that the secondary market has not grown quite as rapidly as the primary market. Many participants in the market buy asset-backed bonds with a view to hold them till maturity. Such 'buy-to-hold' investors tended to form a very large part of the market in the initial years and still constitute a significant fraction of the current investor base. With a significant portion of bonds locked in the portfolio of such investors, the actual volume of bonds available to trade in the secondary market has remained limited. In recent years, the increasing presence of asset managers and leveraged money investors has meant a significant growth in trading of asset-backed bonds. There has also been an increase in the transparency of the market along with the increase in size, with prices and quotes on many bonds now being made available through several sources. These developments have, in fact, tempted even some largely 'buy-to-hold' players to participate in the secondary markets in order to realise mark-to-market gains. As the primary market continues to grow steadily, it is inevitable that the secondary markets will also continue to evolve and expand. In Europe, this trend has started taking hold over the past couple of years and is expected to continue steadily.

Accounting, tax and regulatory issues

The development of the securitisation markets was aided by the accounting and regulatory advantages that it offered. Initially such advantages were magnified by the fact that accounting and regulatory regimes did not factor in securitisation as a financial tool. The sale of assets to a bankruptcy-remote SPV was considered sufficient to remove such assets and the associated risks from the balance sheet of the originator even though they retained a portion of the risk. Over time, both accounting standards and bank regulation have been forced to catch up with this fast growing market. Accounting standards in the United States and, more recently, in Europe, have been updated in order to appropriately handle securitisation. There are now clearer definitions on what constitutes a true sale of assets and on the level of risk transfer that will enable an originator to remove the assets from the balance sheet. Similarly, the new Basel II regulation for banks has an entire section devoted to securitisation, with the accord recognising the lower risks of highly rated asset-backed bonds and also adjusting regulatory requirements depending on the amount of risk transferred (see Exhibit 5.9).

A securitisation uses a bankruptcy-remote SPV and since such a vehicle passes through all cash flows and risks from the assets to the liabilities, it makes no profit or loss. Thus, securitisation vehicles are, to a large extent, tax-neutral in most regimes. Tax regimes, however, do still impact the securitisation market since a sale of assets even to an SPV sometimes leads to a tax on the originator. In Germany, for instance, true-sale securitisations were absent for many years and is still a small market precisely due to this issue of taxation on asset sales. Regulators, recognising the growing securitisation market and its use as a risk management tool, are constantly updating the tax regime to be able to allow securitisations. Thus, more jurisdictions, where securitisations are currently tax-negative, are likely to resolve such issues and join this growing market.

Outlook

What started as a simple financial innovation in the 1970s has now led to the establishment of a multi-billion dollar global market. Securitisation is now no longer a niche product

Exhibit 5.9

Risk weights under Basel II for securitised bonds

External Rating	Risk weights for senior positions and eligible IAA exposures (%)	Base risk weights (%)	Risk weights for tranches backed by non-granular pools, N < 6* (%)
AAA	7	12	20
AA	8	15	25
A+	10	18	35
A	12	20	35
A−	20	35	35
BBB+	35	50	50
BBB	60	75	75
BBB−	100	100	100
BB+	250	250	250
BB	425	425	425
BB−	650	650	650
Below BB− and unrated	Deduction	Deduction	Deduction

*N – number of effective exposures in the transaction.
Source: Basel II publications.

meant for a select few, but is a well understood and sought after asset class by a broad range of institutional investors. As with any financial innovation, some of the advantages of using securitisations that arose from regulatory and accounting loopholes are slowly disappearing over time. However, the core benefits of the product are so well established, that it makes it certain that the market will continue to grow in the coming years. Originators are constantly pushing the boundaries of what can be securitised and how they can be securitised and investors are not far behind in seeking out more innovative risks to invest in. This means that while common asset classes, including residential mortgages and commercial mortgages, will be in regular supply, securitisation will continue to keep throwing up exciting new investment opportunities.

---

[1] American Securitisation Forum – *Hearing on Protecting Homeowners: Preventing Abusive Lending While Preserving Access to Credit*, 5 November 2003.

[2] Tim Nicolle, *Introduction to Securitisation*, 2003.

[3] Meir Kohn, *Government Finance in Pre-industrial Europe*, 2005.

[4] The weighted average life of the bond is the time-weighted average of principal payments the bond is scheduled to receive. Since in asset-backed bonds principal often flows through over different periods the weighted average life gives a better sense of the duration of the bond than a simple maturity date.

Chapter 6

Covered bonds

Heiko Langer
BNP Paribas

Introduction: what is a covered bond?

A covered bond is a senior bank obligation whose interest and capital payments are backed
by a preferential claim on a dynamic pool of assets. The dynamic nature of the pool stems
from the issuer's ongoing obligation to substitute maturing and defaulting assets within the
pool. The assets typically remain on the balance sheet of the issuer or are held by a subsidiary which is consolidated within the issuer's balance sheet. In most cases the main features,
such as cover requirements, preferential claim of the bondholders, matching requirements
and post-bankruptcy procedures, are subject to a specific covered bond law. The covered
bond law can also contain limitations regarding the business activities of covered bond issuers
(special banking principle). Within the last ten years, many European countries have established such covered bond laws, allowing their banks to use covered bonds as a funding tool.
In recent years there has also been issuance of covered bonds without a specific law (see
'Structured covered bonds' in this chapter). With a total outstanding volume of well over
€1tn (end of 2005) the euro covered bond market even exceeds the German government bond
market, Europe's largest government bond market, in outstanding volume. The international
growth of the covered bond market was accompanied by a rising internationalisation of the
investor base. Investors such as central banks, funds, insurance companies and banks are
mainly attracted to the Jumbo market which, with a total outstanding volume of €644bn (end
of 2005), represents the liquid segment of the covered bond market.

The core feature of covered bonds is the investor protection in case of the issuer's
insolvency. In this scenario the pool of assets will be segregated and continues to generate
cash flows in order to pay interest and capital on the outstanding covered bonds. Other creditors of the insolvent issuer have no access to these collateral assets as long as any covered
bond remains outstanding.

In many frameworks the cover assets are entered into a special cover register in order
to distinguish them from other assets on the issuer's balance sheet. This earmarking facil-
itates the segregation of collateral assets in a bankruptcy event. The register is usually kept
by an independent cover monitor (often called 'trustee'), which also ensures that there are
always enough cover assets for the outstanding covered bonds. In cases where there is no
register, either all assets or the whole asset group (that is, all mortgages) on the issuer's
balance sheet act as collateral.

Before the insolvency of the issuer, interest and capital is paid out of the cash flow
generated by the issuer's total balance sheet. Payments to the covered bondholders are not

---

Exhibit 6.1
Covered bonds issued in Europe

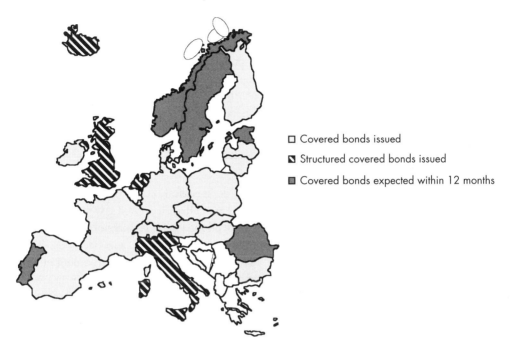

☐ Covered bonds issued

◣ Structured covered bonds issued

◼ Covered bonds expected within 12 months

Source: BNP Paribas.

---

limited to the cash flows generated by the collateral assets. Usually, covered bondholders have a full recourse against the issuer of the covered bonds, that is, there can be no loss under the covered bonds without a prior default of the issuer. During the life of the covered bonds, the issuer has the obligation to provide enough collateral for the outstanding covered bonds. The collateralisation requirement is an essential part of the covered bond framework and can range from a 100 per cent nominal cover to a specified minimum over-collateral-isation. This forms the basis for the dynamic nature of the cover pool. As cover assets mature or default while there are still covered bonds outstanding, the issuer has to add new assets to the cover pool on an ongoing basis in order to meet the cover requirement. Since the issuer continues to bear the credit risk associated with cover assets it is also required to provide the underlying capital, that is, there is no capital relief when issuing covered bonds as there is with other securitisation techniques such as mortgage-backed securities.

Bankruptcy event

In case the issuer becomes insolvent or bankrupt covered bondholders do not participate in the bankruptcy proceedings. Covered bonds and cover assets are segregated from the balance sheet of the issuer and continue to run on their own until the last covered bond has been

93

repaid according to its original schedule. Some frameworks provide for the possibility of early repayment of the covered bonds in a bankruptcy event, but this has to be seen as the exception.

Once the cover pools and the covered bonds have been split from the issuer's balance sheet the pool becomes static. Since substitution of maturing and defaulting assets stops, covered bondholders have to rely fully on the cover pool's ability to generate cash flows for the outstanding covered bonds. If at some point after the issuer's bankruptcy the pool cannot generate enough cash flow to pay interest and capital on the covered bonds the pool would be liquidated and the proceeds distributed among the covered bondholders. If there remain open claims of covered bondholders, they rank *pari passu* with other unsecured creditors of the issuer due to the full recourse of the covered bond holders.

Structured covered bonds

Covered bonds can also be issued where there is no specific law. In the past this has happened in the Netherlands and the UK. These bonds are called structured covered bonds. The word 'structured' refers to the fact that the above-mentioned main features of a covered bond have to be regulated on a purely contractual basis using structured finance methods. Within the structures that have been used so far, the issuer of the covered bonds sells a pool of mortgage loans to a special vehicle that is consolidated with the issuer but does not fall within the bankruptcy procedure in the case of the issuer's insolvency. The vehicle purchases the mortgage loans with funds it has received via an inter-company loan. The issuer issues a senior unsecured bond which benefits from a guarantee (the Covered Bond Guarantee) from the vehicle holding the mortgage loans. The inter-company loan is only to be repaid after all outstanding covered bonds have been redeemed. The guarantee from the vehicle in connec-

Exhibit 6.2

Structure of covered bond issuers (classic and UK/NL model)

'Classic' covered bond structure   **Structured covered bond (UK, NL)**

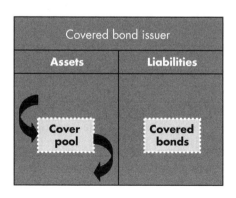

Source: Author's own.

tion with the subordinated inter-company loan provides a comparable protection to the bond-holders as the preferential claim in the case of law-based covered bonds.

Regular asset coverage tests ensure that the quality and quantity of the mortgage pool remains at a sufficient level. Maturing and defaulting assets have to be replaced by the issuer in order to pass the asset coverage test. As a result the cover pool has a dynamic character. On default of the issuer, the vehicle, due to the Covered Bond Guarantee, will take over paying interest and capital to the covered bondholders according to the original schedule. There is no automatic acceleration of the covered bonds. As asset substitution stops, the cover pool becomes static, based on the full recourse of unsatisfied claims of covered bondholders' rank *pari passu* with other creditors of the issuer.

Issuers of covered bonds

Covered bonds have, so far, been issued only by banks or financial institutions. Access to high-quality, long-term assets as well as resources and expertise to conduct an active asset-liability management, make banks suitable for the issuance of covered bonds. Some covered bond frameworks restrict the business activities of the issuing institute mainly to the orig-ination of collateral assets and the issuance of covered bonds. This restriction is referred to as the Special Banking Principle and aims at reducing the issuer's risk profile by concen-trating on selective low-risk business areas.

The level of issuer specialisation differs notably from framework to framework. In extreme cases the issuer is merely a vehicle that acquires the cover assets from its parent company and funds this through the issuance of covered bonds. Extreme specialisation, where the asset side of the issuer consists almost exclusively of cover assets, can negatively affect the value of the covered bondholder's full recourse. Non-collateral assets remain on the parent company's balance sheet and are thus out of reach of the covered bondholder. However, the special bank principle can avoid potential problems in connection with struc-tural subordination of unsecured creditors.

Structural subordination

Structural subordination can occur in a quantitative way if covered bonds are substantially over-collateralised, thus reducing the amount of available assets for unsecured creditors in a bankruptcy event. There can also be qualitative structural subordination if a deteriorating asset base forces the issuer to increasingly substitute assets in the pool which no longer meet the eligibility criteria with performing assets from the rest of the balance sheet. Besides banking supervisory authorities that have been mainly concerned with subordination of deposit hold-ers, rating agencies have also flagged that there could be pressure on the unsecured rating of the issuer as a result of structural subordination. So far, there has been no rating action in connection with structural subordination through the issuance of covered bonds.

Type of collateral assets

The high quality and credit ratings of covered bonds are, to a large extent, based on the quality of the collateral. So far, public sector debt and mortgage loans have been used as collateral for covered bonds. Beside the high credit quality of both asset classes they also tend to have medium- to long-term maturities which is in line with the medium- to long-term focus of covered bond issuance. Both asset classes can be kept either in separate pools or in a mixed pool, depending on the covered bond framework. Separate pools allow a clear distinction between public sector and mortgage covered bonds.

The covered bond frameworks specify which kind of public sector debt or mortgages are eligible as collateral.

Public sector debt

Public sector debt means loans or bonds issued or guaranteed by public sector entities, i.e. central and regional governments as well as municipalities. The respective covered bond framework usually limits the geographical range of eligible public sector debt. Within the defined geographical range there is no minimum rating. However, in some cases only public sector debt with a maximum risk weighting of 20 per cent is eligible as collateral.

Mortgage loans

Mortgage loans used as collateral for covered bonds have to be secured by a first rank mortgage in favour of the issuer of the covered bond. Similar to public sector assets, the geographical range of eligible mortgage loans is limited within the covered bond framework. In addition, there is a maximum loan-to-value (LTV) ratio for eligible mortgage loans which, depending on the covered bond framework, ranges from 60 per cent to 80 per cent. The LTV limit ensures that the value of the underlying property exceeds the amount of the outstanding mortgage loan by a certain percentage (25–67 per cent). Thus, the LTV limit represents a buffer against fluctuations in the real estate market.

Mortgage collateral can be further broken down into residential and commercial mortgages. While some covered bond frameworks do not distinguish between the two mortgage types, other frameworks limit the share of commercial mortgages in the pool or allow only residential mortgages. There is also the possibility to have lower LTV limits for commercial mortgages within the same pool than for residential mortgages.

Mortgage valuation

Valuation methods for the underlying property vary significantly across the different covered bond frameworks. The valuation basis can range from long-term sustainable value to market value or indexation. The less conservative the valuation method is the higher is the need for frequent revaluation. Revaluation intervals differ significantly as well, depending on the framework. They range from monthly revaluation to revaluation on a case-by-case basis if there is a persistent drop in the property value.

Substitute collateral

In addition to the above-mentioned ordinary collateral, the cover pool can also contain to a limited extent (usually capped at 10–20 per cent) substitute collateral. Cash, central bank deposits and high-quality government bonds usually qualify as substitute collateral. Especially in the case of mortgage covered bonds, substitute collateral acts as a buffer against larger unexpected repayments of mortgage loans. Such repayments would result in an increased inflow of cash into the pool (unless a similar amount of covered bonds become due for repayment at the same time) which cannot always be turned into new mortgage loans right away. Technically, such an inflow of cash could otherwise lead to a technical breach of the cover requirements or force the issuer to buy back outstanding covered bonds. Substitute collateral thus increases the issuer's flexibility within the collateral management.

Asset-liability matching

Most covered bond systems show a mismatch in cash flows between cover assets and outstanding covered bonds. Maturities of the cover assets are often longer than those of the covered bonds. Due to the full recourse, the issuer is obliged to pay interest and capital on the covered bonds, even if the cover pool does not produce the necessary cash flows. Thus, the issuer is responsible for the liquidity management. Usually there is no distinction between cash flows generated by cover assets and cash flows coming from other assets of the institute. Obviously, this changes once the issuer becomes insolvent and covered bondholders have to solely rely on the cash flows generated by the pool. The level of asset-liability mismatches at the time of the issuer's insolvency can, therefore, affect the risk of a default of the covered bonds in a post-bankruptcy scenario.

In order to limit potential market risk in a post-bankruptcy scenario, covered bond frameworks contain a variety of asset-liability matching (ALM) requirements. Typically these requirements include the hedging of currency mismatches, limitation of interest rate and duration mismatches, as well as net present value (NPV) matching. The number and strictness of ALM requirements differ significantly across the various frameworks. In several frameworks issuers have voluntarily committed themselves to stricter ALM requirements than those contained in the legal framework. The main aim of this is to enhance investor confidence in the product and to achieve higher covered bond ratings.

Derivatives in the cover pool

When it comes to hedging interest rate and currency risks, derivatives such as swaps play an important role. As we have seen above, hedging of mismatches becomes crucial once the issuer has become insolvent and the pools are static. It is, therefore, important to ensure that the derivative contracts survive a potential insolvency of the issuer and are not terminated upon the default of the issuer. Thus, most covered bond frameworks allow for the inclusion of derivative contracts in the cover pool. This means that derivative counterparts have a preferential claim against cash flows arising from the cover pool which ranks *pari passu* with the claims of covered bondholders. In the case of an issuer's bankruptcy, derivative counterparts continue to receive payments from, and to make payments to, the cover pool according to the terms of the derivative agreement.

Cover monitor

In order to ensure that the issuer of covered bonds complies with the coverage and ALM requirements, an independent cover monitor is appointed for each issuer. In most cases the cover monitor reports directly to the banking supervisory authority. Its main task is to check that assets which are included in the cover pool meet the eligibility criteria and that all outstanding covered bonds are always covered sufficiently. He usually does not act as trustee for the covered bondholders, even though he is sometimes referred to as trustee. Although he usually checks if the valuation of assets has been conducted in line with the regulation, he is not involved in the valuation process itself.

In cases where there is no cover monitor, such as in the Spanish Cédulas framework, the banking supervisory authority itself takes over the supervision of the coverage requirements. The necessity to monitor the cover stems from the dynamic nature of covered bonds, where the composition of the cover pool can change every day. A further level of surveillance comes from the rating agencies, which base their covered bond ratings largely on the composition of the cover pools. However, one has to bear in mind that the legal minimum requirements within the covered bond framework could be lower than the requirements for achieving a triple-A rating.

Rating covered bonds

Based on the high quality of the collateral and the protection provided within the covered bond frameworks, covered bond ratings are usually in the triple-A or high double-A area. Within their rating methodologies Fitch, Moody's and Standard & Poor's (S&P) put a high focus on the quality of the collateral pool and the level of cash flow matching. The three rating approaches mainly differ in the extent to which the creditworthiness of the issuer can influence the covered bond rating.

In case of S&P, the covered bond rating is determined only on the basis of the credit quality of the cover pool and the matching of cash flows (provided that the covered bond framework provides sufficient bankruptcy segregation). The creditworthiness of the issuer only has an indirect impact on the covered bond rating. As long as the issuer can provide the required over-collateralisation, the covered bonds can achieve a triple-A rating. This rating approach is also called the 'de-linked' approach. S&P does not apply the de-linked approach to all covered bond markets. In markets where timeliness of payment is not ensured in a bankruptcy event, or there are doubts regarding the preferential claim of covered bondholders, S&P links the covered bond rating to the creditworthiness of the issuer (notching up).

Within the analysis of Moody's, the quality of the cover pool plays an important role, with the main focus being on credit quality and cash flow mismatches. While the quality of the cover pool determines the expected loss for the covered bondholders, the creditworthiness of the issuer determines probability of default. The issuer's ability to replace assets within the cover pool is also considered when determining the level of over-collateral needed for the desired rating. Timeliness of payment plays a lesser role in Moody's method, at least as long as the probability of default remains low (that is, issuer rating of A1 or better). It is important to note that the link between issuer and covered bond rating is not linear. Changes of the issuer rating in the lower rating area are likely to have a bigger rating impact than changes in the higher rating area.

Fitch determines the level of de-linkage between the covered bond rating and the issuer rating on the basis of the strength of the covered bond framework. If the covered bonds remain unaffected by the issuer's bankruptcy, Fitch does not directly link the covered bond rating to the issuer rating. Where this is not the case Fitch applies a notching approach, where the number of notches between covered bond rating and issuer rating are linked to the level of expected recoveries. The analysis of the cover pool takes into account the asset quality and cash flow mismatches.

Risk weighting

Since covered bonds are issued by banks they generally qualify for a 20 per cent risk weighting. If the covered bonds meet the requirement of Article 22(4) of the UCITS (undertakings for the collective investment in transferable securities) directive, the risk weighting within the EU can be lowered to 10 per cent. The requirements of Article 22(4) of the UCITS directive are:

- the bonds have been issued by a credit institution that has its registered office in the EU;
- the issuer has to be subject by law to a special public supervision;
- sums deriving from the issue of the bonds must be invested in conformity with the law in assets which, during the whole period of the validity of the bonds, are capable of covering claims attaching to the bonds; and
- in the event of failure of the issuer would be used on a priority basis for the reimbursement of the principal and payment of the accrued interest.

In order to benefit from the 10 per cent risk weighting the respective supervisory authority has to notify the EU of the fact that the covered bonds meet the requirements of Article 22(4) UCITS.

Basel II and the Capital Requirements Directive

Basel II itself does not distinguish between covered bonds and unsecured bonds. However, on a European level the new Capital Requirements Directive (CRD) will contain special provisions allowing for a lower risk weighting of covered bonds. In order to benefit from the lower risk weighting, covered bonds have to comply with Article 22(4) UCITS and their collateral has to meet the following requirements (Annex 6 of CRD):

- Exposures to or guaranteed by public sector entities (i.e. central governments, central banks, public sector entities, regional governments and local authorities) in the EU.
- Exposures to or guaranteed by non-EU public sector entities if they qualify for the credit quality assessment step1 (minimum rating of AA−). Non-EU public sector entities that qualify for the credit quality assessment step 2 (rated between A+ and A−) are limited to 20 per cent of the nominal amount of outstanding covered bonds.

- Exposures to institutions that qualify for the credit quality assessment step 1 (minimum rating of Aa3/AA−) if the total exposure to these kind of institutions does not exceed 15 per cent of the nominal amount of outstanding covered bonds.
- Residential mortgage loans with a maximum LTV of 80 per cent.
- Commercial mortgage loans with a maximum LTV of 60 per cent. Commercial mortgage loans with a maximum LTV of 70 per cent are permitted if the covered bond provides for a minimum over-collateralisation of 10 per cent.

The actual risk weighting for covered bonds that meet the above criteria will depend on the approach that the holding institute has chosen. Under CRD there are two main methods: the standardised approach and the internal ratings-based approach.

Standardised approach

Under the standardised approach, the risk weighting of the covered bonds is directly linked to the risk weighting of the issuer. The risk weighting of the issuer itself can either be linked to the risk weighting of the country it is located in (that is, one notch below the country's risk weighting, Option 1) or to the credit rating of the financial institution itself (Option 2) (see Exhibit 6.3).

Internal ratings-based approach

According to the foundation internal ratings-based approach (IRBA) the risk weighting of a covered bond is derived on the basis of the probability of default (PD) of the issuer and the loss given default (LGD) of the covered bond. While the issuer's PD is estimated by the credit institution holding the covered bond (minimum of 0.03 per cent applies), the LGD is given by the supervisory authority. For covered bonds the LGD is set at 11.25 per cent.

Under the advanced IRBA, both PD and LGD have to be estimated by the institution. The main problem with this method will be to get the relevant data on the cover pool in

Exhibit 6.3

Risk weighting of covered bonds under the standardised approach

Option 1			Option 2		
Sovereign rating	Issuer risk weighting (%)	Covered bond risk weighting (%)	Issuer rating	Issuer risk weighting (%)	Covered bond risk weighting (%)
Aaa–Aa3 AAA–AA–	20	10	Aaa–Aa3 AAA–AA–	20	10
A1–A3 A+–A–	50	20	A1–A3 A+–A–	50	20
Baa1–Baa2 BBB+–BBB–	100	50	Baa1–Baa2 BBB+–BBB–	50	20

Source: Author's own.

order to estimate the LGD. The advanced IRBA does not allow the use of data directly provided by the issuer. A possible solution to solve this problem would be to allow institutions to use the foundation IRBA for covered bonds while generally using the advanced IRBA. Otherwise institutions could be allowed to use issuer data on the cover pool for the estimate of the LGD or use data provided by rating agencies for that purpose.

Covered bonds that are outstanding today, in 2006, will keep their preferential treatment under the new regime even if their collateral does not comply with the requirements listed in Annex 6 of the CRD.

The jumbo concept

The jumbo market was created in 1995 in Germany with the main aim being the internationalisation of the investor base for Pfandbriefe. Until then covered bonds were mainly domestically targeted bonds with limited liquidity. At the same time covered bonds were mainly non-rated. Liquidity was improved by specifying a minimum issuance size (DM500m then, now €1bn) and by adding a contractual market making agreement.

Within the market making agreement the underwriters of the Jumbo covered bond agree to quote two-way prices with a defined bid-offer spread. The actual bid-offer depends on the remaining maturity of the jumbo covered bond (see Exhibit 6.4).

Although the commitment to quote prices is directed to investors, it is also conducted between market makers. The interbank market making is an important factor for the liquidity of the Jumbo market. It allows single market makers to cover larger positions relatively quickly and thus price more competitively to investors.

Liquidity is further enhanced by a repo-market making agreement for jumbos with a minimum size of €1.25bn. Within this agreement the underwriting banks commit to quoting prices in the repo market with a fixed bid-offer spread for minimum sizes of €25m.

The jumbo concept proved to be very successful and was the starting point for the internationalisation of the jumbo market. At the beginning of 2006 almost all EU countries had either established, or were in the process of establishing, a covered bond framework. The traditional covered bond market continues to exist and accounts for approximately half of the total covered bond market.

Exhibit 6.4

Bid-offer spreads in the jumbo market making agreement

Remaining maturity (years)	Bid-offer spread (cents)
0–4	5
5–6	6
7–8	8
9–15	10
16–20	15
> 20	20

Source: Author's own

Difference between covered bonds and mortgage-backed securities

Covered bonds are often compared with mortgage-backed securities (MBS), mostly because they are collateralised by a similar type of assets. What differentiates covered bonds from MBS, however, is the full recourse of covered bondholders against the originator of the assets (that is, the issuer) and the dynamic nature of the cover pool. A dynamic cover pool bears the risk of a deteriorating quality in a stressed scenario. An issuer could reduce the level of voluntary over-collateralisation or reduce the quality of the cover assets within the provisions of the covered bond framework. On the other hand, there is an extra level of protection provided by the combination of full recourse and dynamic pool. As long as the issuer is solvent it will cover any credit losses occurring within the pool. Holders of an MBS are fully exposed to the quality of the underlying collateral. It is obvious that the level of the extra protection is linked to the credit quality of the issuer of the covered bonds and its economic and legal ability to substitute cover assets.

While the convergence of risk weightings of MBS and covered bonds under Basel II will probably bring the two products closer together, they are far from becoming exchangeable. With the full reliance on the underlying collateral and the absence of a standardising framework, MBS will continue to show a higher level of heterogeneity than covered bonds. The high liquidity of the jumbo covered bond market and its resulting homogeneity continues to be a main point of differentiation of the covered bond segment.

Chapter 7

Convertible bonds

Moorad Choudhry
KBC Financial Products

Introduction[1]

Convertible bonds have a long history in the capital markets, having been issued by utility companies in the United States in the nineteenth century. Today they are common in all global debt markets including those in Europe, Asia and the Middle East. In 2005 the global convertibles market was estimated at over US$410bn in size.[2] Corporates in the United States are the largest issuer of convertibles, although as a corporate finance tool convertibles are popular with both well-established companies as well as newer institutions in established and emerging markets. Exhibit 7.1 shows the level of issuance in international convertibles during the first four months of 2006, together with the major arranging banks in the market.

A convertible bond is a corporate debt security that gives the bondholder the right, without imposing an obligation, to convert the bond into another security under specified conditions, usually the ordinary shares of the issuing company. Thus, a convertible bond provides an investor with an exposure to the underlying equity, but allied with a regular coupon payment and promise of capital repayment on maturity if no conversion takes place. From the investor's viewpoint a convertible usually presents higher value compared to the dividend stream of the equity, as well as an opportunity to share in any upside performance of the equity. The option represented by the convertibility feature carries value, for which investors are willing to pay a premium. This premium is in the form of a lower bond yield compared to a vanilla bond of equivalent liquidity and credit quality. Because of their structure convertibles display the characteristics of both debt and equity instruments, and are often referred to as *hybrid* instruments.

In this chapter we provide a description of convertible bonds and an overview of issues in their valuation. A glossary of terms is given at the end of this chapter. Chapter 19 of Part II of this book contains case studies looking at two recent convertible issues.

Basic features

Convertible bonds are typically fixed coupon securities that are issued with an option to be converted into the equity of the issuing company under specified terms and conditions. They have been issued as both senior and subordinated securities. The investors' view on the performance of the issuing company's shares is a major factor, because investors are buying into the right to subscribe for the shares at a later date and, if exercised, at a premium on the open market price prevailing at first issue. For this reason the price of a convertible

Exhibit 7.1

International convertibles leading bookrunners

	Managing bank	No. of issues	Total (US$m)	Share (%)
1	Citigroup	12	2,939.40	15.0
2	Credit Suisse	5	2,449.70	12.5
3	Deutsche Bank	13	2,328.20	11.9
4	Nomura	6	2,181.30	11.1
5	Barclays Capital	6	1,699.00	8.7
6	UBS	9	1,397.80	7.1
7	Morgan Stanley	4	966.50	4.9
8	Merrill Lynch	5	923.10	4.7
9	J. P. Morgan	6	690.60	3.5
10	Lehman Brothers	4	647.90	3.3
	Totals	70	19,628.90	

Note: total issuance includes that from banks outside the top ten.

Source: Thomson Financial, IFR. Used with permission.

bond at any time will reflect changes in the price of the underlying ordinary shares; it also reflects changes in interest rates. Convertibles are typically medium- to long-dated instruments with maturities of 5 to 10 years. The coupon on a convertible is below the level payable on the same issuer's non-convertible bond of the same maturity, reflecting the additional value of the equity option element. This is a key reason why issuers favour convertibles, because through them they can raise funds at a below-market (to them) interest rate. The bonds are usually convertible into shares under a set ratio and at a specified price.

The option element in a convertible cannot be stripped out of the bond element, and so is termed an 'embedded option'. The valuation of the bond takes into account this embedded optionality. Note also that unlike a straight equity option, there is no additional payment to make on conversion: the holder simply exchanges the bond for the specified number of shares. One could view the price paid for exercising the option as being the loss of the 'bond' element, which is the regular coupon and redemption proceeds on maturity, but this should be viewed as more of an 'opportunity cost' rather than a payment. This bond element is often referred to as the 'bond floor', which is the straight debt element of the convertible. The bond floor can be viewed as the level at which a vanilla bond issued by the same company would trade, that is, its yield and price. It generally accounts for between 50 and 80 per cent of the total value of the bond.

Some convertibles are callable by the issuer, under pre-specified conditions. These are known as *convertible calls* and remove one of the advantages of the straight convertible – that conversion is at the discretion of the bondholder – because by calling a bond the issuer is able to force conversion, on terms potentially unfavourable to the investor. There are two types of call option. *Hardcall* is non-conditional while *softcall* is conditional. If a bond is hardcall protected for any time after issue then the issuer may not early-redeem the bond.

During softcall protection early redemption is possible under certain conditions, normally that the underlying share price must trade above a certain level for a specific period. This level is usually around 130 per cent of the conversion price.

Investors rarely convert voluntarily. They may do so during an event such as a call or a tender offer, or if the share price has risen by a considerable amount. The main reason why early redemption is not generally in the investor's interest is because it will erode the 'time value' of the option element, as well as remove the yield advantage of holding the convertible. It also removes the downside protection afforded by the bond. That is why soft-call options build in a significant equity upside element before the issuer can redeem early. Issuers will call a bond to effect conversion into shares, at which point the bondholder will convert or simply receive cash for par value. Generally there will be value in conversion at this point so converting is not problematic. Issuers also call convertibles if there is an opportunity to reissue debt at a lower interest rate.

Trading patterns of convertible bonds

The basic premise behind a convertible bond is that it enables the holder to obtain exposure to a company's equity. It follows, then, that a buyer should have a positive view of the company's future prospects. On issue a convertible bond's price behaviour will be a function of the underlying equity price, the credit quality of the issuer and the prevailing interest rate. The price action of the equity determines how an investor will view the convertible. Depending on this price action, convertible bond trade patterns generally follow one of three types. They may move from one type to another during their life, as the fortunes of the underlying equity fluctuate. We discuss the patterns below.

- *Total return investment*: most convertibles are issued as total return instruments, with the investor considering both the bond yield and the conversion premium on the equity. They will continue to trade like this unless the equity moves strongly either up or down. As a total return investment, the bond will exhibit roughly symmetrical conversion premiums. Its price is sensitive to both movements in the price of the underlying equity and market views on the credit outlook of the company. If the share price rises, the conversion option value increases as the conversion premium decreases, although at a slower rate compared to the equity itself. The reverse occurs if the share price falls, but the bond has downside protection so as it approaches its 'bond floor' it outperforms the share and becomes less sensitive to movements in the share price.

  These bonds can behave later like equity investments or yield investments depending on how the share price performs subsequently.
- *Equity exposure investment*: an equity exposure instrument is a convertible that is highly sensitive to the underlying equity, indicating that the underlying equity price has risen and the option element carries high value. The bond price will track the share price closely, as the bond's option element is 'in-the-money'. If the equity price rises high enough, the convertible will become so sensitive to its movements that it will begin to track the equity price on an almost one-to-one basis.

  A negative yield to maturity is common for equity exposure bonds, and indicates that the redemption price is lower than the current bond price and coupon value to redemption.

Notwithstanding this, equity alternatives appeal to investors seeking equity exposure with an element of capital protection if the share price falls. It is much closer to equity as an asset class however, and so is not preferred by investors who require a regular coupon income. Note that a negative yield to maturity is not necessarily 'negative' from the investor viewpoint. Convertibles in these cases are often equity exposure bonds with negligible sensitivity to their fixed-income alternatives. Investors in these bonds focus on the equity upside/downside scenario, and the in-the-money-ness of the bond, rather than any fixed-income characteristics. When the bond is not in-the-money and trading on a negative yield, the investor will be making an equity play but with the benefit of capital protection (issuer credit risk being ignored).

- *Yield investment*: a yield investment is a convertible that trades more like a conventional bond, usually because the share price has underperformed or fallen. It has a high conversion premium and only a low sensitivity to movements in the underlying share price. In this situation the bond will be valued mainly in terms of what it offers as a fixed-income investment. The yield will be assessed relative to the government benchmark yield, with a suitable spread added to reflect the credit risk on the issuer name. This credit spread can also be a function of the share price if the latter falls very low, as this would reflect a worsening view on the company's prospects. So there is often a close correlation between widening credit spread for an issuer name and a decline in its equity price. Another term for convertibles that trade mainly as straight bonds is *busted* convertible, indicating that the conversion option carries effectively no value.

Investor analysis

When evaluating convertible securities the investor will consider the expected performance of the underlying shares, the future prospects of the company itself and the relative attraction of the bond as a pure fixed-income instrument in the event that the conversion feature proves to be worthless. He will also take into account the credit quality of the issuer, the yield give-up suffered as a result of purchasing the convertible over a conventional bond, the conversion premium ratio, and the fixed-income advantage gained over a purchase of the underlying shares in the first place.

Consider a convertible bond issued by hypothetical borrower ABC plc, which confers a right, but not the obligation, to a bondholder to convert into the underlying shares of ABC plc at a specified price during the next ten years (see Exhibit 7.2).

The terms and conditions under which a convertible is issued, and the terms under which it may be converted into the issuer's ordinary shares, are listed in the offer particulars or *prospectus*. The legal obligations of issuers and the rights of bondholders are stated in the *indenture* of the bond.

The ratio of exchange between the convertible bond and the ordinary shares can be stated either in terms of a *conversion price* or a *conversion ratio*. The conversion ratio is given by (1).

$$\text{Conversion ratio} = \frac{\text{Bond denomination}}{\text{Conversion price}} \tag{1}$$

Exhibit 7.2

ABC plc 10 per cent 2009 convertible hypothetical bond terms

Issuer	ABC plc
Coupon	10%
Maturity	December 2009
Issue size	£50,000,000
Face value	£1,000
Number of bonds	50,000
Issue price	£100
Current price	£103.50
Conversion price	£8.50
Dividend yield	3.50%

Source: Author's own

so that for the ABC plc bond it is

£1000/£8.50 = 117.64 shares.

Conversion terms for a convertible do not necessarily remain constant over time. In certain cases convertible issues will provide for increases or *step ups* in the conversion price at periodic intervals. A £1,000 denomination face value bond may be issued with a conversion price of say, £8.50 a share for the first three years, £10 a share for the next three years and £12 for the next five years, and so on. Under this arrangement the bond will convert to fewer ordinary shares over time which, given that the share price is expected to rise during this period, is a logical arrangement. The conversion price is also adjusted for any corporate actions that occur after the convertibles have been issued, such as rights issues or stock dividends. For example, if there was a 2-for-1 rights issue, the conversion price would be halved. This provision protects the convertible bondholders and is known as an *anti-dilution* clause.

The *parity* or *intrinsic value* of a convertible refers to the value of the underlying equity, expressed as a percentage of the nominal value of the bond. Parity is given by (2) below.

$$\text{Parity} = \frac{\text{Share price}}{\text{Conversion price}} \tag{2}$$

or

$$\frac{(\text{Share price} \times \text{Conversion ratio})}{\text{Face value}}$$

The bond itself may be analysed – in the first instance – as a conventional fixed-income security, so using its coupon and maturity date we may calculate a current yield (running yield) and yield-to-maturity. The *yield advantage* is the difference between the current yield and the *dividend yield* of the underlying share, given by (3).

$$\text{Yield advantage} = \text{Current yield} - \text{Dividend yield} \qquad (3)$$

For the ABC plc bond the current yield of the bond is 9.66 per cent, which results in a yield advantage of 6.16 per cent. Equity investors also use another measure, the *break-even* value which is given by (4).

$$\text{Break-even} = \frac{(\text{Bond price} - \text{Parity})}{\text{Yield advantage}} \qquad (4)$$

The *conversion price* is the price paid for the shares when conversion takes place.

$$\text{Conversion price} = \frac{\text{Par value of bond}}{\text{Conversion ratio}} \qquad (5)$$

The *conversion premium* is the percentage by which the conversion price exceeds the current share price. The ABC plc bond has a conversion ratio of 117.64 (that is, 117.64 shares are received in return for the bond with a par value of £1,000) and, therefore, a conversion price of £8.50. If the current price of the share is £6.70, then we have:

$$\text{Percentage conversion premium} = \frac{(\text{Conversion price} - \text{Share price})}{\text{Share price}} \qquad (6)$$
$$= (£8.50 - £6.70)/£6.70$$
$$= 26.87\%.$$

The *conversion value* of the bond is given by:

$$\text{Conversion value} = \text{Share price} \times \text{Conversion ratio} \qquad (7)$$

This shows the current value of the shares received in exchange for the bond. As the current share price is £6.70, the current conversion value is given by:

$$\text{Conversion value} = £6.70 \times 117.64$$
$$= £788.19.$$

If the bond is trading at 103.50 (per 100), then the *percentage conversion price premium*, or the percentage by which the current bond price exceeds the current conversion value is given by (8) below.

$$\text{Percentage conversion price premium} = \frac{(\text{Price of bond} - \text{Conversion value})}{\text{Conversion value}} \qquad (8)$$

In our example the premium value is:

$$\frac{(1035 - 788.19)}{788.19}$$
$$= 31.32\%$$

The premium value in a convertible is illustrated at Exhibit 7.3, which shows the value of the convertible bond minus the conversion feature (represented by the line AB). It is sometimes referred to as the *straight line* value and is the conventional redemption yield measure. The minimum value of a convertible bond is the higher of its straight line value and conversion value.

Investors are concerned with the point at which the ratio of the parity of the bond to the investment value moves far above the bond floor. At this point the security trades more like equity than debt, the 'equity exposure investment' we described earlier. The opposite to this is when the equity price falls to low levels, to the point at which it will need to appreciate by a very large amount before the conversion option has any value; at this point the convertible trades as a yield investment.

Zero-coupon convertibles

Zero-coupon convertible bonds are well established in the market. When they are issued at a discount to par, they exhibit an implicit yield and trade essentially as coupon convertibles. Similarly, if they are issued at par but redeemed at a stated price above par, an implicit coupon is paid and so again these bonds trade in similar fashion to coupon convertibles. A zero-coupon bond issued at par and redeemed at par is a slightly different instrument for investors to consider. With these products, the buyer is making more of an equity play than he is with conventional convertibles, but with an element of capital protection retained.

Exhibit 7.3

Convertible bond and conversion premium

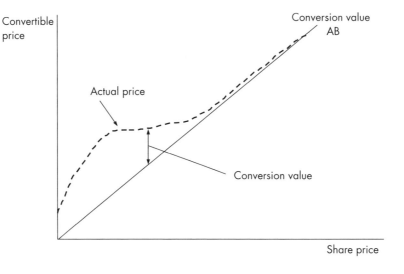

Source: Author's own.

A buyer of a par-priced zero-coupon convertible will have the view that the underlying equity has high upside potential, and will believe that this is worth the negative yield that is earned on the bond. However, the equity will have high volatility, so the convertible route is still lower risk than the pure equity route; the investor pays an opportunity cost in terms of interest foregone in order to retain a greater safety compared to pure equity. The softcall option is often built-in so that the issuer can force conversion if the equity has performed as expected, which caps the investor's upside. In many cases, zero-coupon convertibles are issued in one currency but reference shares denominated in another (less liquid) currency, so that investors can have exposure to the equity without having to hold assets in the less liquid currency.

With par-priced zero-coupon convertibles buyers often are taking a view on equity price volatility, rather than equity price per se, and the value of the note will increase if volatility increases. In such a trade the investor benefits if volatility increases. For issuers, the advantage of zero-coupon par priced convertibles is even greater than that afforded by conventional convertibles: they receive no-cost funding compared to a normal bond or loan. In return they are selling (for them) a cheap route to their equity should the share price perform.

Convertible bond default risk

Default risk is defined as the risk of a corporate failing to meet its contractual obligations regarding the payment of coupon or redemption proceeds. Investors in convertibles will be exposed to a degree of credit default risk.

Credit rating agencies assign a formal credit rating to the individual issue of a corporate, although it is common for the market to refer to, say, a 'double A-rated company'. The ratings fall into two main categories, *investment grade* and *speculative grade*. The main areas that they assess include the debt/equity ratio, the asset base, volatility of earnings per share, and the level of subordination of debt. The agencies analyse published accounting data as well as qualitative data such as the credibility and strength of senior management, and publish forecasts on company performance.

The credit rating of a company is a major determinant of the yield that will be payable by that company's bonds. The yield spread of a corporate bond over the risk-free bond yield is known as the *default premium*. In practice the default premium is composed of two elements, the compensation element specific to the company and the element related to market risk. This is because, in an environment where the default of one company was completely unrelated to the default of other companies, the return from a portfolio of corporate bonds would equal that of the risk-free bond, as the gains from bonds of companies that did not default compensated for the loss from those that did default. The additional part of the default premium, the *risk premium* is the compensation for risk exposure that cannot be diversified away in a portfolio, known as *systematic* or *non-diversifiable* risk. Observation of the market tells us that in certain circumstances the default patterns of companies are related, for example in a recession there are more corporate defaults, and this fact is reflected in the risk premium.

Advantages of issuing and holding convertibles

The main advantage to a borrowing company in issuing convertible bonds is that the cost of the loan will be lower than an issue of straight debt. This is because, as a result of providing an equity option feature with the instrument that carries value, the coupon payable is lower than would be the case with a conventional bond of identical credit quality. The bondholder accepts a lower coupon as the price for being able to share in the success of the company during the life of the bond, without having the direct exposure to the equity market that a holding in the ordinary shares would entail. The yield spread below which a convertible may be sold varies over time and with the quality of the issuer. The second advantage to an issuer is that, under certain circumstances, it may be able to sell ordinary shares at a more favourable price via conversion than through a direct issue in the market. This may occur when, for example, the price of shares in a direct offer is lower because the shares represent investment in a project that is not expected to show returns until a period in the future. The company can issue callable convertibles with a conversion price above the direct market price, and then call the bond at a later date, forcing conversion at the higher price. A third advantage of issuing convertibles is funding diversity. Companies can tap a new investor base that they might not otherwise reach if they issued only straight debt.

For tax and other purposes, equity funds are treated differently to debt funds. In many jurisdictions there is a tax advantage associated with raising funds as debt compared to equity, while on other occasions there will be cost advantages associated with raising equity. For a start-up company it can be advantageous to issue convertibles as these provide debt finance that can later be converted to equity finance. This flexibility is an advantage for the borrower.

A disadvantage of issuing convertibles is apparent when the company experiences a significant rise in its share price; in this case the interest cost may turn out to have been prohibitive and the company would have gained if it had issued shares directly. This, however, is known only in hindsight. The same occurs if there is a substantial drop in the share price after convertibles have been issued; here there is no incentive for bondholders to convert and the company is left with debt on its balance sheet until maturity, when it might have expected to have converted this to equity capital.

The attraction of a convertible for investors lies in its structure being one of a combined vanilla bond and option. Option valuation theory tells us that the value of an option increases with the price variance of the underlying asset. However, bond valuation theory implies that the value of a bond decreases with the price variance of the issuer's shares, because the probability of default is increased. Therefore, attaching an option to a bond will act as a kind of hedge against excessive downside price movement, while simultaneously preserving the upside potential if the firm is successful, since the bondholder has the right to convert to equity. Due to this element of downside protection convertible bonds frequently sell at a premium over both their bond value and conversion value, resulting in the premium over conversion value that we referred to earlier. The conversion feature also leads to convertibles generally trading at a premium over bond value as well; the higher the market price of the ordinary share relative to the conversion price, the greater the resulting premium.

For an investor, holding convertible bonds provides an ability to participate in the fortunes of the company without having to have a direct equity holding. The bondholder has a fixed coupon income stream, together with the advantage (where applicable) of holding senior debt, so it ranks above equity.[3] If the underlying share price rises, the value of the convertible will rise as well, reflecting the increase in value of the embedded option, and if the conversion premium disappears the investor is able to realise an instant gain. This is the upside advantage. There is also downside advantage, because if the price of the underlying share falls, the convertible price will fall only to the point at which it represents fair value for an equivalent conventional fixed interest security (the 'bond floor'). Although the coupon available with a convertible is lower than that available on a conventional vanilla bond, it is generally higher than the dividend yield available from holding the share directly. If there is a rise in interest rates, there is further downside protection available in the time value of the embedded option, which may also add a floor to the price. Therefore, in theory, convertibles offer the downside protection of a debt instrument as well as the upside potential of an equity instrument.

The disadvantages to an investor in holding convertibles mirror the effects of the advantages: the main one is that the investor must accept a lower yield compared to bonds of identical maturity and credit quality. If a convertible is also callable, then this is an additional disadvantage for the investor, as the issuer may force conversion of the bond at its choosing, under potentially unfavourable conditions for the investor. The other disadvantage of holding convertibles is apparent only in hindsight: if the issuer's share price does not appreciate, the investor will have accepted a below-market coupon level for the life of the bond, and possibly a drop in the price of the bond below its issue price.

Different investor classes may be interested in holding convertibles at one time or another. These include equity fund managers who are currently bearish of the market: purchasing convertibles allows them an element of downside market protection, while still enabling them to gain from upside movements. Equity managers who wish to enhance the income from their portfolios may also be interested in convertibles. For bond fund managers, convertibles provide an opportunity to obtain a limited exposure to the growth potential and upside potential associated with an option on equities. An important class of investor is the dedicated convertible bond fund, both outright and as part of hedge funds. Finally, convertibles that reference emerging market shares may be attractive to investors who wish an exposure to this sector but do not wish to hold the shares outright, for liquidity and/or operational reasons.

Convertible bond valuation

Different methods exist of valuing convertibles. Generally the most accurate are those employing an 'embedded option' approach, which views the value of each component as being interdependent on the others. Unlike a plain vanilla equity option, the act of exercising the option does not require additional payment. This is why it is not really accurate to call the conversion share price the 'strike' or 'exercise' price. The investor forgoes part or all of expected coupon income as the price for holding this option.

In early analysis the value of a convertible bond was taken to be the sum of the value of two segments, the straight bond of the issuer and a call option on the issuer's equity. This approach states that, in theory, the fair price of a convertible is the price of the vanilla bond element and the price of the call option, taking into account both the dilution effect of the new shares that are issued and the coupon payments that are saved as a result of conversion. The current approach to convertible bond valuation is to treat the two parts of the bond as interdependent, and recognises that the option cannot be exercised independently of the bond. Intuitively though, it is easiest to grasp a separate valuation where the bond element is priced using the standard yield-to-maturity method and the option element is valued using a binomial or trinomial option pricing model. Descriptions of this approach are given in Connolly (1998), Eales (1999) and Kolb (2000), among others. We present an overview of it in the next section.

Fair value of a convertible bond: the binomial model

The fair price of a convertible bond is the one that provides no opportunity for arbitrage profit, that is, it precludes a trading strategy of running simultaneous but opposite positions in the convertible and the underlying equity in order to realise a profit. Under this approach we consider now an application of the binomial model to value a convertible security. Following the usual conditions of an option pricing model such as Black and Scholes (1973) or Cox, Ross and Rubinstein (1979), we assume no dividend payments, no transaction costs, a risk-free interest rate and no bid-offer spreads.

Application of the binomial model requires a binomial tree detailing the price outcomes from the start period, which is shown in Exhibit 7.4. In the case of a convertible bond this will refer to the prices for the underlying asset, which is the ordinary share of the issuing company.

If we accept that the price of the equity follows such a path, we assume that it follows a *multiplicative binomial process*. This is a geometric process which accelerates as the share price increases and decelerates as the share price falls. This assumption is key to the working of the model and has been the subject of some debate. Although it is not completely accurate, by assuming that market returns follow this pattern we are able to model a time series of share prices that is useful as a means of illustrating the principle behind binomial pricing of an embedded option.

In Exhibit 7.4 the current price of the underlying share is given as P, in period 1 at time t_0. In the next period, time t_1, the share price can assume a price of P_H or P_L, with P_H higher than P and P_L lower than P. If the price is P_H in period 2, the price in period 3 can be P_{HH} or P_{HL}, and so on. The tree may be drawn for as many periods as required.

The value of a convertible bond is a function of a number of variables. For the purposes of this analysis we set parameters required as shown below.

P_{conv} is the price of the convertible bond
P_{share} is the price of the underlying equity
C is the bond coupon
r is the risk-free interest rate
N is the time to maturity
σ is the annualised share price volatility
c is the call option feature
rd is the dividend yield on the underlying share

Exhibit 7.4

Underlying equity price binomial tree

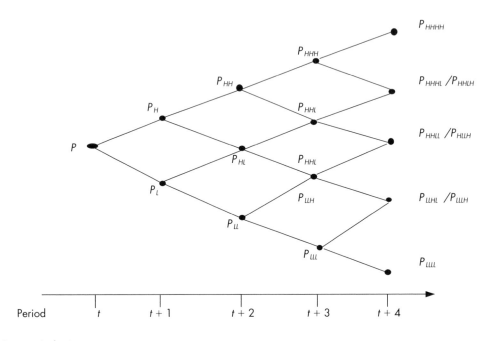

Source: Author's own.

In the first instance we wish to calculate the value of a call option on the underlying shares of a convertible bond. For Exhibit 7.4 if we state that the probability of a price increase is 50 per cent, this leaves the probability of a price decrease as $1 - p$ or 50 per cent. If we were to construct a portfolio of δ shares, funded by borrowing X pounds Sterling, which mirrored the final payoff of the call option, we can state that the call option must be equal to the value of the portfolio, to remove any arbitrage possibilities. To solve for this we set the following constraints:

$$\delta P_H + rX = P_H - E \tag{9}$$

$$\delta P_L + rX = 0 \tag{10}$$

where E is the strike price of the option. If we say that the exercise price is 100 then it will be higher than P_L and lower than P_H. This is illustrated by Exhibit 7.5.

From equation (10) we set:

$$rX = -\delta P_L \tag{11}$$

Exhibit 7.5

Binomial price outcome for call option

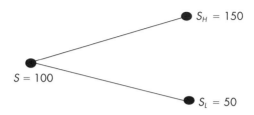

$S_H = 150$

$S = 100$

$S_L = 50$

Source: Author's own.

$$X = \frac{-(\delta P)_L}{r} .$$ (12)

Substituting (12) into (9) gives us:

$$\delta P_H - \delta P_L = P_H - E$$

$$\Rightarrow \delta = \frac{P_H - E}{P(H - L)} .$$ (13)

The number of shares that would be held in the portfolio is δ, which is known as the *delta* or *hedge ratio*.

We use the relationships above to solve for the value of the borrowing component X, by substituting (13) into (10), giving us:

$$\frac{P_H - E}{P(H - L)} \cdot P_L + rX = 0,$$

and rearranging for X we obtain:

$$X = \frac{-L(P_H - E)}{r(H - L)} .$$ (14)

Given the relationships above then we may set the fair value of a call option as (15):

$$c = \delta P + r.$$ (15)

Following Black and Scholes, an estimate of the extent of the increase and decrease in prices from period 1 is given by:

$$H = e^{r + \sigma}$$ (16)

Exhibit 7.6

Hypothetical convertible bond terms

Equity price	100
Conversion price	100
Coupon	5.00% semi-annual
Time to maturity	5 years
Volatility	10.00%
Risk-free rate r	4.00%
Credit-risk rate	6.00%
Time step	6 months
H	calculated below
L	calculated below

Source: Author's own.

$$L = e^{r-\sigma} \tag{17}$$

where r is the risk-free interest rate and σ is the volatility of the share price at each time period.

We are now in a position to apply this analysis to a convertible security. Exhibit 7.6 sets the terms and parameters for a hypothetical convertible bond and underlying share price.

Using the parameters above we may calculate the value of the underlying equity, which is priced at 100 in period 1. Note how we require a value for equity volatility and a current equity price. The volatility is assumed constant at 10 per cent, and the maturity of the bond is five years or 1,825 days. The price is calculated over ten periods, with each time period equal to 180 days. The risk-free interest rate is 4.00 per cent, but under Black and Scholes we require the continuously compounded rate, which is calculated as:

$$r = e^{0.04} = 1.040811$$

or 4.08 per cent.

The one time-period or 180-day equivalent rate is $(e^{0.02}) -1$ or 2.0201 per cent. This is therefore the risk-free interest rate to use. The volatility level of 10 per cent is an annualised figure, following market convention. This may be broken down per time period as well, and this is calculated by multiplying the annual figure by the square root of the time period required. This is shown below:

$$\sigma = \sqrt{t/N} = 0.10 \times \sqrt{0.5/1} = 0.070711$$

This allows the calculation of H and L that is given below.

$$H = e^{0.020201 + 0.070711} = 1.0951726$$

116

Exhibit 7.7

Underlying share price tree

t_0	t_1	t_2	t_3	t_4	t_5	t_6	t_7	t_8	t_9	t_{10}
100.00	109.51726	119.94031	131.35535	143.85679	157.54802	172.54228	188.96358	206.94775	226.64351	248.21377
	95.07451	104.12300	114.03266	124.88545	136.77113	149.78800	164.04372	179.65619	196.75455	215.48020
		90.39162	98.99442	108.41599	118.73422	130.03447	142.41020	155.96375	170.80723	187.06341
			85.93938	94.11846	103.07596	112.88597	123.62963	135.39579	148.28176	162.39413
				81.70644	89.48266	97.99896	107.32578	117.54026	128.72688	140.97815
					77.68199	85.07520	93.17203	102.03945	111.75082	122.38644
						73.85577	80.88482	88.58284	97.01351	106.24654
							70.21801	76.90084	84.21970	92.23511
								66.75942	73.11310	80.07146
									63.47119	69.51191
										60.34492

Source: Author's own.

$$L = e^{0.020201 + 0.070711} = 0.9507451$$

Using these parameters the price tree for the underlying equity, from time periods t_0 to t_{10} under the assumptions given, is shown at Exhibit 7.7. t_{10} is the last period, five years from now.

The valuation now proceeds to the conventional bond element of the convertible. The bond has a coupon of 5.00 per cent payable semi-annually and a maturity of five years. We assume a credit-risk spread of 200 basis points above the risk-free interest rate, so a discount rate of 6.00 per cent is used to value the bond. This credit spread is a subjective measure based on the perceived credit risk of the bond issuer. On maturity the bond must be priced at par or 100, while the final coupon is worth 2.50. Therefore, the value of the bond on maturity in the final period (at t_{10}) must be 102.50. This is shown in Exhibit 7.8. The value of the bond at earlier nodes along the binomial tree is then calculated using straightforward discounting, using the 6 per cent discount rate. For example, at t_9 the valuation is obtained by taking the maturity value of 102.50 and discounting at the credit-adjusted semi-annual interest rate, as shown below:

$$P_{conv} = (102.5/1.03) + 2.5 = 102.01.$$

This process is continued all the way back to time t_0 to give a start price of 98.23 for the bond part of the convertible.

We then take the analysis further for a convertible bond plus its embedded option. Exhibit 7.9 shows the price tree for the conventional bond where the share price and conversion price is equal to 100 in the current time period. Note how the conventional bond element of the convertible provides a floor for its price in later periods.

Exhibit 7.8

Conventional bond price tree

t_0	t_1	t_2	t_3	t_4	t_5	t_6	t_7	t_8	t_9	t_{10}
98.23	98.61	98.99	99.38	99.79	100.21	100.64	101.09	101.54	102.01	102.50
	98.61	98.99	99.38	99.79	100.21	100.64	101.09	101.54	102.01	102.50
		98.99	99.38	99.79	100.21	100.64	101.09	101.54	102.01	102.50
			99.38	99.79	100.21	100.64	101.09	101.54	102.01	102.50
				99.79	100.21	100.64	101.09	101.54	102.01	102.50
					100.21	100.64	101.09	101.54	102.01	102.50
						100.64	101.09	101.54	102.01	102.50
							101.09	101.54	102.01	102.50
								101.54	102.01	102.50
									102.01	102.50
										102.50

Source: Author's own.

Exhibit 7.9

Convertible bond price tree

t_0	t_1	t_2	t_3	t_4	t_5	t_6	t_7	t_8	t_9	t_{10}
110.91	115.54	125.70	145.87	152.08	160.84	173.59	188.96	206.95	226.64	248.21
	106.32	108.73	120.95	134.73	141.27	151.06	164.04	179.66	196.75	215.48
		104.50	106.12	116.40	125.40	133.28	142.41	155.96	170.81	187.06
			102.55	104.39	110.41	115.44	123.63	135.40	148.28	162.39
				101.35	103.29	105.08	107.33	117.54	128.73	140.98
					100.21	102.33	101.09	102.04	111.75	122.39
						100.64	101.09	101.75	102.01	106.25
							101.09	101.54	102.01	102.50
								101.54	102.01	102.50
									102.01	102.50
										102.50

Source: Author's own.

The convertible price accounts for both the conventional bond element and the embedded option element. If we assume the share price in period t_9 is 97.01, then in period t_{10} the share can assume only one of two possible values, 106.25 or 92.24 (see Exhibit 7.7). In these cases the value of the call option c_H and c_L will be equal to the higher of the bond's conversion value or its redemption value, which is 106.25 if there is a rise in the price of the underlying, or 102.50 if there is a fall in the price of the underlying. These are the range of possible final values for the bond, however we require the current (present) value, so we discount this at the appropriate rate.

To determine the correct rate to use, consider the corresponding price of the conventional bond when the share price is 63.47 at period t_9. The price of the bond is calculated on the basis that on maturity the bond will be redeemed irrespective of what happens to the share price. Therefore, the appropriate interest rate to use when discounting a conventional bond is the credit-adjusted rate, as this is a corporate bond carrying credit risk – it is not default-risk free. However, this does not apply at a different share price; consider the corresponding conventional bond price when the underlying share price is 341.25, in the same time period. The position of a bondholder at this point is essentially long of underlying stock and also receiving a coupon. A position equivalent to a risk-free bond may be put on synthetically by holding the convertible bond and selling short one unit of the underlying equity. In the event of default the position is hedged, therefore in this case the correct discount rate to use is the risk-free interest rate. The rate to use at any one time period is dependent on the price of the underlying share at that time and how this affects the behaviour of the convertible. This rate will be either the risk-free rate or a credit-adjusted rate. The adjusted rate can be obtained using equation (18) and indeed all the convertible prices at period $t + 9$ are obtained using equation (18).

$$r_{adjusted} = \delta \cdot r + (1 - \delta) \cdot credit\ adjustment \tag{18}$$

The process is then carried out 'backwards' to complete the entire price tree. At period t_0 with the share price at 100 the fair value of the convertible is seen to be 110.91.

Model parameters

The binomial model reviewed above will calculate the fair value for a convertible where certain parameters have been specified. It is apparent that altering any of the inputs to the model will have an impact on the price calculation. We consider now the effect of changing one of these parameters.

Share price

The price of the underlying share is a key parameter of the model. A change in the value of the underlying share will result in a change in the value of the convertible; specifically a rise in the underlying will result in a rise in the price of the convertible, and a fall in the price of the underlying will result in a fall in the price of the convertible.

The *delta* of an option instrument measures the extent of this change. A partial measure of the change in the price of an option with respect to a change in the price of the underlying equity is given by the delta, which is

$$\delta = \frac{\text{change in note price}}{\text{change in underlying price}} . \tag{19}$$

Exhibit 7.10

Convertible bond price sensitivity

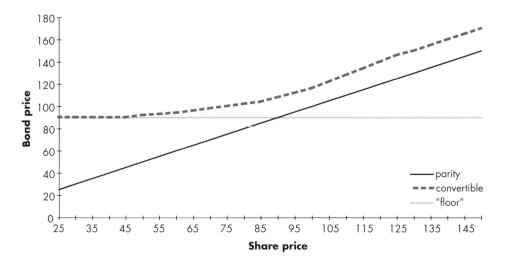

Source: Author's own.

For convertible bonds, delta is defined in terms of the sensitivity of the bond's price to changes in its parity. The parity is given from the value of the underlying equity price. The value of this delta can be gauged from Exhibit 7.10, which illustrates parity and bond floor. The delta is seen from the relationship of the parity and note price.

Exhibit 7.10 depicts a graph drawn from the values in Exhibit 7.7. It shows that when the share price is at low levels relative to the conversion price, the sensitivity of the convertible to movements in the share price is low. However, when the share price is high, this sensitivity (delta) approaches unity, so that a unit move in the price of the share is matched by a unit move in the price of the bond. In the former case the option is said to be 'out-of-the-money', while in the latter case the option is 'in-the-money'. Where the delta approaches unity the option is 'deeply in-the-money'.

The delta is defined as the first derivative of the price of an instrument with respect to the price of the underlying asset. Here we are concerned with the delta being the measure of the change in the price of the convertible bond with respect to change in the price of the underlying share. The value of delta in our illustration is given by the gradient of the convertible price line as shown in Exhibit 7.10. When the option feature of the convertible is deeply in-the-money, the convertible behaves more or less in the same way as the underlying share itself, but one that pays a coupon rather than a dividend.

Volatility

A change in the volatility of the underlying share price will affect the price of the convertible, given that under the binomial model its value has been calculated based on a volatility level for the share. The measure of sensitivity of the convertible price to a change in the volatility of the underlying share is given by *vega*. Put simply, an increase in the volatility of the underlying has the effect that there is a greater probability of nodes on the binomial price tree being reached. This has the effect of increasing the value of the convertible.

Interest rate

A change in the risk-free interest rate will have an impact on the price of the convertible. The measure of sensitivity of a convertible bond's price to changes in the level of interest rates is given by *rho*. The key factor is that the price of deeply out-of-the-money convertibles is sensitive to changes in interest rates, because at this point the convertible behaves similarly to a conventional straight bond. Deep in-the-money convertibles behave more like the underlying equity and are little affected by changes in interest rates.

Dr Moorad Choudhry is Head of Treasury at KBC Financial Products in London.

[1] The author thanks Pascal Paepen, James Walker, Wei Goh, Abbas Siwji, Gavin Robinson and Stuart Turner at KBC Financial Products in London, and Andrew McDonald at KBC Financial Products in New York for review comments and their valuable contributions to this article. Any errors remain the sole responsibility of the author.

[2] Merrill Lynch client research, March 2006.

[3] If the company has issued secured debt, this will rank above senior and subordinated unsecured debt.

Glossary

Call: the right of the issuer to early-redeem the bond before the stated maturity date. A bond may be issued with *call protection*, which means it cannot be called for a specified time after issue.

Conversion ratio: the ratio of the number of shares that each bond can be exchanged into. This is usually fixed on issue.

Conversion price: the price level of the equity at which parity equals the issue price. This is usually set on issue.

Conversion premium: the difference between parity and the convertible price.

Delta: the change in price of the bond for one unit change in price of the underlying.

Exchangeable: a bond that carries the right to convert into the shares of a different company to the issuer.

Greenshoe: the over-allotment option on issue, which can be exercised if there is greater demand for the paper than the initial offered amount.

Issue price: the price per cent of nominal at which the bond is issued.

Issuer: the corporate entity that issues the convertible. This is not necessarily the same corporate entity that is the underlying equity however, which is the case with exchangeable bonds.

Parity: the price of the equity multiplied by the conversion ratio. It is the value of the shares in bond-equivalent terms, a value of what the investor would receive on conversion.

Redemption price: the price at which the bond will be redeemed on maturity. This is frequently par but for many zero-coupon convertibles will be a specified price above par, reflecting the implicit yield.

Running yield: also known as the *current yield*, a simple yield calculation given by

$$rc = \frac{C}{P_d}$$

where C is the bond coupon and P_d is the dirty price.

Warrant: a derivative security that gives the holder the right to purchase securities (usually equity) from the issuer at a specific price within a certain timeframe. Warrants are often included in a new debt issue as a 'sweetener' to entice investors.

Yield-to-maturity: the internal rate of return of the bond, also known as the gross redemption yield. It is the most common measure of bond yield, and is given by

$$P = \sum_{n=1}^{N} \frac{C_n}{(1 + r)^n} + \frac{M}{(1 + r)^n}$$

where

P   bond price
C   coupon payment
n   interest period
N   last interest period
M   redemption payment
r   gross redemption yield.

Bibliography

Black, F. and Scholes, M., 'The pricing of options and corporate liabilities', *Journal of Political Economy 81*, 1973, pp. 637–59.

Choudhry, M., *Advanced Fixed Income Analysis* (London: Elsevier, 2004).

Choudhry, M., *Corporate Bond Markets: Instruments and Applications* (London: John Wiley & Sons, 2005), chapters 8–9.

Connolly, K., *Pricing Convertible Bonds* (London: John Wiley & Sons, 1998).

Cox, J., Ross, S. and Rubinstein, M., 'Option pricing: a simplified approach', *Journal of Financial Economics 7(3)*, September 1979, pp. 229–63.

Eales, B., *Financial Risk Management* (London: MacMillan, 1999).

Kolb, R., *Options, Futures and Swaps*, 2nd edition (London: Blackwell, 2000).

Chapter 8

Instruments for Islamic issuers

Hussein Hassan and Harris Irfan
Deutsche Bank AG

Introduction

The *Shari'a* compliant capital markets have gathered momentum and are now shaping up into an attractive and active market place, especially for borrowers in the Muslim emerging markets. The demand for *Shari'a* compliant securities has been high and is growing, and the supply side is also witnessing increasing activity.

The Islamic prohibition of *riba* (interest) makes it very difficult to structure any pure debt security. The alternative developed by the Islamic finance industry to develop *Shari'a* compliant securities is the *sukuk*.

Sukuk are often wrongly described as Islamic bonds. They are, rather, Islamic investment certificates since they represent the rights of the *sukuk* holders to the underlying assets. One of these rights is the undivided beneficial ownership in the underlying assets. A bond, of course, is a contractual debt obligation. The issuer is contractually obliged to pay the bondholders the principal and any interest on agreed dates. As *sukuk* holders are owners of the underlying assets, their returns arise from revenues generated by the underlying assets as well as sale proceeds of the underlying assets. An analogy may be drawn between *sukuk* and US trust certificates.

The negotiability and tradability of the *sukuk* depend upon the nature of the structure and the underlying assets. Since negotiability and tradability are probably central features of bonds (Islamic or otherwise) it is important to structure *sukuk* such that they do not look like pure debt securities. If the underlying of a *sukuk* is pure debt or mostly debt, the trading of the *sukuk* at a premium or discount will amount to *riba* and is therefore prohibited.

The *sukuk* market has now witnessed a flurry of issues in recent years that have established the *sakk* (sing.) or *sukuk* (pl.) as a credible instrument for tapping liquidity in the Islamic world by sovereigns, corporates and project vehicles.

Indeed, it may even be argued that certain types of *sukuk* structure, such as *sukuk al ijara* (lease-based *sukuk*), may now be considered as belonging to a market approaching maturity. The more forward thinking *Shari'a* scholars, investment banks and law firms are now turning their collective attention to expanding the universe of highly structured *sukuk*, thus enabling the financing of complex cross-border transactions on an Islamic basis. An excellent example of such innovation is the US$3.5bn convertible *sukuk* issued in January 2006 by the Dubai-based Ports, Customs and Free Zone Corporation (PCFC) to partially finance the acquisition of P&O by Dubai Ports World.

Current estimates of the *sukuk* market indicate that approximately US$14bn has been issued to date,[1] with another few billion due to come to market during the course of 2006. Such is the rate of growth, some industry practitioners believe the *sukuk* market may exceed the trillion dollar mark within ten years.

While the earliest *sukuk* were generally sovereign issues (such as Government of Bahrain, Government of Qatar and Malaysia Global *Sukuk*) utilising relatively simple structures, today we see corporates prepared to finance large-scale acquisitions and business expansion through more complex structured issues (such as PCFC *Sukuk*, Gold *Sukuk* (Dubai Metals and Commodities Centre) and Wings FZCO (Emirates Airline)).

We are also witnessing the emergence of a new class of issuer, such as the State of Saxony-Anhalt in Germany, seeking to diversify its investor base through the securitisation of *Shari'a* compliant assets. Conversely, non-Islamic investors are demonstrating interest in *sukuk* in pursuit of both diversification and yield enhancement. At such an early stage of growth in the *sukuk* market, it is difficult to estimate the proportion of conventional investors in this asset class, but anecdotally speaking, sales and syndications desks at global investment banks are spending an increasingly significant proportion of their time discussing new issues with conventional institutions, including hedge funds.

Sukuk structures

As mentioned before, while *sukuk* are generally perceived as being fixed-income securities, and hence bond-like in nature, in theory the singular form of the word, '*sakk*', merely translates as a note or a certificate. In other words, this note represents the monetisation of a *Shari'a* compliant asset using one of over a dozen recognised transaction methodologies.[2] The Bahrain based Accounting and Auditing Organization of Islamic Financial Institutions (AAOIFI), which sets the standard for Islamic financial practices, defines *sukuk* as being: 'certificates of equal value representing undivided shares in ownership of tangible assets, usufruct and services or (in the ownership of) the assets of particular projects or special investment activity. . .'[3]

This standard encompasses a wide spectrum of underlying types of contract which include, *inter alia*:

- certificates of ownership of leased assets (*sukuk al ijara*);
- certificates of ownership of usufruct (*sukuk manfa'a ijara*);
- certificates of rights to an asset being constructed and to be delivered in the future (*sukuk al istisna'*)
- certificates of ownership of a commodity to be on-sold at a known profit (*sukuk al murabaha*);
- certificates of participation in the profits of a specific project or determined activity as a partner (*sukuk al musharaka*); and
- certificates of participation in the profits of a specific project or determined activity as a capital provider (*sukuk al mudaraba*).

This list is not at all exhaustive and, in this chapter, we dwell only on three of the types mentioned above: *ijara* (leasing), *musharaka* (investment partnership) and *mudaraba* (investment management), all of which have significant precedent in the *sukuk* market today.

Let us briefly look at the most common of the *sukuk* structures, *sukuk al ijara*, if only so we can understand its rationale as a precursor to working with more complicated and commercially flexible structures.

Sukuk al ijara

Ijara means leasing and, in the context of *sukuk* implementation structures, it is common to use bankruptcy-remote special purpose vehicles (SPVs) to own the title to the asset and issue notes to the subscribers. Subscription amounts are used to purchase assets such as real estate for the purpose of leasing to end users. The ownership of these assets remains with the vehicle and rentals are charged from the users. Such rentals are the source of income for the vehicle that distributes pro rata to *sukuk* holders.

These *sukuk* represent pro rata ownership by the *sukuk* holders in the tangible assets of the vehicle. The securities are negotiable and can be traded in the secondary market. Secondary market buyers of the *sukuk* replace the sellers in the pro rata ownership of the relevant assets, and all rights and obligations of the primary subscribers are passed on. The *sukuk* price is determined by market forces, and is normally based on profitability of the underlying. A typical *sukuk* al ijara structure is shown in Exhibit 8.1.

Sukuk issues of this nature will normally require qualified investment banks and law firms to structure the transaction, prepare documentation, provide relevant legal opinions,

Exhibit 8.1

Sukuk al ijara transaction

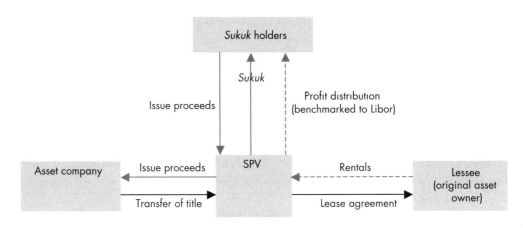

Source: Author's own.

procure *Shari'a* approvals (*fatwa*, or *fatawa* (pl.)) from industry-recognised scholars, and distribute to investors. The *Shari'a* approval process is key to the success of the transaction: the contracts of leasing must conform to the principles of *Shari'a* which may differ from the terms and conditions used in conventional financial leases. Principally, these differences are:

- the leased assets must be of a nature that their use is permissible in *Shari'a*;
- the leased assets must have usufruct, and rental is charged from the point at which usufruct is handed over to the lessee;
- the lessor must undertake the responsibilities related to ownership of the assets;
- the rental is fixed and known in advance to both parties.

If we are to pinpoint one fundamental area in which an Islamic financing differs from a conventional one (and the *sukuk al ijara* structure is a classic example of this), it would be that Islamic financiers do not 'lend' without those monies being underpinned by actual trade or a tangible asset. In other words, it is not enough for the underlying obligation of a bond to be simply the repayment of principal with interest. Instead the profitability of an underlying asset must be the focus, even if the resulting transaction is structured to be compatible from a risk and asset management perspective with conventional fixed-income structures.

However, industry analysts have commented on the limitations of *sukuk al ijara*, and its overuse, as follows:[4]

- *Sukuk al ijara* requires asset-rich companies, with assets not already encumbered;
- asset-rich companies may typically prefer conventional debt and equity solutions over leasing, and may view leasing vehicles as lacking flexibility in pricing, terms, tax and risk management;
- the economic similarities of *sukuk al ijara* with conventional fixed-income products may discourage other less developed *sukuk* variants based on principles of profit and loss sharing (*musharaka* and *mudaraba*); and
- underlying *ijara* transactions may suffer from inadequate legal infrastructure within emerging market Islamic countries, particularly in relation to property or trusts.

Sukuk al musharaka and *sukuk al mudaraba*

Now that we have examined the simplest and most prevalent of *sukuk* structures, let us move away from lease-based transactions (which are predicated on predictable, fixed income-like returns) towards more flexible profit and loss sharing arrangements that may be structured more akin to general corporate bonds, or structured project bonds, or, indeed, quasi-debt instruments with equity-like characteristics.

The concepts of *musharaka* and *mudaraba* provide an Islamic framework for business partners to participate in a given business venture, with a pre-agreed separation of roles and split of profits and losses. *Musharaka* is translated as a partnership, and implies that two or more parties to the venture contribute capital jointly. Profits may be apportioned in any pre-agreed manner among the partners, although losses must be borne in proportion to one's capital contribution. *Mudaraba* is very similar in nature, except that one of the parties acts as the '*mudarib*', or manager of the fund, and is compensated with a pre-agreed portion of the profits. The *mudarib* does not bear any losses (other than the fact his labour has gone in vain).

We may, therefore, loosely translate these two concepts as 'investment partnership' and 'investment management' respectively, and they form the basis for issuing *sukuk* based on profit and loss sharing principles. Both modes of financing can be readily securitised in *sukuk* form, with the *sukuk* being negotiable instruments in the secondary market.

The key difference between such types of *sukuk* and a conventional corporate bond is that the certificate represents a direct pro rata ownership in the assets circumscribed by the *musharaka* or *mudaraba*. As such, as a financing instrument, they are more flexible than a conventional bond. The downside is, of course, that such instruments are not well understood by conventional finance practitioners and regulators, and therefore making them fly for complicated cross-border transactions is as much a demonstration of intellectual capability as it is of sheer persistence.

Risk-sharing *sukuk* can be made to reflect fixed-income type risks and returns by applying a cap to the returns, and enhancing the security package within the venture (for example, through additional collateral). These structures can, therefore, be engineered to meet all kinds of investor expectations.

One of the greatest challenges, however, is to dovetail the requirements of conventional creditors (specifically senior commercial debt providers) with *sukuk* holders, assuming of course that the levels of conventional (interest-bearing) debt are within *Shari'a* acceptable thresholds for the vehicle in question. Once again, we take the example of the US$3.5bn PCFC convertible *sukuk al musharaka* that part-financed the acquisition of P&O by Dubai Ports World, as a case study in the fine art of juggling the needs of conventional debt underwriters, Islamic investors, scholars, and the issuer itself.

The scholar is usually the pivotal point of the transaction, and the most respected among them are also, in themselves, highly accomplished structurers, working alongside the bankers and lawyers on economic structuring and documentation. While there is no single definitive regulatory body for Islamic financial instruments, organisations such as AAOIFI are well regarded as standard bearers for the industry by both scholars and practitioners. Since many financing and commercial contracts associated with an Islamic transaction are often governed by English law, such transactions have a well-precedented framework in which to work, while at the same time adhering to the principles of *Shari'a*.

We will look at the *sukuk al musharaka* structure generically, and then later examine what economic and commercial benefits such a structure may confer on the issuer (see Exhibit 8.2).

Briefly, the SPV issues the *sukuk*, and contributes the proceeds received from *sukuk* holders to a *musharaka*, or joint venture partnership. This *musharaka* is a contractual arrangement between the SPV as capital provider, and the sponsor(s) of the project as providers of capital and/or contribution in kind (such as land or other assets useful to the venture). In addition, the sponsor may act as the managing agent in order to execute the business plan in accordance with the offering circular: this may be formalised via a management

Exhibit 8.2

Sukuk al musharaka transaction

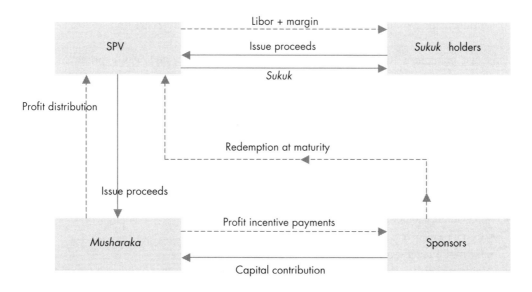

Source: Author's own.

agreement between the *musharaka* partners and the sponsor itself (even though one of the *musharaka* partners is itself the managing agent).

Profit generated from the venture is distributed according to a pre-agreed split between the SPV (that is the *sukuk* holders) and the sponsor. Bond-like economics can be replicated by capping the profit to the SPV, and paying remaining upside to the sponsor in the form of a profit incentive payment. In addition, the security of the vehicle can be enhanced by executing a purchase undertaking between the sponsor and the SPV: the sponsor acts as an obligor to the vehicle (which acts as agent and trustee for the *sukuk* holders), undertaking irrevocably to purchase from the issuer all units in the *musharaka* at maturity.

Now, why is this particular type of structure generating significant interest in the Middle East? After all, could it not be argued by conventional financiers that a *sukuk al musharaka* or *mudaraba* is exposing investors to equity-like risk at bond-like pricing, and without the commercial benefits of being an ordinary equity investor, specifically ownership and voting rights? And don't conventional senior debt lenders require seniority to any *sukuk*, in conflict with the *Shari'a* requirement for any financing to remain *pari passu* within the vehicle?

Indeed, these are valid questions, but they may be addressed by rigorous structuring with a view to:

• ensuring *sukuk* holders are not contractually subordinated to incumbent senior lenders (via, for example, inter-creditor agreements), but instead effectively structurally subordinated through the channelling of cash flows in appropriate ways;

- providing sufficient security within the vehicle via, for example, a purchase undertaking, or additional collateral, perhaps provided by the sponsor, in order to justify bond-like returns; and
- attracting sufficient investor interest via economic incentives, such as tapping the current sentiment for regional equities by convertible or exchangeable structures.

This last point is a fundamental aspect of the PCFC *sukuk*, and was a prime factor in ensuring an initial issue size of US$2.8bn was oversubscribed to the tune of US$11.4bn.[5] The beauty of a profit and loss sharing system in Islamic finance is that there are no hard and fast rules about economics and structures, and therefore the creativity of scholars, bankers, lawyers and their clients is tested to levels we have only previously seen in cutting edge conventional financing solutions, but this time all within the framework of the *Shari'a*.

In the current economic environment in the Middle East, financing corporate acquisition strategies through this form of structure may confer the following benefits on issuers:

- raises finance quickly:
  - by tapping investor sentiment,
  - by minimising exposure to regulatory or legal hurdles;
- avoids expensive sources of finance and instead taps more cost-efficient funding;[6]
- gives maximum flexibility in regards to redemption or pay-off structure;
- establishes a pricing benchmark in the international *sukuk* market and paves the way for future access by the sponsors;
- diversifies the sources of funds; and
- raises the international profile of the sponsors.

The disadvantages are, of course, that a convertible or exchangeable structure may necessitate new equity issuance (either as an initial public offering (IPO), or as a rights issue if the company is already public), and hence a potential dilutive effect for existing shareholders. If the structure allows for the issuer to redeem in cash, the sponsor may be exposed to a significant cash liability, particularly where the strike price is relatively low and the stock outperforms against expectations.

Other potential challenges to be overcome in respect of profit and loss sharing *sukuk* generally are:

- the lack of adequate transparency for sponsors in the emerging markets leading to difficulties in rating issuers;
- lack of investor sophistication and slow development of diversified capital markets;
- poorly developed legal infrastructure in the emerging markets that may make it difficult to enforce security; and
- inadequate tax provisions to accommodate profits from *musharaka* and *mudaraba* transactions, thus favouring the issue of interest-bearing debt.

Now we look at some of the potential risks that *sukuk* are subject to.

Financial risks

Interest rate risk

Sukuk certificates are exposed to interest rate risks indirectly due to the fact that returns earned from the underlying assets of the *sukuk* (like most other *Shari'a* compliant instruments) are calculated using conventional benchmarks. Although the exposure is indirect, it is nevertheless present and is comparable to the risks that conventional bonds face. Unfortunately, whereas in the conventional world the hedging of this risk is bread and butter, the same cannot be said of *sukuk*. *Shari'a* compliant hedging techniques are new, cumbersome and debatable as to their *Shari'a* compliance. The situation is slowly changing with the development of interest rate swaps. These are becoming more widely accepted and used.

Foreign exchange risks

In so far as the currency of the *sukuk* assets is different from the currency of the *sukuk* issue there is a currency risk. Thus, for example, the Islamic Development Bank (IDB) uses the Islamic Dinar as its unit of account. The Islamic Dinar is equivalent to one Special Drawing Right of the IMF. It is composed of a basket of currencies that is weighted 45 per cent in US dollars, 29 per cent in euro, 15 per cent in Japanese yen and 11 per cent in British pounds Sterling. IDB *sukuk* are, however, denominated in US dollars thus giving rise to currency risks.

The industry has tried to mitigate this risk by expecting issuers, through guarantees, to bear the currency risks, thus protecting the *sukuk* holders. However, this transfer of the risk to issuers still needs to be mitigated. As *sukuk* become more structured, larger in size, comprising more international underlying assets and increasingly distributed to international investors, the exposure to currency risk increases.

As with interest rate risks, the market is slowly developing *Shari'a* compliant mechanisms to hedge against currency risk. These include currency swaps, denominating the *sukuk* in multiple currencies and other mechanisms.

Credit risk

Sukuk are exposed more to credit risks due to the nature of the structures used. Thus, for example, *sukuk al ijara* are exposed to the risk of rent default by the tenant, *sukuk al salam* are exposed to the risk of the goods not being supplied on time or as specified, *sukuk al istisna'* involve performance risk, and so on.

Furthermore, the credit risks involved are compounded by the fact that there are restrictions imposed by the *Shari'a* on the penalisation of late payment of debts. The industry has had to come up with other ways of encouraging prompt payment.

Non-financial risks of *Sukuk*

Shari'a compliance risks

The *Shari'a* compliance of the *sukuk* needs to be ensured and maintained until the *sukuk* is redeemed. The redemption itself needs to be conducted in a *Shari'a* compliant manner.

If the status of *Shari'a* compliance of the *sukuk* changes this will probably amount to an event of default and the *sukuk* will have to be redeemed earlier.

The risk that a *sukuk* may be viewed as not being *Shari'a* compliant either at the time of issue or subsequently is enhanced due to the divergent, yet equally valid, views held by different scholars on key issues related to the *Shari'a*. To help achieve some sort of standardisation, AAOIFI has issued certain *Shari'a* standards. These standards, which became effective on 1 January 2004, list a number of acceptable asset classes and the criteria that these asset classes should have in order to be considered *Shari'a* compliant according to AAOIFI. Clearly the list is not, and was not meant to be, exhaustive as innovations are constantly pushing forward the boundaries of *sukuk*. In any case, while many scholars will take into consideration the standards issued by AAOIFI or the decisions of the Fiqh Academy of the Organisation of Islamic Conference (OIC), they are not bound by the standards or by the decisions and they are free to disregard them completely.

Operational risks

The operational risks that *sukuk* are subject to are a combination of risks that are common to bonds, even conventional ones, and some that are specific to *sukuk* due to the unique way in which *sukuk* are structured. The risks specific to *sukuk* include:

- Default risk – for example, in *sukuk al ijara* that the obligor fails to pay the rentals (coupon).
- Asset redemption risk – this arises, for example, in *sukuk al ijara* due to the fact that the originator has to buy back the leased assets. There are also risks that the assets may be lost or destroyed. The industry has come up with mechanisms for insuring against this risk as well as methods for imposing maintenance obligations on the tenant.
- SPV risks – as most *sukuk* are issued by an SPV and incorporate several SPVs in the structure. The SPV is normally a stand-alone vehicle that is bankruptcy-remote from the originator and has the legal title to the assets.

Infrastructural risks

There are a number of risks that *sukuk* are subject to due to the nascent nature of the markets and the legal environment in which they are normally issued. We have touched already upon the lack of binding uniform *Shari'a* standards. This is also true of the regulatory standards themselves in so far as there is no best practice or uniformity. There are also no uniform accounting and auditing standards (although AAOIFI has also issued a number of accounting and auditing standards for the Islamic finance market). The legal framework is also weak, and it is unclear to what extent foreign judgments will be enforced in some of the jurisdictions from which *sukuk* are issued.

These are some of the main risks to which *sukuk* are subject, and of which issuers and investors need to be aware.

The industry and those advisers who have been involved with most of the previous issues have amassed valuable experience in relation to the following:

- tax implications, if any, of the *sukuk* issuance;
- choice of domicile of the SPV/trust;
- the relevance of external regulations such as the US Regs 144; and
- appropriate *Shari'a* compliant methods of providing credit and/or liquidity enhancements.

Conclusion

It is clear that *sukuk* are playing a crucial role in meeting the financing needs of issuers and the liquidity management needs of investors. In 2005, the *sukuk* market reached and then exceeded the US$10bn mark and it is clear that significant demand remains unfulfilled. This year, that aggregate figure may double.

Issuers who wish to tap this demand should keep in mind that investors are demanding more from *sukuk*. While the days of the plain vanilla *sukuk al ijara* are far from over, the more attractive *sukuk* are those that offer more than pure bond-like returns. This may be in the form of subscription rights (as in the Safa Tower *Sukuk*), or time shares (as in the Zamzam *Sukuk*), or guaranteed allocation in forthcoming IPOs (as in the PCFC *Sukuk*).

We are sure to see more of this type of *sukuk* as all those involved, from issuers to investors to the *Shari'a* scholars, regulators and other professionals contributing to the *sukuk* market get more comfortable with complicated structures.

---

[1] Source: Liquidity Management Centre B.S.C., Global Sukuk Table, 19 March 2006.

[2] *Shari'a* Standard No. 17 (May 2003), Accounting and Auditing Organization For Islamic Financial Institutions (AAOIFI).

[3] Ibid.

[4] Adam, Nathif J. and Thomas, Abdulkader, *Islamic Bonds – Your Guide to Issuing, Structuring and Investing in Sukuk*, Euromoney Books (2004).

[5] Source: *Arab Press Digest*, 13 January 2006.

[6] If we examine US and European convertible bond issuances, in some cases per annum coupon savings versus a straight bond issue can be as much as 800 basis points, depending on maturity, volatility of the underlying and strike price (source: Deutsche Bank Equity Capital Markets internal document, unpublished, February 2006). In the case of the PCFC *sukuk*, the coupon was paid as 7.125 per cent p.a. if an IPO were to take place at maturity, or 10.125 per cent if no IPO took place – this pricing was at the high end of the range as a result of the innovative nature of the transaction.

Chapter 9

Ratings

Gerry Rawcliffe
Fitch Ratings

Introduction

Credit ratings have been around for about 100 years with all three of the major international rating agencies bearing the names of the original industry pioneers; Messrs Poor (Standard & Poor's), Moody (Moody's Investor Services) and Fitch (Fitch Ratings). However, their significance has increased exponentially over the last decade. This is especially the case in the European context with the introduction of the euro in 1999, and the subsequent rapid evolution of the European credit markets, together with even more explosive growth in the global credit derivatives market.

The credit rating agencies

As noted above, credit ratings are provided primarily by independent private sector entities, with the three agencies named above having built up genuinely global franchises, assigning ratings across all of the different credit asset classes in all the major (and, indeed, in many minor) financial markets. Issuers generally choose which rating agency(ies) to use on the basis of the degree of investor/lender acceptance of those ratings in the market(s) in which they seek to raise debt finance. All of the major rating agencies, and indeed most, if not all, of the numerous regional or sector specialist agencies are profit-maximising (optimising) organisations. Various attempts over the years to establish state-owned or state-sponsored rating agencies have met with little success. As a result of this predominant ownership format it is important to recognise that the principal revenue stream of the major agencies is made up of fees paid by borrowers to have their debt rated. Such fees can vary widely in scale, from US$1,000 to US$750,000 per issue. In certain cases, a rating agency might rate all or a number of issues issued by a particular issuer, or insured or guaranteed by a particular insurer or guarantor, for a single annual fee. Such fees are expected to vary from US$10,000 to US$1.5m. A secondary revenue stream accrues to the agencies from investors who subscribe to the underlying research that the agencies produce to support their rating assessments. Note that the ratings, themselves, tend to be freely available, either on the agencies own websites, or from third party data providers such as Bloomberg or Reuters. Although there would appear to be a conflict of interest as a result of providing a supposedly independent rating in exchange for a fee, this risk is fully mitigated by the market discipline imposed by the need for investor acceptance of the ratings. While most of the agencies' ratings are initiated and paid for by the issuer, a minority have been assigned by the agencies in different marketplaces at different times at the agency's initiative, usually to satisfy investor demand, but also when seeking to establish breadth of coverage in a new market. Fitch Ratings currently maintains global coverage of 5,387 financial institutions, 1,279 corporate issuers, 96 sovereigns, and 117 sub-sovereigns and maintains surveillance on over 7,970 structured finance transactions.

What are credit ratings?

Credit ratings provide an opinion on the relative ability of an entity to meet financial commitments, such as interest, preferred dividends, repayment of principal, insurance claims or counterparty obligations. Credit ratings are used by investors as indications of the likelihood of receiving their money back in accordance with the terms on which they invested. As such they are a component in the pricing decision and, therefore, help set the cost of debt finance for borrowers. Changes in ratings over time, therefore, can and do impact a borrower's cost of funding. Credit ratings cover the global spectrum of corporate, sovereign (including supranational and sub-national), financial, bank, insurance, municipal and other public finance entities and the securities or other obligations they issue, as well as structured finance securities backed by receivables or other financial assets.

The use of credit ratings defines their function: 'investment-grade' ratings (international long-term, 'AAA' to 'BBB–'; short-term, 'F1' to 'F3') indicate relatively low to moderate credit risk, while those in the 'speculative' or 'non-investment-grade' categories (international long-term, 'BB+' to 'D'; short-term, 'B' to 'D') signal either a higher level of credit risk or that a default has already occurred. Credit ratings express risk in relative rank order, which is to say they are ordinal measures of credit risk and are not predictive of a specific frequency of default or loss.

Depending on their application, credit ratings address benchmark measures of probability of default as well as relative expectations of loss given default. For example, issuers are typically assigned issuer default ratings that are relative measures of default probability. Similarly, short-term credit ratings (assigned in most cases to obligations with an original maturity of less than 13 months) place greater emphasis on the liquidity necessary to meet obligations in a timely manner. Short-term ratings are primarily used in the commercial paper market. Securities, however, are rated taking into consideration probability of default, and loss given default. As a result, for entities such as corporations security ratings may be rated higher, lower or the same as the issuer rating to reflect expectations of the security's relative recovery prospects, as well as differences in ability and willingness to pay. While recovery analysis plays an important role throughout the ratings scale, it becomes a more critical consideration for below investment-grade securities and obligations, particularly at the lower end of the non-investment-grade ratings scale where Fitch publishes actual recovery ratings, which are complementary to the credit ratings.

Typically, structured finance ratings are assigned to each individual security or tranche in a transaction. Each structured finance tranche is rated on the basis of various stress scenarios in combination with its relative seniority, prioritisation of cash flows and other structural mechanisms.

The definition of default and rating time horizon

Default generally is defined as one of the following:

- the failure of an obligor to make timely payment of principal and/or interest under the contractual terms of any financial obligation;
- the bankruptcy filing, administration, receivership, liquidation or other winding-up or cessation of business of an obligor; or
- the distressed or other coercive exchange of an obligation, where creditors were offered securities with diminished structural or economic terms compared with the existing obligation.

For structured finance, the rating horizon is generally recognised as being the life of the transaction.

Ratings in corporate and public finance address entities which usually have no finite lifespan or immutable operating boundaries. As such, the ratings are subject to a wider array of exogenous and event-driven risks than is the case for structured finance. Consequently, these ratings are generally referred to as having a time horizon of three to five years, being the period of greatest 'visibility' for that entity's performance.

That said, corporate and public finance ratings will incorporate some elements that are potentially very short-term in nature (liquidity position, crisis management performance), but also some risk elements that have a much longer-term impact (for example, potential technological obsolescence, exposure to long-cycle volatility). So, while the rating horizon is often referred to as three to five years for such entities, the ratings actively include considerations that are unlikely to occur within five years, but which still present a material threat, or support, for the entity concerned. Equally, they may be driven by events of a much shorter-term nature, particularly where these affect issuer-specific or systemic liquidity problems.

The rating process

Initiating ratings

Each rated entity or transaction is assigned to a lead analyst and also, typically, a secondary analyst. For corporate and public finance ratings, the lead analyst is responsible for leading the rating process and formulating a recommendation and is typically also responsible for the continuous surveillance of the ratings during the life of their publication. For structured finance transactions, the lead analyst is responsible for bringing the initial transaction rating to committee, and for the transfer of the rating information to a dedicated surveillance analyst. The surveillance analyst is then responsible for the ongoing surveillance of the ratings assigned to the transaction.

In all cases, ratings are initiated and reviewed using a committee process. Generally the quorum for a rating decision is four analysts, including one analyst titled Senior Director or above. In practice, most rating committees comfortably exceed this minimum quorum.

The ratings are established in accordance with the methodologies and criteria applicable to that sector, and the definitions of the rating scales or scores applied. Any material deviation in either methodological terms or the scope of the rating is noted to the committee and in any prepared commentary.

Monitoring ratings

Analysts in all groups consider and, where necessary, respond to a change in business, financial or operational condition of a rated entity or transaction at the time that change is noted. Consideration is not deferred until a formal review date. As such, the review process for all published ratings is continuous/ongoing. Ratings are also subject to formal periodic reviews, where there has otherwise been no observed change in business, financial or operational condition.

Ratings are assigned using a committee process. The committees are convened in accordance with the requirements of the relevant Analysts Reference Guide (ARG). The committees consider the information contained in the committee package, and a consensus decision is reached on an appropriate rating, including a 'rating outlook' or 'rating watch' designation where appropriate.

The methodologies employed by analysts, and the criteria that determine rating levels within each major methodology, are created and revised by the analytical teams. New and revised criteria documents are reviewed by the agency's four global criteria committees (Corporate Finance, Structured Finance, Public Finance and Emerging Markets). The criteria committees are composed of senior analysts from each asset class, drawn from a balanced selection of different international offices.

Under certain circumstances, new criteria which affect multiple asset classes or propose a new rating scale are additionally submitted to the multi-disciplinary Credit Policy Board (CPB), the 14-member senior analytical and procedural decision-making body of the agency.

Input from rated entities

Ratings are assigned based upon a threshold for information received from all sources, both public and non-public. Public disclosure has improved greatly in virtually all markets over recent years. Many issuers publish very detailed strategic plans as part of their investor relations outreach to equity and bond markets, and more than ever the role of senior management and treasury officials extends to presenting their financing and strategic plans in public forums.

Ratings are prepared using this publicly available financial, operational and strategic information. The rating process often also incorporates information provided directly by the rated issuer, which may include management or treasury meetings, forecasts, site visits, additional documentation, feedback on proposed research and other communications. The process may also incorporate data and insight gathered by analysts in the course of their interaction with other companies across their sector of expertise.

Rating analysts regularly have access to confidential information, and the agencies, therefore, operate strict confidentiality policies. Typically, it is not the value of any particular piece of non-public information that is important to the rating process, but that access to such information and senior management may assist in forming a qualitative judgement about a company's management and prospects. While access to such non-public information and senior levels of management at an issuer is beneficial, in many jurisdictions, an objective opinion about the creditworthiness of an issuer can be formed based solely on information in the public domain.

Corporate finance ratings

Non-bank corporate ratings

Quantitative inputs
The key variables employed vary significantly, but can be grouped into two main classes – first, balance sheet- or capital model-driven variables, of most use in looking at financial institutions and insurance companies; and, secondly, cash flow-driven variables, of most use in looking at industrial and utility companies. Common themes used in the ratio analysis to differentiate between entities include measures of leverage, liquidity and profitability or sustainability.

For quantitative information, Fitch uses a mixture of internally and externally prepared data. Internal data is taken directly from the issuer's financial statements and other reports, and entered into proprietary databases by the analysts or by a dedicated inputting department. External data is sourced from various market-standard providers (Bankscope, Bloomberg, Thomson Worldscope, and so on), and used to provide market data, or for background, sectoral or comparative purposes.

There are no standard quantitative assumptions, linked in part to the ordinal nature of the ratings (that is, agencies do not establish target default frequencies to which individual issuers' ratings are benchmarked). There is some correlation between individual ratios and rating categories within sub-sectors (i.e. within a discrete rated segment, certain levels of ratio may correlate with certain rating categories). However, typically, such sub-sectors will be small in size (that is, there are no 'one-size fits all' ratios), and the rating process remains subject to substantial qualitative weighting.

Qualitative inputs
The quantitative analysis is reviewed alongside the business risk of the issuer. While there are a multitude of considerations, they can generally be summarised within two broad areas of investigation.

First, what influence does the business risk exercise on the rating profile, irrespective of financial condition? Does the business risk, for example, indicate a floor or ceiling to the creditworthiness of the entity, if an issuer is in a highly volatile sector, or their sector benefits from strong government or external systemic support?

Secondly, within a given business sector, where does the individual issuer sit? (For example, is the issuer a start-up? An established player with substantial market share?)

There is no pre-determined weighting between quantitative and qualitative factors in arriving at any of the traditional public debt ratings. Pronounced strengths or weaknesses in elements of one can override strengths or weaknesses in elements of the other.

Strategy can be viewed as the pathway from the business and financial risk profile today to that of the future. As such, it is central to agencies' consideration of corporate finance issuers, each of which generally has a high degree of flexibility to reconfigure their business and finances over a given period. Fitch and other rating agencies consider data provided by management through public domain disclosure, market presentations, and direct meetings with management. Analysts also consider the exogenous events that could affect the company, and that are outside the company's direct control, such as the strategy of competing companies, general market dynamics for the company's sector, and the pressures exerted upon a company's strategy by equity, capital or bank markets, or by other interested parties (for example, state ownership, regulated industries).

While Fitch's and other rating agencies' rating process does not include an audit of a company's financial statements, it examines accounting policies and the extent to which they accurately reflect a company's financial performance. Relevant areas are consolidation principles, valuation policies, inventory costing methods, depreciation methods, income recognition and reserving practices, pension provisions, treatment of goodwill and off-balance sheet items. The overall aim is to judge the aggressiveness of the accounting practices and restate figures, where necessary, to make the company's financials comparable with those of its peers. Rating agencies also analyse the various differences among national accounting standards and the effect these differences have on financial results of companies within the same industry but domiciled in separate locations.

Bank ratings

Quantitative inputs

It might appear at first glance that the nature of banking as a business lends itself particularly well to quantitative analysis. However, as laid out in the following section, qualitative factors also play a key role in arriving at any given bank rating. Nevertheless, quantitative analysis is important and can be broadly split into three levels: the economy (or increasingly, multiple economies) of domicile, the banking system and the bank itself.

The economy in which a bank operates has a significant bearing on its financial performance, and it is essential to take into account any economic risk that may affect its creditworthiness. Agencies, thus, look at the basic economic indicators of the country in question, (generally derived from the sovereign risk analysis undertaken by their Sovereign Ratings departments) such as the size of its economy, GDP growth, inflation, growth in consumer lending, savings and investment, trends in unemployment, exchange rates, bond yield and national and/or regional property price indices.

The next level of data relates to the banking system itself. Data relating to the banking system in which the bank in question operates and to the place of the bank within that system are collected and analysed. This process includes analysis of the relevant national banking market and of existing and potential competition in that market and also of the degree of concentration within it.

The final level of data relates to the bank itself and Fitch employs a broad range of balance sheet, profitability and liquidity metrics, each of which is viewed in the context of a relevant peer group of banks. These peers may be fellow domestic institutions, but increasingly larger, more sophisticated banks are viewed in the context of relevant international peer groups. Undoubtedly the most important of these metrics relate to risk appetite and risk management, in particular exposure to credit and market risk. Of course, risks cannot be viewed in isolation from the returns that they generate and from the capital that a bank holds to absorb both expected and unexpected volatility to those returns. Although Fitch has followed closely, and commented regularly upon, the Basel II capital adequacy process, it does not, at this point in time, employ a capital model approach to deriving its credit ratings for banks.

However, to add a formulaic, non-intuitive element to the rating decision and thereby to help ensure greater consistency, Fitch banking analysts do use score sheets on which they have assigned scores to the bank for profitability, credit risk, market risk, operational risk, funding, liquidity and capital, as well as non-quantitative factors such as franchise and diversification, management and strategy, economic, regulatory and banking environment, size and potential outside support. Other rating agencies employ similar methods.

Qualitative inputs
In addition to the qualitative inputs common to all corporate finance ratings – those relating to business risk and strategy – banks, and concomitantly their ratings, are subject to two further qualitative considerations which, arguably, are closely related.

The first is regulation and supervison, of which banking has the most significant burden of all industrial and commercial sectors. This should not be surprising given the pivotal role it plays in economic systems as intermediaries between savers and borrowers and as key components in national and international payment systems.

Fitch analyses the role and functions of the banking supervisory authorities in the country of domicile of each rated bank (and generally has regular meetings with these authorities), of the degree of state control of that country's banking system, of the requirements for public reporting by banks and of the accounting practices that lie behind the figures publicly reported by banks. This is standard practice for most rating agencies. Increasingly, it is also necessary to extend this examination beyond the frontiers of the country in question to take in such phenomena as the EU's 'single banking market' and its bank capital adequacy, accounting and consolidated supervision Directives, including the recent 'Conglomerates' Directive. On a still wider scale, it is necessary to take into account the capital adequacy guidelines of the Basel G10 Committee, most notably those laid down in the 1988 Basel G 10 Capital Accord and its subsequent amendments, as well as those in the proposed new Basel Accord (Basel II).

The corollary of the degree of regulatory oversight to which banks are subjected is the significant degree of external support that is available to them when they run into difficulties. Uniquely among the major rating agencies Fitch has been explicitly assessing and rating this component of bank risk for the last 25 years via its Support ratings, which complement its assessment of the stand-alone, intrinsic risk profile of any given bank. These Support ratings present (on a scale of 1 to 5) Fitch's assessment of the likelihood that third-party support will be made available to a bank should it be required in order to prevent a default. The source of support can either be a sovereign (or its agent, such as a central bank) or an institutional shareholder, the latter being increasingly important on a cross-border basis.

Public finance ratings

Quantitative inputs

A wide range of economic and financial variables are incorporated into sovereign and public finance (sub-sovereign) ratings. Key quantitative inputs for sovereign rating analysis can be placed into three broad categories: macroeconomic stability; public and external debt sustainability; and vulnerability of external and public sector balance sheets to economic and financial 'shocks'. Quantitative measures of macroeconomic stability include the history, volatility and outlook for (consumer price) inflation, exchange rates, economic growth, and quality of the banking sector (using measures such as credit ratings of major financial institutions, system-wide capital adequacy and non-performing asset/loan ratios, as well as trends in credit growth). Indicators of the sustainability of public and external debt include debt interest payments to government revenues/expenditures and to exports of goods and services in the case of external debt (public and private), effective and marginal cost of borrowing, debt structure (share of short-term debt in total debt and measures of 'liquidity' such as stock of international reserves held by the central bank), stock of public and external debt relative to GDP and government revenues and exports of goods and services, and primary fiscal and external balance required to stabilise or reduce public and external debt ratios compared to the current and prospective balances, as well as source and type of funding (non-debt-creating sources of funding, such as foreign investment and privatisation proceeds, as well as access and reliance on local and international capital markets). Measures of vulnerability to 'shocks' include the share of public and external debt denominated in foreign currencies, maturity and interest rate structure of debt, and sensitivity of tax and export proceeds to adverse changes in commodity prices.

Ratings of public finance entities, such as provinces and cities, draw on similar quantitative measures of fiscal flexibility and debt sustainability, such as the ratio of debt and interest payments to revenue, as well as a detailed analysis of key revenue and expenditure items (diversity and mandatory vs discretionary spending respectively), and measures of liquidity (for example, size of cash deposits relative to debt service).

For sovereign analysis, data sources for the quantitative inputs are, in most instances, publicly available from international financial institutions such as the IMF, European Commission and OECD, and national sources such as central banks and key government departments (ministries of finance and economy, debt management offices (DMO) and Treasury departments) and national statistical agencies. Often the DMO and Treasury departments will be requested to provide more detailed and up-to-date information on public debt and debt service than is available in the public domain. Subnational authorities are the principal source of data on their public finances.

Qualitative inputs

Qualitative inputs primarily seek to capture the 'willingness to pay', which for sovereign and sub-sovereign issuers is an important aspect of the credit and rating assessment. 'Willingness to pay' relates to the political will and capacity of the policy authorities to formulate and effectively implement measures that will be sufficient to mobilise resources necessary to honour debt obligations. In the case of sub-sovereign ratings, the qualitative factors include the characteristics of the institutional and legal framework, political factors associated with inter-governmental relations and the socioeconomic profile of the city/region. Qualitative inputs into the sovereign rating assessment will include the transparency and predictability of economic and budgetary policies, rule of law and governance environment more generally, as well as an assessment of broader 'political risk' that includes the likelihood of internal or external conflict, including war, as well as 'regime change' that could disrupt debt service or even result in the repudiation of debt incurred by a previous regime. Indicators of 'willingness to pay' include debt service record, political and social stability (for example, incidence of peaceful transition of power from one regime to the next, democratic or otherwise), indicators of governance (such as those provided by the World Bank and Transparency International) and indicators of demography and income (for example, level of income inequality; population growth and structure).

Structured finance

Quantitative inputs

The key variables and their relative importance may change from asset class to asset class. Broadly they include: default rate of securitised assets; loss severity of securitised assets; timing of asset defaults; time to recovery after asset default; level of excess spread; asset values; transaction counterparty risks; transaction market risks (if not hedged). Structural variables are also key, such as: issuer capital structure; the level or absence of various triggers, typically based on events or ratios. These triggers may, for instance, amend priorities; trap or divert cash flows; cause amortisation to commence, and so on.

Historic pool or asset data are typically provided by the originator or arranger, sometimes these are sourced from the market. Market data such as interest rates, asset prices, FX rates or indices are also used. Fitch ratings of transaction counterparties are used. Other rating agencies will use their own data.

As with all of our ratings, Fitch assumes that data provided by arrangers and originators are correct – we do not 'audit' the data. The data are stressed according to Fitch criteria for a given rating category. Assumptions are sometimes made, and described in the Issuer Report, regarding, for example, short or otherwise sub-optimal data sets and the analytical compensations applied.

Quantitative techniques

These involve forms of deterministic or stochastic modelling. Asset models establish the portfolio default and recovery characteristics and a cash flow model then incorporates asset model results and structural (liability) features to determine whether the liability tranche to be rated defaults under the respective stress. Models are also used to project future trends in market variables.

For each of the asset groupings within which a core methodology is applied consistently (for instance, structured finance, public finance, or commercial entities, as mentioned above), a high-level description of qualitative inputs, in particular the scope of qualitative judgement, for example, regarding the strategy, business plans of the rated entities, and so on.

Qualitative inputs

Features of the transaction structure, including the use of special purpose vehicles, ownership, priorities of other creditors (if any), method of asset transfer and cash flow through the structure, are key qualitative inputs. The integrity of these structural features is supported by the transaction legal opinion which might be considered a qualitative input. Much of the qualitative input for structured finance ratings comes via operational risk assessments of servicers, asset managers and other transaction counterparties. Other qualitative inputs would include the impact of macro trends on pool asset quality and the historic performance of similar transactions managed or originated by the same parties.

Qualitative judgement is also used, for instance where data are sub-optimal or agencies' criteria are not wholly applicable. This is usually exercised through consensus of expert opinion in a rating committee or, in cases with wider analytical implications, through a transaction screening committee.

Project finance

Fitch has rated or reviewed many different types of project finance transactions in the international markets, including telecommunications, power projects, toll roads, airports, mines and pipelines. Fitch generally breaks down the analysis into the following areas: sponsors, precompletion risk, operation risk, offtake risk, country risk and structural aspects. While these factors can be applied to most project financings, the relative importance of each in the analysis will vary by project. Other rating agencies use similar methods.

The popularity of project financings in the international markets has increased significantly in recent years. This is in large part a result of the demand for infrastructure projects in emerging markets experiencing exponential growth. The increased popularity of BOOT (build-own-operate-transfer), BLT (build-lease-transfer), BOO (build-own-operate) and other structures, has resulted in an increase in the use of project finance as a means of financing the infrastructure needs in countries throughout the world.

Historically, these projects have been financed by a combination of equity, internally generated cash flows and debt, which has generally been provided by commercial banks, export credit agencies and multilaterals. The capital markets have not been widely used to

143

raise debt for infrastructure projects. Recently, there has been increasing interest in the capital markets as a source of funding for infrastructure projects. There are a number of reasons for this. First, the demand for infrastructure projects in emerging markets is increasing at a rapid pace, and, at the same time, governments are facing increasing financial constraints. Secondly, the commercial banks are not a natural source of financing for these projects due to the relatively long term of the loans required by the projects. Finally, the analysis of these transactions takes a significant amount of time and resources due to their complexity. With increased exposure to these transactions, parties are better able to analyse the allocation of risks.

In international projects, it is especially important to have strong economics, since the environment in which they operate can be untested or uncertain. Projects with strong economics provide incentives to the participants involved. Strong projects can achieve investment-grade ratings. Projects that have received investment-grade ratings include projects with construction risk. In these cases, a large part of the construction risk was assumed by the contractors and/or sponsors.

Typically, the rating of a project will be constrained by the rating of the sovereign. However, Fitch has reviewed a number of transactions that have attempted to mitigate certain sovereign risks and achieve a rating above that of the country. These have included transactions with political risk insurance as well as transactions structured to take advantage of the preferred creditor status of certain multilaterals and export credit agencies. Finally, projects that generate hard currency offshore may be able to be structured to reduce transfer and convertibility risk. In rating projects in international markets, Fitch uses analysts with a variety of backgrounds. Typically, this would include the involvement of the international structured and project finance group; industry analysts, which vary with the type of project being rated; sovereign analysts; and analysts from the Fitch affiliate office in the country in which the project is located. This is common to all rating agencies.

Part II

Applications

Chapter 10

Commercial paper issuance
Financial institutions and corporates

Andrew Ellis
Goldman Sachs

Introduction

The purpose of this chapter is to provide some real-life indicators to the drivers of behaviour in today's global commercial paper markets. Complementing our earlier analysis of the technical and regulatory aspects, as it were, of operating a commercial paper programme, the objective of this chapter is to provide the student of the short-term debt markets with a clearer understanding of how and why the markets behave in the way that they do currently.

Basic definitions

In its simplest form, commercial paper is an unsecured promissory note, or debt security, with a fixed maturity. Commercial paper is zero-coupon debt, which means that it is sold to investors at a discount to its face value (or par). An investor will typically hold the paper until it matures. Over the life of the security the investor earns interest income based on the difference between the price at which it is bought and the face value. At any particular time a number of important factors will influence the absolute price at which an issuer can place its paper into the market with investors, the most critical and immediately visible of which is the issuer's credit rating. Other factors that will play a role in determining how much an issuer has to pay to investors to maintain debt outstanding in the commercial paper markets are the price paid by relevant peers with a comparable credit rating, the size of programme outstandings (the amount of an issuer's commercial paper in issuance in the market at a particular point in time) at any given time relative to other issuers in the same ratings category, and the frequency with which the issuer seeks to access the commercial paper market – meaning, how visible is the programme to investors; for example, we find that programmes whose average level of outstanding paper in issuance is less than US$1bn or equivalent may fall under the radar screen for certain investors whose investment criteria may permit approvals to buy paper from programmes who can demonstrate regular average issuance levels of US$1bn or more over time. Anything less and the investor may not feel compelled to conduct the necessary credit work to have the programme approved.

When we consider the current market for commercial paper as a whole, the reality is that we are, in the main, examining the trends and evolution in the two largest and most liquid commercial paper markets: these are the US and Euro-commercial paper markets (USCP; ECP). That said, the student of the short-term debt markets should not ignore or forget the existence of stand-alone domestic markets for short-term debt around the world such as exists, importantly, in France, for example. It is certainly the case that some international borrowers continue to supplement their sources of liquidity by establishing debt programmes that allow them access to relevant markets such as France, whose indigenous investor-base would otherwise be closed to them. In the case of France, this is due to the existence of barriers to entry and regulatory impediments that currently mitigate against the free purchase of ECP by domestic French investors. In brief, this is because the French regulator regards ECP as being unregulated and ineligible (therefore restricted) for investment by French SICAVs (mutual funds). It therefore limits the amount of ECP that a French SICAV can purchase. At the time of writing, this is an impasse that may be cleared if the establishment of commonly recognised standards of supervision for ECP are adopted and accepted by national regulators across the EU – an initiative that is being sponsored by the European Central Bank. Nevertheless, generally when we talk about commercial paper markets these days, the focus tends towards the steadily growing capacity, flexibility, maturity and sophistication of the US and Euro-commercial paper markets.

Some statistics and issuer characteristics

The US and ECP markets have evolved at different speeds, of course. As the older of the two, the USCP market today also dwarfs its more recent cousin in terms of the number of active issuers and size of total outstandings. At the end of March 2006, in the United States active issuers of USCP were collectively responsible for US$1.7tn of total issuance, as measured by actual month-end outstandings. Readers who are interested to understand more about commercial paper issuance patterns in the United States and Europe, and who have a mind for statistical analysis, would be well-served by referring to the excellent data and statistics resources maintained on the US Federal Reserve's website and the Euroclear website.

By contrast, at the same date in the Eurocommercial paper market the number of active programmes was about 350 and the absolute level of total outstandings was US$573bn. The fact is that it has only really been during the course of the past six years, and more precisely since the advent of the euro as the single currency of the Eurozone in 1999, that the ECP market has begun to represent a meaningful, that is, liquid and dynamic, source of liquidity for international issuers. A second sea-change that has provided additional momentum for the impressive growth of this market since the start of the new millennium has been the gradual acceptance of the use of the debt capital markets, both long- and short-term, by issuers, especially in Europe, who for many decades had relied upon the banks, and each other, for funding purposes. With the evolution of the ECP market, and the growing demand for paper generated by an increasingly sophisticated and risk-aware international investor-base, issuers of all complexions have flocked to establish their own programmes in order to take advantage of the growing wall of liquidity available to them at very reasonable pricing.

While, of course, it is clearly evident that the sheer size and scale of the USCP commercial paper market is far greater than the ECP market, when we consider the types of issuer who utilise the markets, it is then that we can see a greater degree of similarity and synergy. Both markets, for example, count among their list of participants issuers which can be broadly categorised under the following headings:

- corporations;
- financial institutions;
- asset-backed commercial paper issuers (secured, rather than unsecured, debt); and
- supranationals, sovereigns and government agencies.

Over the years, depending on the vibrancy of the economy in terms of individual issuers' economic activity or an issuer's need for liquidity, the overall share of outstandings maintained by each sector as a percentage of the total market aggregate outstandings, has ebbed and flowed. Exhibit 10.1 provides a time-stamped synopsis of the share by issuer type, as measured by total outstandings, as at the end of the first quarter of 2006.

The importance of ratings and pricing

Earlier in this chapter we learned that a key determinant of the price at which an issuer can place its paper into the market – of fundamental importance, obviously, to a treasurer or head of funding in order to keep a firm control of the overall practical cost of borrowing for their institutions – is an issuer's credit rating. These days, international investors in the capital markets will base their investment decisions on a thorough examination of an issuer's business, its reports and accounts and the independently awarded credit rating. For an issuer in the commercial paper markets, as with all the capital markets, the maintenance of a strong

---

Exhibit 10.1

Ratings categories in main commercial paper markets

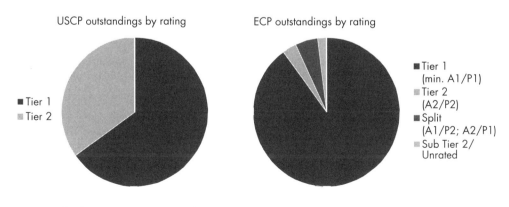

Source: Federal Reserve, CPWare, April 2006.

---

credit rating is of genuine importance, and the level of the rating can have a profound impact on the overall cost of funds to an issuer. Should a credit event occur that negatively impacts a particular issuer, it may well give rise to a credit downgrade in its rating that will, in turn, have an immediate impact on pricing and access to investors. Sometimes, if the downward ratings movement is particularly aggressive, it may prevent the issuer from borrowing in the commercial paper markets at all.

While the actual rating itself is important, since it provides a general benchmark for investors to compare credits, what is equally important for the issuer looking to make good use of the commercial paper markets is the price for its paper relative to similarly rated credits. While the absolute level of active participation by investors in the commercial paper markets has continued to grow, powered particularly in the United States by the steady evolution of the hugely powerful and well-funded 2a-7 stable net asset value money market fund industry (total assets at the beginning of April 2006 in this asset class were over US$2tn, for example), the actual amount of investible liquidity on any one day is governed entirely by the amount of cash investors have to spend. In a sense, issuers are therefore fighting to access available liquidity on any one day, and treasury or funding managers must be cognisant of the need to offer pricing (the levels at which they post in the market) that makes their paper attractive when compared to a similarly rated credit. Since the most active part of the trading day in the commercial paper market is generally the early morning, investors with cash to invest will tend to want to have found a target for their investible cash during this period of the day. Therefore, the issuer who either posts uncompetitive levels, or who is marginally late in communicating its levels, may well have to revert to other sources of funding, for example the interbank market, to satisfy its funding needs on that day. As a remedial activity this can often be more expensive and less flexible.

Discernible patterns and trends

Regardless of market and rating (though one should not be too cavalier in dismissing the importance of an issuer's credit rating or, indeed, the role the ratings agencies play in determining the fate of an issuer in the international debt capital markets), are there any discernible patterns or trends for us to consider in terms of the types of issuer which utilise the commercial paper markets, be it the USCP market, the ECP market, or both?

From our earlier chapter in this publication, readers will by now be familiar with the essential requirements for the establishment of a commercial paper programme by which a borrower can access either the USCP or ECP markets, or indeed both (by way either of two stand-alone programmes giving access to each market separately, or through the establishment of one single global commercial paper programme). In all cases commercial paper in the USCP and ECP is normally issued pursuant to a full legal documentation process, underpinned by supporting disclosures about the issuer for the benefit of investors.

It is important to note that issuance and programme utilisation patterns will differ according to issuer borrowing requirements, and their ability to obtain funding in the market at levels that they find competitive. Whether one looks at the USCP market or at the ECP market, the single biggest issuer type in the international commercial paper markets has long been financial institutions. In the case of the ECP market, issuance by financial institutions of unsecured commercial paper accounts for more than 50 per cent of total market outstandings (end of March 2006). Often, the biggest banks and insurance companies will have access to all the major commercial paper markets simultaneously to generate sufficient liquidity to fund themselves and will subsequently maintain a level of market outstandings of many billions of US dollars or euros. If we also consider that many of these same financial institutions have sought to make their balance sheet even more efficient by moving assets into off-balance sheet entities such as asset-backed commercial paper programmes (these, in turn, issue secured commercial paper, the proceeds from which are used to fund further asset acquisitions), one can see that, overall, a bank's exposure to the short-term debt markets is necessarily extremely broad. Exhibit 10.2 provides some further colour, by market, of the key issuers in both the USCP and ECP markets, measured by actual outstandings, as at the end of March 2006.

Generally speaking an issuer's use of the market, taking for granted for a moment that there is a natural demand for the paper from investors, is driven by the need for liquidity, on the one hand, and cost of funds on the other.

Thoughts on corporate issuance

Turning to the importance of liquidity, one thing that becomes strikingly clear is the fact that (surprisingly to some perhaps) the overall level of issuance of commercial paper by corporate issuers is low in comparison to issuers from other sectoral groupings. Though Exhibit 10.2 illustrates a point-in-time analysis of the situation, the fact of the matter is that the two single biggest catalysts for growth in both the USCP and the ECP markets, especially in recent years, has been issuance activity by banks, on the one hand, and by asset-backed commercial paper vehicles on the other (as measured by outstandings in the market). This is of course not to say that corporate, or industrial, issuers have been absent from the market, as a quick look at the tables will illustrate. Rather, their relative usage has been lower, and this is because a corporate's funding needs and demands are of a different nature and magnitude from those of a bank.

A corporate issuer will typically issue commercial paper to meet its working capital and short-term funding requirements. Looking back over the issuance patterns of corporates since the start of the new millennium, one observes a gradual diminution in the relative importance of the corporate sector in terms of percentage share of aggregate market outstandings. Interestingly, and this is particularly pronounced when one studies the evolution of the ECP market over the past few years, the absolute level of issuance by corporates/industrials, in comparison with an analysis of their issuance relative to other issuer types, has actually remained fairly constant. Put another way, while the growth in total market outstandings has been fuelled, as we have observed earlier, by the needs of banks and asset-backed commercial paper issuers in particular, the actual amount of corporate/industrial supply has remained constant.

Perhaps a further reason why the commercial paper markets have not experienced a period of explosive growth in corporate/industrial issuance over the past few years is because,

Exhibit 10.2

The leading commercial paper programmes – ECP/USCP – April 2006

(a) Top 10 ECP corporate programmes (as of 31 March 2006)

	Issuer	Outstanding (US$m)
1	Unilever NV	3,241.98
2	GE Capital UK	2,618.23
3	RWE AG	2,590.41
4	E.ON AG	2,280.95
5	Telefónica	1,588.98
6	Nestlé Germany	1,306.27
7	Pfizer Inc.	1,263.35
8	Vodafone Group	1,232.22
9	TotalFinaElf	1,213.19
10	Toyota Netherlands	1,187.92

Source: CPWare, April 2006.

(b) Top 10 ECP bank programmes (as of 31 March 2006)

	Issuer	Outstanding (US$m)
1	BFCM	8,770.18
2	DePfa Bank plc	8,332.25
3	HBOS Treasury	6,746.26
4	Macquarie Bank	6,681.36
5	NAB	5,569.16
6	Ulster Bank	5,438.73
7	Barclays Bank plc	5,434.25
8	Dexia FP	5,300.50
9	UBS AG (London)	5,075.99
10	BCP Finance Bank	4,868.47

Source: CPWare, April 2006.

(c) Top 10 USCP programmes (as of 1 March 2006)

	Issuer	Outstanding (US$m)
1	GECC	58,515
2	Goldman Sachs (Japan) Ltd	37,601
3	UBS Fin.	35,600
4	Morgan Stanley	31,008
5	Grampian Funding LLC	24,649
6	Citigroup Funding Inc.	21,093
7	Park Granada	18,538
8	DePfa Bank plc	18,305
9	Amstel Funding Corp	17,821
10	Silver Tower Funding Ltd	17,434

Source: Bloomberg, April 2006.

in common with the rest of the debt capital markets (particularly in Europe), corporate investment-grade new debt issuance has been quite subdued. A number of factors combined to precipitate a slowdown in the issuance of corporate debt, including a general economic slowdown soon after the turn of the new millennium, the loss of confidence in credit markets by investors in the wake of the storm caused by the accounting scandals at companies such as Worldcom, Enron and Parmalat, and a subsequent move towards balance-sheet repair and cash accumulation by shell-shocked CFOs. It has really only been over the course of the past few months that we have begun to see any degree of pick-up in new issuance by corporate and industrial borrowers in the commercial paper markets specifically. It is, perhaps, no surprise that this seems to be coinciding with a dramatic upturn in merger activity on both sides of the Atlantic. In particular in the United States, where issuers in the USCP markets continue to find that they can fund themselves more cheaply and in greater depth than in the ECP markets, we have seen a number of high-profile commercial paper ramp-ups in outstandings by issuers which have elected to use commercial paper as an acquisition or bridging finance tool in merger and acquisitions activity. This has yet to replicate itself in the ECP market, though the past few months in the corporate/industrial sector have been marked by the return to the market of some of the more high-profile issuers from among the telecommunications sector, including Deutsche Telekom, France Telecom, BT, Telefónica and Telenor, to name some of the more obvious examples. As economic confidence returns and corporates adopt a more aggressive and expansionist business strategy after the more recent pattern of retrenchment and scotching on bigger growth ambitions, the likelihood is that the first place they will look to fund their expansion plans will be the commercial paper markets. Assuming their pricing is attractive, and their credit rating is sufficiently robust to support their use of these markets, then the commercial paper markets should continue to offer them a reliable, liquid and cost-effective source of funding.

Overall, the short-term debt capital markets in Europe and the United States provide stable yet dynamic sources of funding for financial institutions and corporations alike. While the needs of each sector, and consequently the issuance patterns of participants in the market from each sector, are necessarily quite different, the fact of the matter is that an issuer can enter or re-enter the market with the minimum of fuss, in a very short time space, and be up and active in issuance terms very efficiently. Whether a programme gets off to a flying start or not will depend on the right things being done on market entry: investor marketing and communication, attractive pricing and a robust credit rating, supportive of borrowing in the commercial paper markets.

Programme management

In practice, issuance strategies adopted by issuers in the markets will differ. They will often differ between the same issuer's USCP and ECP programmes. As an originator of commercial paper programmes myself, I find that probably the single most important factor that is discussed with a prospective issuer in the market (other than pricing) is the relevant programme management strategy for that issuer.

The fact of the matter is that an issuer, be it a financial institution or a corporate/industrial issuer, will adopt a different programme management strategy from market to market.

Let us take as one facet of a programme management strategy: the appointment of a panel of dealers. Getting the right mix of proactive dealers, with the optimal degree of access to the widest possible investor base, is of critical importance to the success of an issuer's commercial paper programme. Although an issuer can obviously manage its dealers through a regular formal review process, or by sanctioning reverse enquiry dealers on a 'dealer for the day' basis, it is still the case that selecting the correct balance of dealers at the outset is most important.

There are subtle differences in the way in which an issuer will select its dealer panel, based often on both objective and subjective criteria. Broadly speaking, what one tends to find is that long-established corporate/industrial programmes in the United States (and such issuers are often capable of maintaining a large amount of commercial paper outstandings, measured by the actual programme limit) will operate through two dealers, chosen from among the top two to three dealers in the market (in terms of size of commitment to the commercial paper/money market business through trading, sales, origination and marketing). Compare this approach to that more prevalent in the ECP market where the instance of programmes on which multiple dealers have been appointed is much more common. It is fair to say that 15–20 years ago, in the early, more formative years of the ECP market, there was a more widespread view that the market and particularly the investor-base was a good deal more fragmented than in the more homogeneous USCP market. This view was correct at the time, but arguably the situation has evolved over the past five or so years, largely precipitated by the advent of the euro, as investors have become bigger and more sophisticated and as the technical and operational evolution of the ECP market has slowly eroded barriers that once existed to the smooth passage of business (such as the introduction of overnight paper trading in the ECP market), and the ECP market has subsequently become more transparent. At the time, however, the developed view was that to ensure one's programme got as broad an access as possible to indigenous investors across Europe in particular, in what in many ways were still local, domestic markets, it was appropriate for an issuer to appoint dealers which could offer access to regional investors. However, as the marketplace has become more transparent, and as some of the barriers to cross-border investment in Europe have continued to be eroded by the passage of EU regulation aimed at harmonising mutual fund investment in particular, it has become easier for dealers to claim that they offer a greater degree of pan-European (and often further afield) investor penetration than was the case a decade ago. These days, therefore, particularly in the ECP market, it is more usual to experience panels of, perhaps, closer to three or four dealers.

Close

In summary, let us step back and reflect: the global commercial paper markets are in a period of sustained growth and evolution. Both in the US and Europe this growth pattern is emphasised by the regular attainment of record amounts of debt outstanding as measured by month-end statistics. New issuers and new programme types continue to test the flexibility and sophistication of the markets, and the availability of a broad and deepening pool of investors continues to offer fundamentally attractive liquidity, available in large size in an operationally straightforward manner, to those issuers who need it. For issuers, their ability to access the commercial paper markets will only be hampered, as we have observed, if they fail to maintain the optimal level of visibility and frequency in the market, with the best credit rating possible at that moment in time, and at the right price. These simple home truths are equally applicable whether one is a global bank or a regional corporate.

Source material: Allen & Overy, Banque de France,
Bloomberg, CIBC World Markets, CPWare, Euroclear,
Euroweek Euro-MTNs Handbook, Federal Reserve, Goldman Sachs

Chapter 11

Syndicated loans – acquisition finance

Rebecca Manuel
The Royal Bank of Scotland

Introduction

Acquisition finance is one of the most dynamic and exciting areas of the syndicated loan market. With its combination of demanding timeframes, large risk positions and integration with other capital markets instruments, acquisition financings can pose challenges for even the most experienced loan market professionals. This chapter will discuss the main areas of acquisition finance – high grade, cross-over and leveraged – and present several case studies that illustrate the basic structures and processes of acquisition deals in today's market.

Background

As discussed in Chapter 2, the syndicated loan market offers borrowers tremendous flexibility across a wide array of uses, largely because the loan market is a private market and the participants are sophisticated banks or institutional investors who are able to assess risk and take decisions quickly. In acquisition finance, however, the syndicated loan market truly demonstrates its ability to add value to financial market transactions because of its unmatched abilities in the three 'S' categories: size, speed and secrecy. Large amounts can be raised in a matter of days from one or a small number of lead banks, thus preserving the confidentiality of the bidder's intentions with regards to the target. These traits have enabled the syndicated loan market to play a critical role in the growth and development of mergers and acquisitions (M&A) activity globally.

The period 1995–2000 represented historic records for M&A activity, fuelled by the dot-com boom. Post-2002, the debt and equity markets underwent a significant retrenchment, as corporates focused on de-levering their balance sheets and rebuilding credit quality. In 2005, the markets experienced a resurgence in global M&A activity, as acquirers with strong balance sheets took advantage of low long-term interest rates in the United States and Europe and seemingly limitless liquidity in the debt capital markets to pursue ground-breaking acquisitions in terms of size and structure (see Exhibit 11.1).

The syndicated loan markets have been a key contributor to the growth in M&A activity, as both new and existing lenders/investors have become increasingly active in acquisition finance transactions. In Europe, 17 of the 20 largest European transactions in 2005 were funded in whole or in part by syndicated loans. In total, global M&A deals announced in 2005 totalled US$2,611bn, which represented a 33 per cent increase on 2004 M&A levels.

Exhibit 11.1

EMEA syndicated loan investment-grade M&A volume

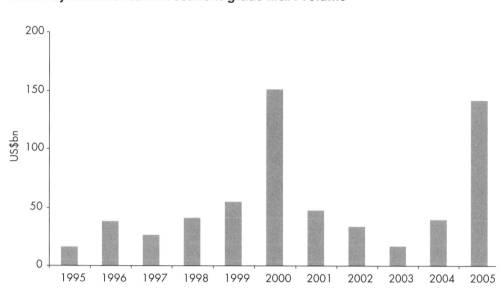

Source: Thomson Financial.

Many of these transactions were made possible by the depth of the syndicated loan markets, as unprecedented amounts of debt financing allowed companies to finance ever-larger trans-actions. In addition, the willingness of lenders to consider a wide range of transactions, from solid investment-grade deals to crossover and highly leveraged transactions, broad-ened the scope of the syndicated loan market considerably. The Telefónica £17.7bn takeover of O$_2$, financed by a £18.5bn syndicated debt facility, the c.€11.7bn takeover of TDC (the Denmark public telephone company), financed by a €12.2bn syndicated debt facility, and the €5.57bn acquisition of Gecina (a French property company) by Metrovacesa, financed by a €7.57bn syndicated debt facility are just three examples of record-breaking deals across the credit spectrum that contributed to the M&A growth.

The strength of the syndicated loan markets carried into the beginning of 2006, although the number of deals was substantially reduced from Q1 2005. The first quarter of 2006 saw only 67 refinancings with US$65.8bn in volume compared to 98 deals and US$148bn in Q1 2005. Nevertheless, the appetite for lending to these transactions continues unabated, as evidenced by transactions such as E.On's (German utility) €32bn facility for the takeover of Endesa (Spanish utility), the €14bn facility for the takeover of Schering (German pharma) by Bayer (German pharma), and the US$6.8bn facility to support the takeover of P&O by Dubai Ports. Other potential transactions on the horizon include the planned takeover of BAA (UK airports) by a consortium led by Ferrovial (Spanish construction), which would likely be a multi-billion pound financing.

Exhibit 11.2

Western European investment-grade M&A by rating, 2005

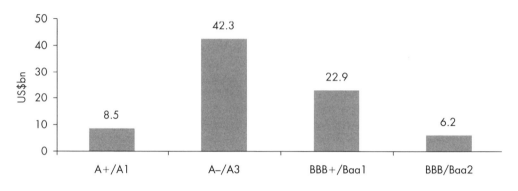

Source: LoanConnector/Reuters LPC.

As noted above, the syndicated loan markets for acquisition debt financing have grown significantly in the last 18–24 months, and have clearly become the financing method of choice for any meaningful acquisition financing need. The markets have not only become deeper in terms of liquidity, but also increasingly more sophisticated in terms of risk/return analysis and in analysing or adapting to new or complex structures. While lending to investment-grade borrowers for acquisition financing has always been a staple of the syndicated loan market, the often multi-billion euro/Sterling/dollar sizes have pushed the participants to a new level of analysis and focus on the overall depth of the market. Likewise, the influx of new money in search of yield has driven the highly leveraged market to test new boundaries both in terms of structures and volumes. Finally, 2005 saw the emergence of a new type of financing, the 'crossover' credit transaction. Again, with deal sizes in the multi-billion range, the crossover credit, covering issuers from previously investment-grade 'fallen angels' to previously highly leveraged companies on the road to de-leveraging and credit stability, to companies with highly leveraged balance sheets but very stable utility-like, long-term cash flows ('crossover infrastructure'), saw increasing activity and looks to become a permanent part of the syndicated loan market landscape.

Each of these market sectors has its unique characteristics and participants as seen below, although at the lead arranging levels, there is some degree of overlap:

• Investment-grade transactions
  • generally for publicly rated companies BBB–/Baa3 or better;
  • arranger/investor relationship is with corporate borrower;
  • typically jumbo deals, with range of up to €50bn, structured as bridges to public debt capital markets, that is, short tenors (1, 3, 5 years), pricing with step-ups (for example, margin increases by 10–15 per cent over time if not refinanced) or tied to percentage of deal outstanding;
  • all senior unsecured debt;

- margins generally in the 12.5–40 basis points (bp) over London interbank offered rate (Libor) range and tied to public ratings;
- can include some element of amortising debt, but primarily bullet repayment;
- pricing generally includes an 'acquisition premium' to compensate for size as well as any potential short-term deterioration in credit quality;
- reliant on core group of relationship banks to drive liquidity for transaction, with potential for ancillary business key part of lead lender decision criteria;
- also taps into investment-grade retail lenders who invest for yield with no ancillary business requirements to fill out transaction;
- in EMEA (Europe, Middle East and Africa), in 2005, this accounted for c.€374bn of total syndicated loan activity, with c.250 investors participating.

- Crossover transactions
  - generally for unrated companies, or companies with ratings in the BB–/Ba3 to BB+/Ba1 range;
  - arranger/investor relationship may be with corporate borrower or with financial sponsor;
  - deal size can range from €500m–€15bn, structured as longer-term debt (that is, 5–7 years) with some expectation of refinancing risk at maturity;
  - pricing generally in the 100–200 bp over Libor range, with some margin reduction tied to de-leveraging;
  - generally includes some element of amortising debt or cash flow sweeps to facilitate de-leveraging;
  - generally senior secured debt, though can be unsecured depending upon credit profile;
  - reliant on emerging group of banks that invest in crossover credits, generally driven by corporate lenders in search of higher-yielding assets;
  - some ability to attract institutional lenders at higher end of margin spectrum, with potential liquidity increased if in possession of public ratings;
  - In EMEA, in 2005, this accounted for c.€103bn of total syndicated loan activity, with c.225 investors participating.

- Highly leveraged transactions
  - generally for unrated companies, or companies with ratings in the B+/B1 and below range;
  - arranger/investor relationship is with financial sponsor(s);
  - deal size can range from €200m–€15bn, typically structured as long-term debt (7, 8, 9 years) with both contractual amortisation and bullet structures, albeit limited refinancing risk assumed at maturity;
  - always senior secured debt, usually with some element of subordinated debt, that is, second lien, mezzanine or high yield;
  - pricing generally in the 225–325 bp over Libor range for senior debt, and c.250–350 bp higher for subordinated debt;
  - reliant on the institutional investor market as well as banks specialising in leveraged finance lending;
  - in EMEA in 2005, this accounted for c.€137bn of total syndicated loan activity, with c.200+ banks and institutional investors participating.

Telefónica – investment-grade case study

Acquisition of O_2

As an investment-grade acquisition case study one would be hard placed to find a more notable example than Telefónica S.A.'s £18.5bn facility to back up its acquisition of O_2 plc. The transaction represented the largest cross-border acquisition and syndicated financing by a Spanish company in Europe. At the time of the acquisition the offer was the second largest cash deal in the past ten years behind Cingular's takeover of AT&T Wireless in the United States in 2004. It also represented the largest European telecom acquisition facility since France Telecom's €30bn loan that backed the £25.1bn acquisition of Orange. On completion the transaction consolidated Telefónica's position as the second largest listed international telecoms group by market capitalisation behind Vodafone plc.

The transaction also claimed the titles of:

- largest European all-cash acquisition;
- largest-ever acquisition loan financing;
- largest-ever corporate loan;
- largest-ever Sterling loan; and was
- voted Best Western European Loan and Most Impressive Loan in Euroweek 2005 awards.

Background

Citigroup, Goldman Sachs International and The Royal Bank of Scotland plc jointly provided an underwritten financing of £18.5bn to Telefónica Europe B.V. (a wholly owned subsidiary of Telefónica S.A.) to enable Telefónica S.A. to satisfy in full a cash offer (the 'Offer') of 200 pence in cash per O_2 share. This represented a premium of 22 per cent (over the middle market price of an O_2 share of 164.25 pence at the close of business on 28 October 2005, being the last dealing day before this announcement). The offer, which launched on 31 October 2005, facilitated the negotiations of an irrevocable undertaking from O_2 directors in respect of their 2,820,573 O_2 shares and their ultimate recommendation of the offer.

It was Telefónica's ability to present a convincing business plan and carefully select its timing to launch the offer, together with a fair premium to shareholders that enabled it to avoid having to face competitive bidders. It was evident from the outset that acquiring O_2 was a logical step for Telefónica in pursuing its strategic goal of providing its shareholders with both growth and returns. The transaction drivers included accelerating Telefónica's growth profile relative to its peers; providing enhanced scale by entering Europe's two largest markets – Germany and the UK – with critical mass; balancing Telefónica's portfolio across businesses and regions; and the generation of significant synergies by 2008 while being immediately accretive to earnings, cash earnings and free cash flow per share. Importantly, it continued to enable Telefónica to preserve its stated shareholder remuneration policy based on dividends and share buybacks.

The syndicated loan product's ability to provide certainty of funds subject to acquisition related conditions precedent (in this case such as the regulatory requirements and UK standard acceptance conditions) made it the debt instrument of choice. This was further enhanced by the company's ability to take advantage of highly liquid financial markets.

Business description

Telefónica, previously the monopoly telephony operator in Spain, is a global leader in the telecommunications sector with a presence on three continents. The company provides a vast array of telecommunications services ranging from fixed-line and wireless communication access, internet and data transmission services to residential and corporate customers. Outside of Europe, it is the leading operator in Brazil, Argentina, Chile and Peru and has substantial operations in Colombia, Ecuador, El Salvador, Guatemala, Mexico, Morocco, Nicaragua, Panama, Puerto Rico, Uruguay and Venezuela.

Prior to the acquisition of O_2, for the year ended 31 December 2005, Telefónica reported revenues of €37.9bn, EBITDA (earnings before interest, tax, depreciation and amortisation) of €15.3bn and earnings per share of €0.913 per Telefónica share. As of 31 December 2005, Telefónica reported shareholders equity of €16.2bn.

With respect to the target, O_2 has 100 per cent ownership of mobile network operators and a leading mobile internet portal business in the UK, Germany and Ireland. At the time of acquisition O_2 had approximately 26 million customers and some 15,000 employees. For the year ended 31 March 2005 it reported revenues of £6.683bn, EBITDA of £1.768bn and net assets of £10.281bn. As of September 2005, O_2's reported customer base grew to 25.7 million, turnover grew to £3,615m and EBITDA grew to £975m. These increases are 17 per cent, 12 per cent and 15 per cent greater than the same period the previous year.

Facility overview and structure

Under the terms of the Facility Agreement dated 31 October 2005 Telefónica Europe B.V. as borrower with Telefónica S.A. as guarantor was provided with a £18.5bn dual-tranche multi-currency term loan facility.

Two-thirds of the facility was structured as a £12.33bn 364-day term loan ('tranche A') and the remaining third as a medium-term debt piece in the form of a £6.16bn three-year term loan ('tranche B'). Given strong investor demand in the public capital markets for a credit such as Telefónica, the company anticipated repaying a significant portion of the facility through debt capital market take-outs and, as a result, tranche A was structured (1) with two extension options to provide borrower flexibility; and (2) to incentivise such repayment and subsequently reduce the refinancing risk on termination.

The first extension option allowed up to 100 per cent of Tranche A to be extended for a further 365 days while the second provided for a maximum of 50 per cent of Tranche A to be extended for a further 180 days. The first extension option was subject to an extension fee depending on the amount extended, 2.5bp for less than 50 per cent and 5bp for more than 50 per cent respectively. A 5 bp extension fee was applied in relation to the second extension. The structure further supported such repayment by the inclusion of a pricing reduction mechanism whereby the applicable margin was reduced by 5 bp in the event that drawn amounts were equal to or less than 50 per cent commitments. The initial applicable margin for each facility was linked to ratings, with tranches A and B paying 32.5 bp and 37.5 bp as the out-of-the-box margin respectively.

Commitment fees of 27.5 per cent and 30 per cent of the applicable margin were applied in relation to tranches A and B.

Unlike the full suite of financial covenants expected in leverage and cross-over acquisitions, this facility did not benefit from any financial covenants. It did, however, include a restriction on financial indebtedness of the group. This is consistent with the strength of the Telefónica credit, indications from the ratings agencies that the company would maintain an investment-grade rating, and a confidence in the reduction of the refinancing risk through the strong representations regarding debt capital market issuances for the group.

Syndication strategy

RBS, together with its joint-bookrunners and the company, undertook a two-phase syndication strategy. The first phase – a sub-underwriting phase – focused on reducing the underwriters' commitments and was launched on 16 November 2005. Given the quantum of the transaction it was evident that successful syndication would be dependent on a successful sub-underwriting phase. The transaction was overwhelmingly well received by banks with in excess of £40bn being raised from 40 banks. Sub-underwriters signed into the transaction on 14 December 2005. Despite the fact that adequate funds had been raised, a second phase – a smaller general or retail syndication – was launched on 11 January 2006. This second phase targeted Telefónica's smaller relationship banks and resulted in 18 banks from nine different countries committing and raising approximately €1.7bn. These general syndication banks were signed into the facility on 10 February 2006.

In summary participant banks were invited at the levels shown in Exhibit 11.3.

Exhibit 11.3

Invite levels of participant banks

Invite level	Sub-underwriting amount (£m)	Take and hold (£m)
Mandated lead arranger	1000	700
Senior lead arranger	700	500
Arranger		200
Lead manager		100
Manager		50

Source: RBS.

The geographic spread of the syndicate represented the diverse global operations of the Group's business with significant take-up from the market being at Mandated Lead Arranger level. The graphs below depict the sub-underwriter split by role (and amount), country as well as depict a similar country split for those banks committing in general syndication (see Exhibit 11.4). From a lender's perspective key investment considerations included Telefónica's leading position in the fixed line telephony and mobile

Exhibit 11.4

(a) Sub-underwriter breakdown by country

(b) General syndication breakdown by country

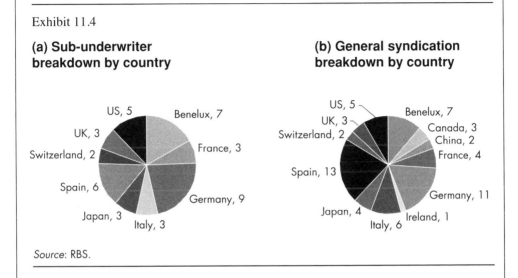

Source: RBS.

telephony businesses which represented the company's core operating segments. The geographic operational diversity of the business in approximately 40 countries and the company's profitable growth orientated strategy provided additional attraction to investors, as did the diversified product and client portfolio. Ultimately, however, a strong capital structure, an excellent track record of successful acquisitions and a strong, experienced management team provided lenders and the viability of corporate bond take-outs with the comfort levels they required to support the transaction.

Conclusion

This landmark transaction highlights the key benefits of the loan market product, the flexibility it offers and the short timeframe under which financing can be secured. While the sheer quantum could have been deemed daunting, the unique balance between appropriate pricing and structure, positive credit metrics and strong market dynamics provided the ingredients for an overwhelmingly successful deal. Telefónica has continued to deliver in line with its financing strategy and has since tapped the corporate bond market for US dollar, euro and Sterling bond issuances greater than US$14bn (equivalent value) in part to refinance the initial acquisition loans.

Metrovacesa – cross-over acquisition case study

Metrovacesa is an example of the growing sophistication in risk/return analysis leading to a more complex structure. The deal occupies the 'cross-over' space, with high leverage (but stable cash flows funding an ongoing de-leveraging of this) and an overall sub-investment-grade rating, while retaining a more typical senior financing structure.

Acquisition of Gecina

Background

Metropolitana Vasco Central (Metrovacesa) was formed in 1988 from the merger of Compania Inmobiliaria Metropolitana, Urbanizadora Metropolitana and Inmobiliaria Vasco-Central. Together these businesses developed buildings for lease in Spain. In 2003, Metrovacesa merged with the real estate company BAMI to further develop the property group. Metrovacesa is now Spain's largest property company with an equity market capitalisation of €7.3bn at the end of June 2006. The group has expanded organically and through the selective acquisition of landbank in addition to the transformational merger with BAMI.

Metrovacesa had a total gross asset value (GAV) of €5.5bn as at December 2004 (net €2.45bn), total revenues of €805.4m, and EBITDA of €325.5m (its EBITDA is achieved through rental activities (43 per cent), residential development (32 per cent) and land sales and management activities (25 per cent)). Metrovacesa is a member of the IBEX 35 (the reference index of the Spanish stock exchange).

Metrovacesa operates three businesses:

- *Commercial property letting*: Metrovacesa owns and manages real estate worth €3.3bn (59.5 per cent of the 2004 GAV). Metrovacesa has a diversified rental portfolio with 1.24 million square metres of property primarily comprised of offices, shopping centres and hotels.
- *Residential property development*: the development of real estate projects for the sale of housing – both permanent and second homes – worth €0.8bn (16 per cent of the 2004 GAV).
- *Land sales*: at the end of 2004, Metrovacesa's land reserves stood at 2.46 million square metres worth €1.4bn. The company actively manages this Landbank with significant acquisitions and disposals every year allowing it to manage its exposure and concentration risk.

Deal background

In mid-2004, Metrovacesa appointed RBS to lead arrange an €2.7bn financing in respect of their offer for Société Foncière Lyonnaise ('SFL'), which they narrowly lost to their main Spanish competitor, Colonial. RBS underwrote €2.4bn of the €2.7bn financing, with Banco Popular underwriting the balance. Despite the missed opportunity, Metrovacesa continued to search for acquisition opportunities.

Transaction overview

In March 2005, Metrovacesa acquired a 30 per cent stake (31.5 per cent of the voting rights) in Gecina at a cash price of €89.75 per share, with payment deferred until December 2005. An unconditional guarantee for the payment was required during this period and arranged by the Royal Bank of Scotland. A cash offer for all remaining shares at the same purchase price was made in December 2005.

Exhibit 11.5

Sources and uses

Sources	€m	Uses	€m
Tranche A1	5,273.2	Financing acquisition of shares of Gecina by Metrovacesa and any acquisition costs	5,673.2
Tranche A2	1,000	Refinancing Metrovacesa's existing debt	600
Tranche B1	800	Refinancing Gecina's existing debt*	800
Tranche B2	500	Working capital requirements	500
Total	7,573.2	Total	7,573.2

Source: Metrovacesa.

Exhibit 11.6

Financing/facility overview

Facility size and type	€7,573,200,000 term and revolving facilities agreement			
Tranches	Tranche A1	Tranche A2	Tranche B1	Tranche B2
Tranche types	Amortising term loan	Bullet term loan	Bullet term loan	Revolving credit facility
Amount (€m)	5,273.2	1000	800	500
Maturity	7 years	7 years	5 years	5 years
Pricing				
Commitment fee	25	25	15 subject to a step up to 35	15 subject to a step up to 40
Initial margin	175*	220*	100*	100*
*Margin ratchet	The margin for each tranche is subject to adjustment. In relation to tranches A1 and A2, this is by reference to the ratio of net debt to GAV and in relation to tranches B1 and B2, this is by reference to Gecina's long-term credit rating by S&P. While any default is continuing the margin shall revert to the highest of the relevant rates for that particular tranche.			

Source: RBS.

Metrovacesa mandated The Royal Bank of Scotland plc, Morgan Stanley Bank International Limited, Banco Popular Español, S.A. and Calyon Sucursal en España to arrange €7.573bn facilities to finance the acquisition and to refinance certain existing debt in both Metrovacesa and Gecina. Following the acquisition, Metrovacesa became the largest real estate company in Continental Europe with increased scale and diversification through access to the more liquid French real estate market.

Exhibit 11.7

Primary investor breakdown by country

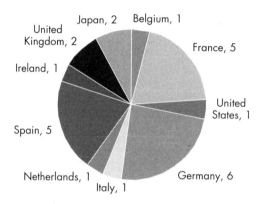

Source: RBS.

Syndication summary

At the time, this was the largest cross-border acquisition and syndicated financing by a Spanish company in Europe. The deal was highly levered at > 70 per cent net debt/gross asset value, with pricing between 100 and 220 bp for maturities ranging from 5–7 years.

The transaction was structured to enhance liquidity and pricing with significant incentives to de-lever the facility for the company. The deal was highly successful, with 48 lenders raising over €8.5bn at the sub-underwriting phase. No general syndication was required, with significant scale-back to sub-underwriters.

LBO acquisitions

Debt bankers, by the very nature of the business in which they work, that is, lending money, are not risk takers in its purest meaning. If money is lent then a calculated assessment will have been undertaken to ensure that the borrower's business can support the repayment of the loan. By their core characteristics leverage buyouts ('LBOs') are inherently more risky than other acquisition structures given the amount of debt funding in the overall capital structure. Based on this it is an interesting recent trend to see the popularity and volume of financial sponsor LBO transactions continuing to grow (see Exhibits 11.8 and 11.9).

Exhibit 11.8

EMEA sponsored LBO syndicated loan volume

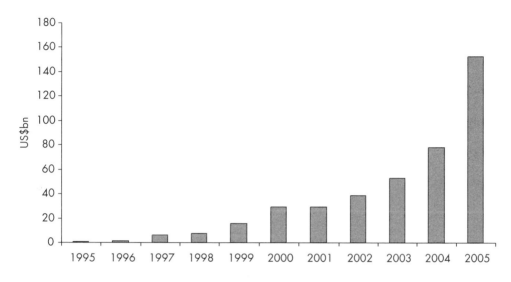

Source: Thomson Financial.

Exhibit 11.9

Sponsor vs. corporate leveraged loans

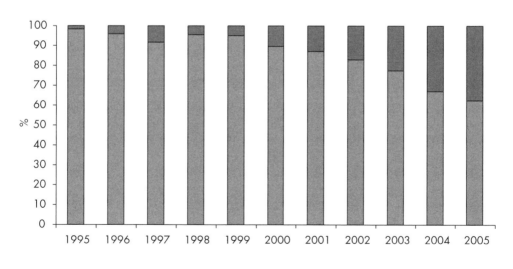

Source: Thomson Financial.

By way of background and before discussing recent trends in the leverage/LBO market and presenting a leverage acquisition/LBO case study, it is important to understand the basics of what an LBO is. An LBO can be defined as a debt-financed transaction funded typically via bank loans whereby a private equity house/financial sponsor ('financial sponsor') takes control of a company and the company's assets are used as security for the loans required to finance the purchase. Typically the debt component in the capital structure is 70–80 per cent, with equity from the financial sponsor being the funding balance. The return (profit) of the company will be 'leveraged' to the equity capital and produce a large return on equity (ROE) for the owners risking their money. The loan capital is borrowed through a combination of prepayable bank facilities and/or public or privately placed bonds, which may be classified as high-yield or 'junk' bonds. Often, the debt will appear on the acquired company's balance sheet and the acquired company's free cash flow will be used to repay the debt. The capital structure of an LBO generally consists of some or all of the following instruments: (i) senior debt, (ii) senior subordinated debt, (iii) subordinated debt, (iv) mezzanine financing, (v) bridge financing and (vi) equity layers.

An LBO can either be an acquisition of a public company, taking a public company private and delisting it from the stock exchange or financing a secondary, or tertiary LBO acquisition as was a growing trend in 2005.

The significant reliance on debt to finance the acquisition magnifies the risk of the transaction; consequently, the potential return to the buyer upon subsequent exit is increased. Possible exit strategies for LBOs include (i) initial public offering, which allows investors to liquidate their ownership interest, (ii) re-capitalisation, which allows equity holders to realise a return by taking a sizable dividend, and (iii) outright or partial sale to another strategic or financial buyer.

History

The LBO market started in the 1970s in the US but as an acquisition financing concept it didn't really take off in Europe until the late 1980s and early 1990s. In the early days in Europe, LBOs were primarily 'club' deals with wide equity syndications targeted onto UK acquisitions and with few LBO banks providing the debt funding with large take and hold positions distributed among this small circle of LBO banks. The LBO banks in this early period were primarily the UK banks, namely The Royal Bank of Scotland, Bank of Scotland, NatWest and Barclays.

In the mid-1990s and early 2000s, the European LBO model had developed along with the increasing sophistication and evolution of the debt capital markets. As a result of the attractive yields and range of LBO acquisition targets, financial sponsors were expanding their investment activities across Europe with increasing numbers of new funds, larger private equity funds being established and the liquid European investor base being able to support larger transactions, which required wider debt syndication and less equity syndication. Another key development in the structuring of LBOs since their initial days in the 1980s was the movement from the EBITA (earnings before interest, tax and amortisation) metric to the now commonplace EBITDA metric.

More recently the LBO market has been characterised by (i) the establishment of mega private equity funds (see Exhibit 11.10), (ii) jumbo consortium LBO transactions in order for a mega equity cheque to be provided, (iii) acceptance of secondary LBO transactions, and more recently tertiary LBOs (see Gala case study in this chapter), (iv) sell-side staple financing, (v) recapitalisations, (vi) opco/propco structures to assist in funding the increasing valuations of LBO transactions, (vii) increasing investments in LBO's by hedge funds, and (viii) market-wide acceptance and utilisation of 'run rate' EBITDA/Proforma EBITDA metrics.

Exhibit 11.10

New funds raised by private equity (Europe)

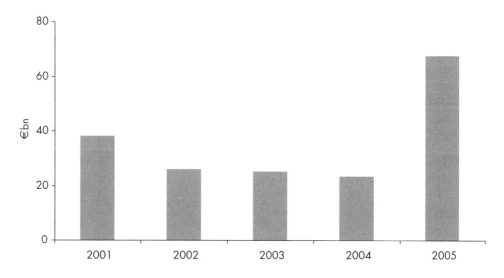

Source: European Private Equity and Venture Capital Association (EVCA)/Thomson Venture Economics/Pricewaterhouse Coopers.

Standard & Poor's LCD (Leveraged Commentary and Data) reported that for the first time ever the total value of European LBO deals topped €100bn in 2005, at €103bn, which was more than double the 2004 volume of €43.8bn, and more than equalled the total combined volumes of 2002, 2003 and 2004. Another key metric achieved in 2005 was that the volume of €1bn plus deals reached its highest level with 33 deals valued at over €1bn, which was up from 16 deals in 2004 (source: Thomson Financial). LBO deals of €1bn plus accounted for 14.6 per cent of the total number of 2005 LBO deals which was up from 5.3 per cent in 2004. The mid market remained the largest contributor to the European LBO market in 2005 with deals in the 'less than €250m' size range accounting for 42 per cent of the total number of LBO deals executed in Europe (see Exhibit 11.11).

Exhibit 11.11

Growth of jumbo leveraged loans

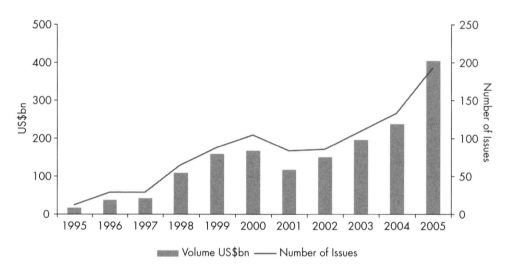

Source: Thomson Financial.

Other key trends identified by Standard & Poor's in their LCD Leveraged Lending Review of the 2005 European Loan Market were:

- Increasing leverage multiples as leverage, in itself, allows for deal values to increase with the same amount of equity investment from private equity sponsors. This, in turn, brings more sellers into the market. For new LBOs of €250m to €1bn, structures were the most aggressive at 5.8× total debt and 4.8× senior debt to EBITDA.
- Telecoms, services and leasing, chemicals and retail sectors attracted the highest level of private equity investment in 2005 and accounted for 43 per cent of the volume of the €103bn of LBOs executed in 2005.
- Significant increase in secondary buyouts: 69 secondary buyouts comprised €27.7bn or 47.1 per cent of the €59bn of new LBO volumes and 60.5 per cent of new LBOs in terms of number of deals.
- Public to private buyouts had their best year yet in terms of volume, with €11.9bn in loans accounting for 20.3 per cent of new-issue LBO volume. This compares to €5.3bn in 2004 and €4.6bn in 2003.
- Historically, it used to be the case that in the US market institutional investors bought *c*.70 per cent of the leveraged debt and in Europe it was the reverse, however this trend is starting to change.

Based on these trends and the buoyant leverage/LBO market in 2005, it was no surprise to the market that Gala decided that 2005 was the right year to execute its largest acquisition to date.

Gala – LBO acquisition finance case study

In terms of an LBO/leverage acquisition case study we will review the successful purchase by Gala Group Limited ('Gala') of Coral Eurobet Limited ('Coral') in October 2005, with the continued support of the financial sponsors Candover Partners Limited ('Candover') and Cinven Limited ('Cinven'), who were the equity houses in the March 2003 tertiary LBO, and funds advised by Permira Advisers Limited ('Permira') who acquired a stake in the Gala business in August 2005. Funds advised by Permira, under the terms of the transaction, invested c.£200m in order to become joint and equal investors in Gala alongside Candover and Cinven.

Before looking into this case study in detail, it is probably worth looking at the key drivers and criteria for LBOs and leverage acquisition candidates as these underlying factors remain virtually unchanged for every LBO and leveraged acquisition (see Exhibit 11.12).

Exhibit 11.12

Core LBO/leverage acquisition candidate criteria

Typical LBO candidate criteria	Additional candidate criteria for leverage acquisitions
Steady and predictable cash flow	Target is EBITDA accretive
Clean balance sheet with little debt	Acquisition assets are complementary and expand diversification
Strong and defensible market position	Additional asset value for loan collateral
Limited working capital requirements	Synergy benefits with existing business
Minimal future capital requirements	Strengthens market share and market position
Heavy asset base for loan collateral	
Divestible assets	
Strong management team	
Synergy opportunities	
Potential for expense reduction	
Viable exit strategy	

Source: RBS.

Background

Gala is no stranger in the leverage acquisition and LBO financing markets having completed its tertiary LBO in March 2003 and the £2.18bn LBO acquisition of Coral in October 2005. Gala underwent a management buy-in backed by PPM Ventures Ltd and Royal Bank Development Capital in December 1997 and its second LBO occurred in March 2000, which was led by CSFB Private Equity and with PPM Ventures Ltd and Royal Bank Development Capital also investing new money in Gala. The latest tertiary LBO involved Candover and Cinven acquiring Gala for £1.24bn. Since its first

LBO, Gala has grown its EBITDA from £36.0m in FY97 to £159.3m (pre-joint venture and exceptional items) in FY05 and has increased its bingo market share to 40 per cent in 2005. The strong Gala business model, experienced management team, positive market dynamics and strong cash flows with high cash conversion ratios, has meant Gala has remained an attractive LBO target since the mid-1990s. In addition to all the LBO transactions Gala has undergone since 1997, Gala itself has also undertaken a series of acquisitions to strengthen its underlying business and expand its market presence. The most notable acquisitions undertaken include Ritz in 1998, Jarglen in 1999, Riva in 2000, Ladbroke Casinos (from Hilton plc) in 2000 and New Generation Bingo in 2005.

Business description

Gala is the leading UK gaming operator in the high-volume, low-stake segment of the market, with the largest licensed bingo business in the UK and the third largest casino business in the UK. In FY05 Gala had a 40 per cent share of the ticket sales of the National Bingo Game and the largest bingo chain with 167 clubs. In its casino operation Gala has 30 outlets serving $c.1.3$ million members, which has established a market share of 20 per cent.

Coral, itself, is also no stranger to acquisitions and has been the target of two LBO transactions. Originally founded in 1926, Coral was first acquired by Bass in January 1981 and then by Ladbrokes in December 1997. Coral's first LBO was executed in December 1998 by Morgan Grenfell Private Equity. In September 2002, Coral underwent its secondary LBO with private equity house Charterhouse acquiring Coral from Morgan Grenfell Private Equity. As at FY05, Coral was a leading provider of both off-course and online betting and gaming products and is a natural complement for Gala's existing bingo and casino businesses. Coral offers odds and takes bets on horseracing and other sporting events, as well as numbers betting, FOBT (fixed odds betting terminals) and AWP (amusement with prizes) machines through its national network of 1,267 licensed betting offices.

Overview of the Coral acquisition

On 7 October 2005, Gala agreed to acquire Coral for a total consideration of £2.18bn. The acquisition closed and funded on 27 October 2005. This transaction was an important strategic move for Gala as it transformed Gala into the pre-eminent integrated betting and gaming franchise in Europe in the high-volume, low-stake segment of the market with a total capitalisation of over £4.0bn. As at FY05, the combined company operates the UK's largest bingo business (167 bingo clubs), third largest casino business (30 units), and third largest bookmaking business (1,267 licensed betting offices), as well as a leading online betting and gaming platform, altogether serving more than 2.2 million active customers.

Financing summary and facilities overview

Gala's £2.18bn acquisition of Coral was financed by total funded debt of £2.56bn, a total new cash equity contribution of £862m and a significant rollover equity contribution with total equity accounting for 37.5 per cent of the capital structure. The Royal Bank of Scotland ('RBS') and Lehman Brothers ('Lehman') were mandated as the mandated lead arrangers ('MLAs') and joint bookrunners to arrange and underwrite the acquisition financing facilities. The acquisition facilities consisted of £1.95bn of funded senior term debt facilities, £50m revolving credit facility, £200m capital investment facility, £150m second lien facility and a £460m subordinated mezzanine facility. The capital structure yielded the following highlights:

- high level of interest cover;
- rapid net de-leveraging of the business from the opening net leverage of 6.9x; and
- rapidly reducing ratio of Net Total Debt/(EBITDA – Normalised Capex).

The principal terms of the facilities are summarised in Exhibit 11.13.

Exhibit 11.13

Summary facility terms

Facility	Amount (£m)	Maturity	Repayment	Initial margin[3] (%)
Term loan A	530.0	7 years	Amortising	2.25[1]
Term loan B	710.0	8 years	Bullet	2.50[1]
Term loan C	710.0	9 years	Bullet	3.00
Capital investment facility[2]	200.0	7 years	Amortising	2.25[1]
Revolving credit facility[2]	50.0	7 years	Bullet	2.25[1]
Second lien facility	150.0	9.5 years	Bullet	5.00
Mezzanine facility	460.0	10 years	Bullet	4.00% Cash pay/ 5.00% PIK

Notes:
1 Subject to margin ratchet.
2 Undrawn at closing.
3 Pre-reverse flex.

Source: RBS.

In terms of Gala and the financial sponsors' decision on the selection of banks to lead the deal, RBS and Lehman were relatively obvious choices given their long-term relationships with Gala and Coral respectively. RBS was jointly mandated with Merrill Lynch in quarter 1 of 2005 to arrange £1.025bn of financing to support the planned refinancing of Gala's existing debt following Permira's purchase of a 29 per cent equity stake in Gala. This transaction was superseded by the Coral acquisition transaction. In January 2005 Lehman Brothers, along with Bank of Scotland, Deutsche Bank and UBS, was mandated to arrange £1.045bn of senior and £200m of mezzanine facilities to support a recapitalisation of the Coral business.

This leveraged acquisition financing achieved a number of milestones for the European LBO market, at the time it was (i) the largest Sterling LBO done to date, and (ii) the largest mezzanine tranche done to date. These achievements had knock on implications for the syndication strategy for RBS and Lehman as it meant that there was going to be a large syndication to manage as the invitation list of traditional banks and institutional investors ('funds') would have to be sufficiently long to ensure a successful syndication. In order to achieve this and to capitalise on the strong liquidity in both the traditional bank and funds markets, the MLAs decided that a one phase syndication was the best selldown strategy to execute with an underwrite joint lead arranger ('JLA') ticket on offer at the same time as three general syndication phase tickets (see Exhibit 11.14). By offering three general phase tickets, the MLAs were able to tap into a wider investor base and to approach investors who might not be able to commit to the larger take and hold tickets.

Exhibit 11.14

Syndication ticket invitations

Title	Underwrite (£m)	Final hold commitment (£m)	Upfront fee (bp)
Joint lead arranger	100	70	100
Lead arranger	N/A	55	70
Arranger	N/A	40	60
Co-arranger	N/A	20	50

Source: RBS.

As a result of the growth in the funds market over 2005 and the significant liquidity in this market at the time of the deal launch for a strong credit such as Gala/Coral, it was decided that 60 per cent of term loan B and term loan C would be sold via a carve-out to funds. As a result of the 60 per cent carve-out equating to £426.0m in each of the term loans B and C, this represented the largest institutional carve-out up to this point in time.

The syndication, which closed in December 2005, resulted in all of the facilities being significantly oversubscribed with the second lien and mezzanine facilities oversubscribed the most. As a result, a reverse flex was proposed and was well received across the committed investors to reduce the second lien margin from 500 bp to 462.5 bp and the mezzanine facility margin from 400 bp cash interest/500 bp PIK interest to 400 bp cash interest/425 bp PIK interest. With investors chasing attractive assets, reverse flex has become a relatively common occurrence among leveraged loans. In Europe, 48 leverage loans in 2005 successfully reverse flexed compared to only 14 reverse flexes of leveraged deals in 2004 (source: Standard & Poor's LCD). This highly successful syndication was well received in the investment banking community and the market recognised the £2.18bn Gala transaction in the 2005 Euroweek Loans Poll by awarding it the Best LBO Loan in 2005.

Conclusion

While the outlook for the overall capital markets is becoming more cautious, the use of the syndicated loan markets to support acquisition financing, be it generated by corporate borrowers, private equity sponsors, or infrastructure players, will continue due to the syndicated loan market's speed of execution, level of sophistication and depth of liquidity, and its ability to maintain a high level of confidentiality. Given the flow of money into private equity firms, the strength of corporate balance sheets, and the amount of liquidity in the global syndicated loan markets, expectations for the continued strong relationship between the syndicated loan markets and acquisition financing remain high.

Chapter 12

Project finance

Richard Cole and Paul Eardley-Taylor
HSBC

Introduction

Synopsis

This chapter seeks to provide a broad reflective practitioner overview of key project finance considerations. After defining the subject, we outline parties' motivations in using project finance before reviewing a transaction's process sequence. We then analyse the structural underpinning of transactions before commenting on the risks analysed and mitigated in concluding a project financing. In providing such overview, we have attempted to minimise jargon and inherently trade off detail against an overview.

Definition

Each book on project finance offers an alternative subject definition. The authors' own definition is:

> the raising of finance for a major capital investment for which repayment (either largely or exclusively) of the lenders relies on the cash flow generated by that investment (for which the lenders are granted an associated security package).

Project finance is a form of structured, highly leveraged 'sole recourse' lending usually advanced to a special purpose vehicle (SPV). The SPV borrower is usually an entity formed by the 'project sponsors' solely to build (or acquire), own and operate the project (noting that many project financings are concluded without the SPV owning the project). In many markets (with the United States and Australia as exceptions) project finance is not usually tax driven, with a natural exception for project lease transactions.

Exhibit 12.1 compares project finance to corporate lending.

Project finance has some resemblance to leveraged buyout (LBO) finance. Both are highly leveraged financings with tight covenant packages. However, LBO borrowers only secure funds for completed projects and although borrowers are usually single industry, they usually have multiple corporate operations/revenue centres. In contrast, project finance borrowers are usually single industry *and* single business activity, with lenders asked to take construction risk upon that single business activity.

Exhibit 12.1

Comparison between corporate lending and project finance

Aspect	Corporate lending	Project finance
Borrower	Existing company	SPV formed for project
Leverage	Lower, with corporate gearing often 30%–75%	Higher. Median debt to equity ratios of 70:30 (233% gearing) to 80:20 (400% gearing).
Repayment	Dependent on the company's corporate revenue generating capacity (with spreading of repayment risk)	Solely from the free cash flow of the individual project
Recourse	An undoubted guarantee needed if the borrower is a poor credit	Save for certain pre-defined circumstances (such as equity funding), no recourse to project sponsors, meaning sole recourse to SPV
Security	Generally realisable and of value	As granted over a single purpose asset, may have little 'cashable' value
Credit analysis	Centred upon corporate financial statement/projection analysis	As sole recourse lending, detailed assessment made of technical and contractual structure and bespoke financial projections

Source: Author's own.

Industrial sectors and countries

Project finance was traditionally used to fund larger (or lumpy) capital investments in the older economy, for example, power generation or petrochemical plants. More recently, public private partnership (PPP)/private finance initiative (PFI) activity has brought project finance techniques into large areas of public sector infrastructure. Exhibit 12.2 shows an apportionment of 2005 project finance transactions by industrial sector.

A project's industrial sector, for example, Liquefied Natural Gas (LNG) has implications for its contractual structure (see section on commercial contracts, in this chapter) and for the associated transaction risks that must be satisfactorily addressed to achieve financial close (see section on risk analysis and mitigation, in this chapter).

Exhibit 12.3 shows an apportionment of the leading 2005 project finance loans (by country), which were reasonably spread between the global economic regions.

Exhibit 12.4, though, shows that on a regional basis the market trend between 2004 and 2005 was clear.

Motivation

Investors have many debt financing options to fund their capital investments. The authors argue 'tender authorities', project sponsors and lenders are key stakeholders within project finance who may use or provide project finance for the following reasons.

Exhibit 12.2

Transactions by sector

Sector	Value US$m	%	Sector	Value US$m	%
Industry	6,690.3	4.9	Ports	3,317.7	2.4
Leisure and property	5,776.4	4.2	Power	34,673.5	25.2
Mining	7,854.8	5.7	PPP	11,569.2	8.4
Oil and gas	18,200.1	13.2	Telecoms	14,500.8	10.5
Petrochemicals	8,599.1	6.2	Transport	26,404.8	19.2

Source: Project Finance International Magazine.

Exhibit 12.3

Transactions by country

Country	Value US$m	%	Country	Value US$m	%
United Kingdom	16,925.4	12.0	Australia	8,904.0	6.3
Spain	16,147.6	11.5	Oman	5,671.3	4.0
Qatar	14,076.0	10.0	South Korea	4,575.2	3.3
USA	12,999.3	9.3	India	3,123.1	2.2
Italy	9,824.7	7.0	Brazil	3,060.6	2.2

Source: Project Finance International Magazine.

Exhibit 12.4

Transactions by region

Country	Value US$bn 2004	Value US$bn 2004	% change
Europe, Middle East and Africa	51.3	94.3	83.8
Americas	28.0	21.0	(25.0)
Asia-Pacific	36.0	24.9	(30.8)

Source: Project Finance International Magazine.

Tender authorities

In certain sectors, such as PFI social infrastructure, tender authorities trigger an eventual project financing through issuing a request for proposal (RFP) to the private sector requesting offers to finance, build, own and operate specific infrastructure projects. This method is used because:

- in many markets (for example, the Arabian Gulf states) it is an excellent way to procure public infrastructure at a lower cost than previous procurement alternatives; and
- it is a suitable method of passing construction and operating risks to the private sector in return for the provision of new social infrastructure.

Project sponsors

Project sponsors (the SPV investors) are the bidders for/developers of projects and the customers for project finance lenders. In addition to the above circumstances, project sponsors may select project finance because:

- in joint venture projects (for example, LNG projects) it can be an excellent means for partners of potentially different credit standing to fund a project while minimising individual financial exposure;
- it enables cash constrained (or risk averse) sponsors to separately incorporate companies and raise higher debt amounts than through corporate borrowing while retaining traditional equity benefits (such as dividends, repayment of shareholder loans and the ability to sell shares); and
- it enables sponsors to leverage general banking relationships to potentially increase their corporate borrowing capacity, access a wider pool of funding sources and longer-term funding (for example, tenors of around or over 20 years).

Project sponsors can be crudely divided between occasional users of project finance (such as the super-major oil companies) who mainly use project finance when required by joint venture partners or jurisdiction, and the serial users of project finance (such as PFI contractors).

Supplier motivation

The main suppliers within project finance are lenders and contractors. In consideration for providing long-term (compared to corporate lending) funding to projects, lenders wish to make adequate returns and, to lend, require adequate project sponsor equity contributions, mitigated construction risk, appropriate offtake arrangements as well as a free cash flow priority towards debt service obligations.

Contractors' (construction and operations and maintenance) motivation is to make a profitable sale. In doing so in a project finance structure, contractors must sign tight contracts with the SPV and permit the lenders to have direct contractual rights in the event of an SPV default. The other main supplier category are third-party professional advisers (such as financial, legal, technical, insurance and sector-specific advisers), whose motivation is to provide their individual good or service and who play a major role in executing transaction due diligence.

Pros and cons

General pros and cons of project finance as a product are shown in Exhibit 12.5.

Exhibit 12.5

Pros and cons of project finance

Pros	Cons
Excellent means to fund larger projects, joint venture investments and public infrastructure investments, including the matching of an investment's repayment term to its cash flows	Higher transaction costs due to execution time required and involvement of multiple parties.
Allows many investors to access more optimal debt financing terms than they could individually secure, encompassing the matching of debt profile to cash flows	Project finance all-in debt cost often higher than corporate borrowings and highly restrictive once in place (tight financial covenants). Project finance is rarely used for 100% owned investment
Controls imposed by project finance (and lender monitoring) ensures efficient SPV management	High disclosure requirements in relation to use of proceeds and commercial details

Source: Author's own.

Process sequence

The project finance process sequence typically takes one of two simplified forms although it always involves competitive tendering.

Investment tender

In the example investment tender schedule shown in Exhibit 12.6 (often seen in the PFI sector), tender authorities' RFP issue leads to bids from potential project sponsors. Herein, project sponsors face bid risk and lenders face bid on bid risk (as they must find a project sponsor to work with and their project sponsor must achieve bid success). For larger tenders, the total process sequence can take between 12 and 24 months.

Exhibit 12.6

Investment tender schedule

Activity	Months	Activity	Months
RFP development	0–4	Winning bidder selection	11
Pre-qualification	1–3	Commercial negotiations	11–14
RFP issue	4	Commercial signature	14
Bid preparation	4–9	Financing negotiations	13–16
Bid submission	9	Financing signature	16
Bid evaluation	9–11	Financial close	17–19

Source: Author's own.

If project finance is used in a project acquisition/disposal transaction, the process sequence must shorten to meet the vendor's timetable (this is possible as due diligence requirements are lower for completed projects). For example, in a 2005 UK power sector acquisition financing, there was only a four-month period from bank selection pre-bid through to financial close.

Supplier tender

In the example supplier tender schedule shown in Exhibit 12.7 (often seen in the oil and gas sector), project sponsors individually develop a project, for which they tender for suppliers (such as contractors and lenders).

In this schedule, a project sponsor would develop its commercial arrangements in the earlier phases (but keeping in mind key finance market requirements) before, in later phases, securing and closing the project financing.

Managing the process

Project finance has certain resemblances to project management, being a details business with many transaction stakeholders (each of whom have different objectives to be reconciled), an extensive involvement for third-party consultants (who must be engaged, instructed and managed), with the transaction core being a large, high-value capital investment.

In managing the process, principals are advised to closely monitor projects under development and negotiation, have a firm idea of what they strategically want from the project, know the constraints they face in project bidding and execution and know the points that can be negotiated to achieve project closure.

For the key principals (tender authorities, project sponsor and lender) there is some commonality of process. Each is working on the same transaction, with the same technical proposition and host jurisdiction, meaning they will encounter similar issues. Secondly, each stakeholder is commercially reliant upon the results of a financial model that outlines, from

Exhibit 12.7

Supplier tender schedule

Activity	Months	Activity	Months
[Tender of JV partners]	0–6	Lead bank selection	15
Development of commercial structure/agreements	6–12	Signature of commercial agreements	15
[Tender of contractor(s)]	10–13	Financing negotiations	15–17
Lender RFP issued	12	Financing signature	17
Lender offers submitted	14	Financial close	18–21
Evaluation of lender offers	14–15		

Source: Author's own.

their perspective, the project's projected financial performance and must have the confidence and ability to manage the financing process (including developing the financial plan, financial modelling and subsequent negotiations). Thirdly, each stakeholder has to clear a similar hurdle of decision-taking gatekeepers to close the individual project. For a project, tender authorities must pass the tender analysis committee or tender board, project sponsors must pass their investment committee and/or Board of Directors while lenders' must gain the approval of their credit committees.

Relevant structures

Commercial contracts

The provisions of the underlying project commercial contracts are pivotal to a successful project financing. Given its sole recourse nature, such contracts are often the basis of lenders/investors repayment. As example, Exhibit 12.8 shows a schematic contractual structure for a

---

Exhibit 12.8

Schematic contractual structure

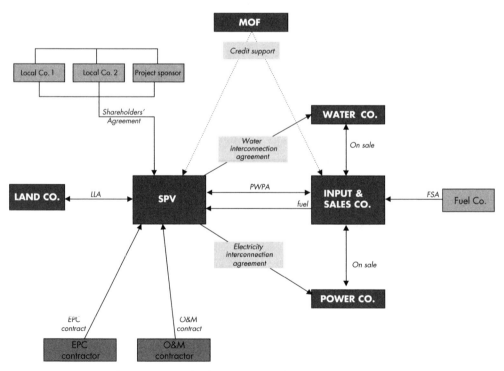

EPC: Engineering, Procurement and Construction; FSA: Fuel Supply Agreement; LLA: Land Lease Agreement; MOF: Ministry of Finance; O&M: Operations and Maintenance; PWPA: Power and Water Purchase Agreement

Source: Authors' own.

---

power and water project. The SPV (also the borrower) is the key contractual counterparty to analyse with key contractual arrangements noted below.

Ownership arrangements

In a project's development phase, ownership arrangements may be contained within a Development or Consortium Agreement which would outline the parties' intent concerning, *inter alia*, the nature of the corporate vehicle, the percentage of shares owned, methods of SPV funding and decision-making.

Subsequently, ownership arrangements are codified in a formal shareholders agreement (see Exhibit 12.6) (or Joint Venture or Partnership Agreement). This document codifies all matters relating to the control, corporate governance, funding, ownership, share transfers and potential termination of the SPV.

Land access

The SPV will require unencumbered access to the project site for the project duration. This will usually be granted through a Site Lease, Land Lease Agreement (LLA) (see Exhibit 12.8) (or equivalent) which provides the SPV with site access (and permission to carry out site works) over a specified term in return for rental payments.

Input and sales arrangements

A project's input and sales arrangements represent the core of a project's creditworthiness (noting that long-term operational free cash flow will repay lenders and pay dividends to the project sponsors).

'Input arrangements' covers, *inter alia*, gas/fuel supply agreements, alumina or steam supply agreements, tolling agreements (where the party purchasing the output is also responsible for providing the inputs) or, in the case of wind farms, the wind itself.

Similarly, 'sales arrangements' can cover power (and water) purchase agreements (see Exhibit 12.8), steam purchase agreements, project agreements, offtake agreements (on a fixed price and/or volume basis), tolling agreements, terminal use agreements, renewable energy purchase agreements, hedging contracts or, in the case of traded commodities, selling into the marketplace. In assessing such contracts, key issues to assess are:

- the contractual term (longer than the debt? If not, there is contract renewal risk);
- the rigidity of the SPV's purchase/sale obligations (are contracts supply or pay/take or pay?);
- the basis of sale (is product sold if it is available for consumption (that is, it does not have to be dispatched or physically sold) or only if it is actually sold in the marketplace?);
- the price of inputs/outputs (are they fixed (subject to indexation) or subject to market movements over time?);
- the risk of external events (how are they borne by the parties under the arrangements?); and
- what is the governing law and what are dispute resolution procedures?

Finally, as shown in Exhibit 12.8, in order to sell its product, an SPV may require to be connected to national utility networks.

Credit support

Given the importance of input/sales arrangements, project sponsors and lenders place a major focus on supplier/purchaser credit quality. For example, if the purchaser is of insufficient credit standing (for example, no independent investment-grade credit rating) and there are no alternative methods of redress (such as statutory protection for its contractual liabilities), credit support will be required for their supply/payment obligations.

In contracted transactions, payment guarantees from investment-grade counterparties (such as the national government (see Exhibit 12.8) or ultimate parent company) are typically provided for supply/payment obligations. In market risk-based transactions, letters of credit may be accepted as a form of revolving credit support (as with a tradable commodity, purchaser default could permit a swift redirection of output to alternate customers).

Build and operate/maintain

A project's construction and operational arrangements represent major credit concerns only slightly less important than the input/sales arrangements.

Construction arrangements are typically carried out under a single EPC contract as shown in Exhibit 12.8, or in the case of complicated industrial process plants or renewable energy projects, two to three separate individual contracts. Given the risk concentration upon the contractor, the contractor's experience and credit standing are key project sponsor/lender concerns.

Post-completion, a project may be operated under an operations and maintenance ('O&M') Agreement (see Exhibit 12.8), service contract, facilities management contract or similar. Frequently, the operator is also an SPV shareholder (seen as a credit benefit).

Behind the scenes

Finally, in order to prevent potential future problems, sponsors and lenders may also need to be mindful of underlying or behind the scenes obligations (notwithstanding that the SPV may benefit from primary sales arrangements). In Exhibit 12.8, separate national bodies are responsible for fuel supply and water and electricity transmission/distribution activities and so each concludes contracts with 'Input & Sales Co.' (the SPV's primary obligor for input and sales arrangements).

Financing matters

Equity

Project sponsors typically contribute their percentage of funding in one of three methods:

- share capital;
- shareholder loans (the motivation being to reduce 'trapped cash' due to a potentially insufficient distributable reserve); or
- equity bridge facilities (EBF) (loans borrowed by the SPV but severally guaranteed by the SPV shareholders and repaid by one of the two above methods).

Low-risk infrastructure sectors such as PFI tend to have gearing up to 90 debt:10 equity, contracted power plants may have gearing of 80:20, whereas more market risk sectors (such as petrochemicals or merchant power) have gearing in the range of 70:30.

Sources of debt finance

Dependent on variables such as project jurisdiction, debt requirement, sponsor bank relationships and transaction risk profile, project sponsors can choose from a number of debt financing sources to provide their project finance. Absent transaction specifics, a sponsor's choice will usually be driven by what is the most economic source for that transaction (for example, the lowest all-in price (fees, premia and margins), the lowest percentage amortisation by maturity and the longest term before maturity so as to maximise the sponsor's net present value (NPV) of their investment).

Exhibit 12.9 shows in headline form key sources of project finance debt.

Globally, syndicated commercial loans (provided by banks) finance the largest percentage of transactions (in 2005, 84 per cent of all project finance), although bonds and term B facilities (provided by institutional investors) are more widely seen in the United States (in 2005, being used as much as bank loans). In more emerging markets, export credit facilities still play a leading role in financings, although recent years have found them to be 'priced out' of many markets for medium-sized transactions. However, in the largest transactions, combinations of a number of the above facilities (multi-sourcing) are used to provide the required liquidity. For example, a 2006 US$2.5bn Saudi Arabian transaction saw a combination of syndicated loans, Islamic finance, two export credit agency tranches and EBF.

Typically, the majority of debt finance raised will fund construction costs. However, depending on the project's sector, additional facilities may be raised to fund working capital, debt service reserve requirements as well as to provide credit support to third parties. In terms of refinancings, syndicated commercial loans are again the most widely used funding source although in lower-risk sectors, capital markets issues are more regularly seen (which bonds may be wrapped by an insurance company).

Documentation and security

Financing documentation codifies the commercial deal between the SPV and its lenders and seeks to ensure, from lender perspective, an appropriate control regime is in place to give the greatest assurance of repayment. This is supplemented by, to the extent available in an individual jurisdiction, a comprehensive security package.

Exhibit 12.9

Key sources of debt finance

Source	Source
Syndicated commercial loans (international and local)	Lease finance
Bonds (mainly private placement and wrapped (by insurance companies))	Term B loans
Export credit agency (under OECD consensus and direct tranches) and multilateral agency tranches	Islamic finance

Source: Author's own.

Key documentary provisions could include:

- Financial covenants
  - at financial close, looking forward over each calculation date until final maturity a minimum required ratio (for example, 1.25×) of cash flow available for debt service to debt service (debt service coverage ratio or 'DSCR');
  - during the project's operating period, upon any calculation date, a minimum DSCR test (for example, 1.15×) must be passed before any surplus cash flows (following debt service) are released to the project sponsors.
- Non-financial covenants
  - no additional indebtedness;
  - no disposals;
  - negative pledge;
  - controls over expenditure outside agreed budgetary parameters.
- Amortisation
  - supplementing scheduled amortisation, the use of cash sweep mechanisms to protect the lenders and encourage refinancing.
- Accounts
  - lender control of SPV bank accounts (which, depending on project jurisdiction, may be located outside the host country);
  - specified funds flow priority (waterfall) with debt payments made following payment of operating expenses and taxes.
- Direct agreements
  - in the event of SPV default under a commercial contract, direct contractual access to that underlying commercial agreement (to 'step-in' to the SPV's rights and obligations).
- Security
  - pledge/lien over shares in the SPV;
  - mortgage over project site and assets;
  - assignment of SPV's contracts with third parties;
  - assignment of intellectual property and receivables;
  - charge over SPV bank accounts and insurance proceeds.

Such documentation will be drafted by the lender's legal advisers and negotiated by the SPV's legal advisers.

Cash flow

Project finance is linked to capital budgeting and financial economics. Project sponsors will only invest in projects to the extent they are economically viable and can reasonably be expected to generate a positive NPV (that is, a projected internal rate of return in excess of the sponsor's requirement). Project sponsors will seek to maximise the NPV of a project's future cash flows, for example, determining and sourcing their financing plan on that basis.

Project commercial analysis will be centred upon a financial model and in transactions there may be as many as three models (one for each of the tender authorities, project sponsors and lenders). The model is required to contain all material costs (capital and operating, including debt service and taxation) and revenues pertaining to the project and is usually independently audited prior to financial close. The financial model is also used to calculate the lenders' required financial cash-flow ratios, the DSCR we have mentioned above and other ratios often used include the loan life coverage ratio (LLCR) and the project life coverage ratio (PLCR).

Note the 'debt to EBITDA' ratio seen in LBOs or the 'interest cover' ratio seen in corporate lending are not widely seen in project finance which tends to rely on purely cash flow-based coverage ratios.

Risk analysis and mitigation

Introduction

As project finance is sole recourse lending/investing, extensive risk analysis (encompassing third-party due diligence) and subsequent risk mitigation is required to close a project financing. The scale of the due diligence requirement depends upon the project's scale and industrial sector. For example, integrated multi-billion LNG value chain projects require more due diligence than a £30m portfolio of primary school refurbishments.

To make a deal bankable, project finance risk management philosophy states that risks must be identified, analysed and allocated to the party best able to hold it. In contractual terms, if a risk is assumed under a head contract (for example, construction risk), it should then be transferred (or back to backed) under a subsequent sub-contract (for example, an EPC contract).

Project risks are typically divided into construction phase risks and operations phase risks and often analysed through a risk matrix.

Construction phase risk matrix

As an example, Exhibit 12.10 shows a summary risk matrix relating to the construction phase of a power plant.

Regarding construction risk, different sectors have different norms as to its allocation. For example, complex petrochemical projects usually have multiple construction contracts (carrying interface risk), typically mitigated by the project sponsors' provision of a project completion guarantee. In contrast, wind farms have neither a single construction contract not a completion guarantee from the project sponsors.

Operations phase risk matrix

As example, Exhibit 12.11 shows a summary risk matrix related to the operational phase of a power plant.

Exhibit 12.10

Construction phase risk matrix

Risk	Mitigant
Delay in completion	SPV to execute construction contract with experienced, creditworthy contractor containing financial penalties (liquidated damages) for completion delay, to be secured by bonding. Technical consultant to advise lenders on construction contract provisions and schedule.
Completion of local infrastructure	Either forms part of construction contract per above or is the responsibility of the local sales counterparty.
Performance shortfall (output and efficiency)	SPV to procure reliable equipment (proven in similar conditions). Project to be handed over from contractor to SPV only when technical performance tests have been passed, with liquidated damages to be payable to SPV in the event of tested underperformance. Technical consultant to advise on plant design, equipment reliability and testing provisions.
Cost overrun	Technical consultant to confirm expected technical adequacy of budget (including contingency funding). Committed standby debt and equity funding to be available from financial close in an amount determined by industry sector risks (and also reviewed by the technical consultant).
Force majeure	Extensions of time and relief from liability if parties are unable to work due to force majeure. SPV to seek financial protection (against asset damage and revenue loss) from commercial insurance (reviewed by insurance consultant).
Sponsor credit risk	Adequate investment-grade credit rating (such as BBB+) needed for lenders to assume a clean sponsor equity contribution risk failing which project sponsors would be required to provide letters of credit as security against equity contribution risk.

Source: Author's own.

Conclusion

Project finance is a form of sole recourse investing/lending that requires extensive upfront due diligence and financial engineering to structure transactions that achieve mutually acceptable risks and rewards for all project stakeholders. Although not suitable for all investor financing requirements, it is highly suitable for many large capital investments, joint ventures and public infrastructure procurements.

Developing and executing project finance transactions requires substantial work upon project contractual structures and risk management considerations, with the typical payoff for tender authorities, project sponsors and lenders being an efficient financial structure capable of raising large sums of money over a long tenor, thus achieving parties' financial objectives.

Exhibit 12.11

Operations phase risk matrix

Risk	Mitigant
Fuel supply	Input fuel to be supplied at specified prices under a term contract by creditworthy supplier in adequate volume for plant operations. Supplier to have access to adequate reserve base and supply contract to provide relief against force majeure risk.
Sales/Offtake:	
Contracted	Term sales contract to specify sales of project capacity/output at specified volumes and prices, to be concluded with, or guaranteed by a creditworthy counterparty, and to provide relief against supply obligation during force majeure.
Non-contracted	Sales made on market basis (potentially to be hedged for a 1–2-year period looking forward) under an agreed trading strategy to be supported by appropriate security against counterparty default risk. Independent market study must demonstrate acceptable market size, supply/demand balance, prospects and volume/price projections for project duration.
Availability and O&M	Term O&M contract with experienced operator (potentially also a SPV shareholder) in accordance with good industry practice. Contract to contain liquidated damages in the event of performance shortfalls (such as output or efficiency). Maintenance arrangements may be sub-contracted to original equipment manufacturer under a 'long-term maintenance agreement'.
Political risks (including regulatory and permitting)	In non-public sector transactions, political risks (such as change in law) to lead to contractual relief in a similar manner to force majeure. In public sector transactions, risks such as adverse change in law or regulatory change should lead to SPV receiving commercial relief (for example, deemed availability or tariff adjustment).
Force majeure	As for construction phase matrix.
Cash flow	Base case financial model to contain all project assumptions and required to demonstrate pre-financial close adequate financial ratios (to be independently audited and technical assumptions independently confirmed). The model will also be required to demonstrate acceptable 'downside' coverage ratios under sensitivity analysis (changing individual/combined assumptions). Financing may include 6-month reserve account to fund 'blips' in financial performance.
Currency/inflation	Currency risk to be largely mitigated by securing project debt in the same currency as project revenues. In contracted transactions, inflation risk to be assumed by sales counterparty. In non-contracted transactions, inflation risk to be included as a financial model assumption.
Interest rates	SPVs with contracted revenue streams typically place interest rate swaps at financial close hedging a larger percentage of interest rate exposure. SPVs with market-based revenues tend to hedge less.
Environmental/ emissions	Project to comply with local/national requirements. In addition, many lenders require projects over US$50m value to demonstrate compliance with the 'Equator Principles', a global framework of environmental and social requirements (including emissions/permitting) for project finance transactions.

Source: Author's own.

Richard Cole is Chief Executive of HSBC Holdings plc's (HSBC) global Project and Export Finance Division within which Paul Eardley-Taylor is a Director, specialising in Power & Utilities projects. In 2005, HSBC was selected by Project Finance International as 'Global Adviser of the Year'. This chapter naturally represents the authors' own views and not those of HSBC.

Chapter 13

SES Global's billion dollar private placement

Michael Thilmany
HSBC

Precursor to a private placement

In July 2003, SES Global issued, what was at the time, the largest private placement in the United States. The Group's decision to tap the private placement market to raise funding was the result of a number of considerations and perceived advantages that this route has over more 'traditional' methods. The amount raised – US$1.045bn funded by a total of 39 institutional investors – reflects the greater flexibility and considerable potential that this market offers corporations looking to raise debt.

SES Global is the world's leading satellite group operating over 40 satellites throughout the world. SES operates mainly through SES ASTRA in Europe, SES AMERICOM in North America and New Skies Satellites in Africa, South America, the Middle East and parts of Asia. The Group also holds strategic participations in satellite operators AsiaSat, SES SIRIUS, QuetzSat, Ciel and Star One as well as in a number of satellite service provision companies.

SES provides customers with unrivalled market expertise, the highest audience figures year upon year, and an unmatched level of service excellence. The Group offers truly global coverage with the world's largest satellite fleet reaching 95 per cent of the world's population.

At the time of the American acquisition at the end of 2001, a large syndicated bank loan was put in place, primarily as an 'acquisition facility', based on floating rates and with specific requirements and covenants attached to the deal. However, with the then relatively low global interest rates and with the possibility of an uptick in the foreseeable future, SES Global started thinking about refinancing this arrangement.

The company is a highly capital-intensive business. Running costs are relatively low but building and launching a satellite is an expensive business, costing, on average, €250m. Satellites have an average working lifetime of 15 years. To this point, the company's growth has been both organic and through acquisitions. The Group was then entering a phase of business development at the time, consolidating operations and focusing predominantly on organic growth, for which the Group had specific capital requirements.

SES looked at fulfilling these requirements in January 2003, with an attempt to raise finance in the Eurobond markets, but without success. Nothing was wrong with the 'credit' per se, but the pricing of the potential bond issue didn't meet the company's expectations and there was no pressing need for them to raise finance at that time. Readers should bear in mind that no satellite operator had ever approached the Euromarkets before, so credit analysts there were unfamiliar with the media value chain in general or fixed satellite service providers in particular. World financial markets, particularly the public debt and equity markets, sat anxiously on the sidelines watching the run-up to the war in Iraq.

Thus, SES decided to pull out of the Eurobond market. Within an hour of making that choice, the company got a call outlining the possibilities of using the private placement market. Even in times of distress in the capital markets, there are always players in the private placement market looking to invest. Indeed, during difficult times, it is business as usual for the US private placement market. During previous crises such as the crash of 1987, the Asian crisis of 1997, the Russian crisis of 1998 or the attacks of 9/11, the US private placement market has steadily provided a reliable alternative for issuers of debt and equity. Although SES did not have a specific need for financing at the start of the year, it was clear that there would be the potential for fund raising, whenever they chose to go back to the market. So persuaded, the company went on a roadshow in July to explain their business model to potential investors.

The company's business model has some specific advantages when appealing to investors through the private placement market. Operating margins are among the highest credit analysts would ever see. Furthermore, SES has long-term contracts with broadcasters. Ten years is typical, where broadcasters are contracting to use transponder capacity for ten years, or even longer in some cases. These long-term contracts ensure secure earnings flow – what is referred to as the 'contract backlog' – and SES has the biggest contract backlog in the sector, currently worth over €7bn.

Decision to approach the private market

Why did SES go to the private placement market? First, as mentioned previously, reliability. Secondly, in contrast to the Eurobond market, there is a high level of confidentiality. An issuer can talk to potential investors, but the deal is not made public until it is closed. Thirdly, SES's financing needs are predominantly in US dollars so the company looking to raise US dollar finance and having a pool of US-based potential investors was another major attraction. The company imagines that it could one day issue in the US public markets: many of those investors would already be well-educated SES investors. Fourthly, the timing was perfect from an interest rate point of view. Ten-year interest rates had hit 3.10 per cent in June so SES was motivated to lock in historically low US dollar rates.

Transaction execution

The company appreciated the simple, transparent and straightforward process, which took about nine weeks in total.

SES hired two banks, HSBC and Barclays as agents. One, in conjunction with SES, wrote the private placement memorandum and investor presentation using the company's publicly available information and the banks' sector expertise. The other agent worked with pre-appointed lenders' counsel to craft the note purchase agreement out of the termsheet the second agent wrote in conjunction with both SES and its US legal counsel. The investor presentation was derived from the company's equity presentation which eliminated shareholder-focused information and added useful credit information typical to the market and often found in bank presentations. The termsheet, and by extension, the note purchase agreement (which used the Private Placement Enhancement Project's Model Form No. 2 as a framework) drew heavily from SES's syndicated bank loan referenced in relation to the AMERICOM purchase. Since this was an acquisition facility, the agents were able to reduce covenants and ratios on behalf of SES while at the same time complying with market standards (after the private placement closed, the company refinanced the syndicated bank loan and commanded much easier terms from the banks due to the successful dilution of covenants in the private placement documentation).

The three offering documents – the private placement memorandum, investor presentation and note purchase agreement – were prepared in about three weeks.

In the final week of offering document preparation, the banks held a 'lottery' to choose the investors that each agent would exclusively market to. Investor totals were in excess of 50. Once done, each agent contacted all of their names to schedule roadshow meetings. Upon completing the private placement memorandum and note purchase agreement, each agent sent the documents, along with a joint letter from each agent, to the investors, effectively launching the transaction. Investors had a few days to a week to begin researching the credit and familiarising themselves with the transaction before the roadshow.

The SES roadshow

The roadshow was very extensive, consisting of visiting investors, both in groups as well as one-on-ones, across 12 US cities in the course of one week, from east coast to west coast plus London. Meetings lasted from one and a half to two hours each. SES's Finance Director (since retired) and Group Treasurer, Walter Dilewyns, presented the company. For those investors who were either unable to personally meet with SES management or were located in inconvenient cities, the company held a (recorded) conference call where the company spoke uninterrupted for about 50 minutes followed by a similar amount of time of individual investor questions.

Even before the roadshow began, a lot of the questions that came out of this were dealt with immediately by the company or their advising banks. While the company enjoyed the group meetings and the conference call, SES found that communicating with small groups was a much better way of getting their message across. Their experience was that investors were much more demanding in the questions they asked when presenting for a private placement, compared to, say, a public offering. The private placement investors do their own credit analysis and make their own estimates of the creditworthiness of a particular company. Nevertheless, they will still look at credit ratings when they are available and compare them with the National Association of Insurance Commissioners' (NAIC) ratings. The NAIC assigns a rating to every fixed-income investment held by a US insurance company. As it was, SES was already rated BBB by Standard & Poor's and Baa2 by Moody's, and between pricing of the deal and the due diligence visit, S&P upgraded their rating to BBB+, which was good news for investors.

The agents provided investors price guidance at the conclusion of the roadshow. Since there were no direct investment-grade public comparatives to guide the market, the agents had to refer to various BBB public media comps to justify the maturities and pricing SES expected to command.

Circling and pricing

Although SES put US$300m on the cover, offering 7-, 10- and 12-year maturities, the transaction was getting very intense attention from the entire market and it was obvious by the end of the roadshow that SES would enjoy a blowout reception. Bids were due about three days after the last roadshow meeting. Knowing that demand would reach record levels, SES quickly checked with key board members about increasing the transaction. Given the company's refinancing requirements and objectives, SES was able to immediately utilise the additional funding, and decided to conclude the fundraising at US$1.045bn. The company felt that the pricing was very attractive and there was a willingness on the part of all the parties involved to go to this higher figure.

On the morning following bids, bonds were allocated to the 39 investors across the 7-, 10- and 12-year maturities. The agents fixed the coupons and executed the relevant swaps within a few minutes, thereby eliminating any further interest rate or market risk for SES.

Investor due diligence

Arrangements were then made for all interested investors to visit SES's head office at Chateau de Betzdorf in Luxembourg. Investors were treated to a tour of the facilities and received further presentations on pre-defined areas of further interest to investors. A convivial dinner hosted by senior management served as the starting point for the direct relationship SES has developed with the investors over the years. Investors greatly value this direct access to management that public investors lack. Investor due diligence is, therefore, of benefit to both the company as well as investors.

Finalisation of documentation

Documentation was finalised a few weeks after due diligence and funding occurred on the date agreed at the time of coupon setting, about a month previous. While T + 5 settlement in the public markets is the norm, the private placement market can provide up to one year delayed drawdown, a valuable option for issuers in steep yield curve environments. SES took advantage of the then-prevailing steep US dollar yield curve and saved itself basis points by executing forward starting swaps at the time of pricing. Customarily, investors are often willing to provide up to three months' delayed funding free of charge.

Successful execution

The result was the biggest private placement deal at that time and SES felt this was a very positive outcome for their group in particular and the sector in general. Insurance companies had been particularly interested in what they were offering, because they tend to have longer-term liabilities and are, therefore, looking for longer-term investments. The fact that

SES contracts are typically of 10- or 15-year duration means the company is ideal for that type of investment. Another advantage of opting for a private placement is that an issuer can have a large degree of flexibility over structuring the repayment terms. An issue can have bullet payments or amortise, with SES having chosen to use both for different tranches of their placement.

The private placement process is also relatively straightforward from a reporting aspect. It is not necessary for an issuer to report under US GAAP (generally accepted accounting principles) and not being required to publicise the deal was important to SES after pulling out of the proposed issue in the Eurobond market. Nor is there any need for Securities and Exchange Commission (SEC) registration. Similarly, there is no formal requirement for a company to have a long-term debt rating in order to raise money via a private placement, though having one is undoubtedly an asset.

In a private placement, there is no agent between the company and the investors. In the future, an issuer's relationship can be direct with their investors. Of course, this also means an issuer has to be highly effective in communicating with investors, but this relationship should help with any future fundraising activity.

Choosing professional advisers is still a key part of the process and the chemistry between the company and its advisers and among the advisers is very important. In SES's case, they chose two banks, where the individuals crucially had a sound knowledge of the industry. It is particularly important that the chemistry is right when dealing with more than one party. The vital question to ask is 'Can they sell to the right people?'.

SES enjoyed a positive experience in the US private placement market.

Chapter 14

Hybrid bonds for corporates

Jean-François Mazaud and Franck Robard
Société Générale

Introduction to Hybrid Corporates' Bond

Hybrid capital is the generic name of a class of financial instruments that incorporates elements both from debt and equity, and includes embedded option elements.

Hybrid capital instruments are constructed to optimise benefits of debt (fixed remuneration, no dilution, no voting rights and tax deductibility) and those of equity (equity value from ratings agencies, equity accounting, favourable impact on leverage ratios and equity for banks or private placement covenants). They are even more powerful as they allow the issuer to diversify its capital base and have a positive impact on cost of capital and net income.

The specifics of hybrid capital vary between jurisdictions due to legal and tax differences, but basically:

- their ranking is between debt and equity with regards to rights upon liquidation;
- they are a permanent component of the capital base of the issuer thanks to perpetual tenor or very long dated maturity, even if a synthetic maturity is materialised by call and step-up features; and
- distributions can be deferred or cancelled without default.

Market take-off in 2005

The corporate hybrid securities market has taken-off thanks to significant developments over the last 18 months. The year 2005 has seen the emergence of an asset class in the Euro Institutional Investors market driven first by a clarification of the accounting and rating benefits of these instruments, and secondly by investors who see these products as a means to gain additional yield in the current low interest rate and credit spreads environment. In the past 12 months more than ten European corporates have used this new opportunity to issue equity-like debt instruments for a total amount close to €10bn and debt capital market participants expect more to come (see Exhibit 14.1).

Types of bonds

The idea behind the architecture of a hybrid instrument is to start with a debt-like security and to twist it into an equity security by playing on three main criteria: ranking, maturity

Exhibit 14.1

Hybrids for corporates: a quick take-off

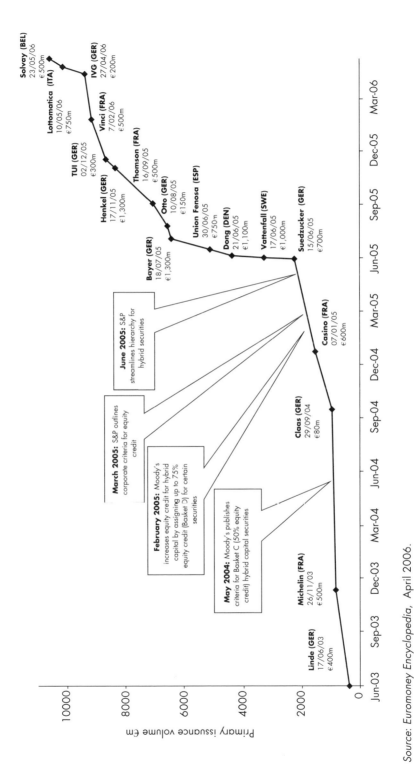

Source: *Euromoney Encyclopedia*, April 2006.

Exhibit 14.2

'Basket C' structures

	DONG (BBB+/Baa1)	THOMSON (BBB+/Baa1)	VINCI (BBB+/Baa1)	Solvag (A/A2)
Instrument	Subordinated Capital Securities	Deeply Subordinated Bond	Deeply Subordinated Bond	Subordinated Capital Securities
Ranking	Deeply subordinated notes – only senior to all classes of shares capital	Deeply subordinated notes – only senior to all classes of shares capital	Deeply subordinated notes – only senior to all classes of shares capital	Deeply subordinated notes – only senior to all classes of shares capital
Issue date	21-Jun-05	19-Sep-05	07-Feb-06	23-May-06
Maturity	1,000 years	Perpetual	Perpetual	98 years
Coupon	5.50% until year 10. €3m + 320 bps thereafter	5.75% until year 10. €3m + 362.5 bps thereafter	6.25% until year 10. €3m + 375 bps thereafter	6.375% until 10. €3m + 335 bps thereafter
First Call	At the make whole amount in June 2010 + replacement language / At par in June 2015	At par in Sept 2015 + replacement language	At par in Nov 2015 + replacement language	At par in June 2016 + replacement language
Step-up	Yes 100 bps after June 2015	Yes 100 bps after Sept 2015	Yes 100 bps after Nov 2015	Yes 100 bps after June 2016
	Optional at any time. Deferred interests are non cash cumulative but can be settled by common shares or similar securities (paid in kind)	Optional coupon deferral at Thompson's discretion except if a dividend was paid or shares bought back in the previous 6 months	Optional coupon deferral at Vinci's discretion except if a dividend was paid or shares bought back in the previous 6 months	Optional at any time, non cash cumulative (but compounded)
Interest payment mechanism	Deferred interest has to be settled before paying a dividend on ordinary shares or redeem, repurchase or acquire share capital	Any interest not paid on such date shall be forfeited and no longer be due and payable to the issuer (non cumulative)	Any interest not paid on such date shall be forfeited and no longer be due and payable to the issuer (non cumulative)	ACSM within 12 months following a payment on Junior or Parity Securities

ACSM	Yes	No	No	Yes
Special event redemption	Yes call if tax event	Yes call if tax event	Yes call if tax event or accounting event	Yes call if tax event
Change of control clause	No	Yes	No	No
Rating (notches below corporate credit rating)	BBB–/Baa3 [-2/-2]	BBB–/Baa3 [-2/-2]	BBB–/Baa3 [-2/-2]	BBB+/Baa1[-2/-2]
Equity credit	Intermediate (S&P)/50% (Moody's)	Intermediate (S&P)/50% (Moody's)	Intermediate (S&P)/50% (Moody's)	Intermediate (S&P)/50% (Moody's)
Price guidance	ms + 210/235 revised 220/235	ms + 250/270	ms + 275 bp area	ms + 235 bp area
Size/Re-offer spread	1.1bn/ms + 220	500m/ms + 262.5	500m/ms + 275	500m/ms + 235
IFRS treatment	Equity	Equity	Equity	Debt
Size of the book	Over 3bn	€1.3bn	Over 1bn	Over 1.4bn
Over-subscription	2.7	2.6	2	2.8

Source: Société Générale.

Exhibit 14.3

'Basket D' structures

	VATTENFALL [A- /A2]	SUEDZUCKER [A- /A3]	BAYER [A/A3]	HENKEL [A-/A2]	Lottomatica [BBB wn/ Bal [prospective]]
Instrument	Capital Securities	Deeply Subordinated Bond	Deeply Subordinated Bond	Deeply Subordinated Bond	Subordinated Capital Securities
Ranking	Deeply subordinated notes – only senior to all classes of shares capital	Deeply subordinated notes – only senior to all classes of shares capital	Deeply subordinated notes – only senior to all classes of shares capital	Deeply subordinated notes – only senior to all classes of shares capital	Obbligazioni Ranks junior to all other unsubordinated and subordinated creditors but senior to ordinary, savings and preference shares
Issue date	17-Jun-05	15-Jun-05	18-Jul-05	17-Nov-05	10-May-06
Maturity	Perpetual	Perpetual	100 years	99 years	60 years
Coupon	5.25% until year 10. €3m + 295 bps therafter	5.25% until year 10. €3m + 310 bps thereafter	5% until year 10. €3m + 280 bps thereafter	5.375% until year 10. €3m + 285 bps thereafter	8.125% until year 10. €3m + 505 bps thereafter
First call	At par in June 2015 + replacement language	At par in June 2015 + replacement language	At par in July 2015 + replacement language	At par in Nov 2015 + replacement language	At par in March 2016 + replacement language
Step-up	Yes 100 bps after June 2015	Yes 100 bps after June 2015	Yes 100 bps after July 2015	Yes 100 bps after Nov 2015	Yes 100 bps after Mar 2016
	Compulsory if dividend on share capital or junior securities or if the issuer has redeemed, repurchased or acquired share captal	Compulsory if dividend on share capital or junior securities or if the issuer has redeemed, repurchased or acquired share capital	Compulsory if dividend on share capital or junior securities or if the issuer has redeemed, repurchased or acquired share capital	Cumulative optional; if aj. Cash flow/adj. Debt is lower than 20%	Optional coupon deferral at Lottomatica's discretion
Interest payment mechanism	Cumulative Optional deferral otherwise	Cumulative Optional deferral otherwise	Cumulative Optional deferral otherwise	Non cash cumulative mandatory non payment if adj. Cash flow/adj. Debt is lower than 15%	Cumulative non compounding. To be settled in cash at the earliest dividend payment. If unpaid

	Non cumulative mandatory non-payment if FFO + interest paid/interest <2.5%	Non cash cumulative mandatory non-payment triggered when FFO/revenues is below 5%	Non cash cumulative mandatory non-payment triggered when gross cash flow/sales is below 7%	Non cash cumulative if a trigger (FCF before dividends and debt service/interest expense <1.35) is breached	after 5 years, can only be settled as mandatory deferred interests
ACSM	No	Yes	Yes	Yes	Yes (pre-emptive ACSM)
Special event redemption	Yes call if tax event	Yes call if tax event	Yes call if tax event	Yes call if tax event	Yes call if tax event, withholding tax
Change of control clause	No	No	No	No	Yes
Rating [notches below corporate credit rating]	BBB–/Baa1 [-3/-2]	BBB–/Bac2 [-3/-2]	BBB/Baa2 [-3/-2]	BBB–/Baa1 [-3/-2]	BB+ wn/Ba3 [prospective]
Equity credit	Intermediate (S&P)/75% (Moody's)	Intermediate (S&P)/75% (Moody's)	Intermediate (S&P)/75% (Moody's)	Intermediate (S&P)/75% (Moody's)	Intermediate (S&P)/75% (Moody's)
Price guidance	ms + 187.5/200	ms + 200/220	ms + 185/195	ms + 185 bp area	8.25%/8.50%
Size/reoffer spread	1bn/ms + 195	500m/ms + 210 + 200m tap/ms + 205	1.3bn/ms + 180	1.3bn/ms + 185	750m/ms + 405
IFRS treatment	Debt	Equity	Debt	Debt	Debt
Size of the book	Over 2bn	750/800mios + tap	Over 5bn	Over 3.75bn	Over 4bn
Over-subscription	%2	%1.5	%3.8	%2.9	%5.3

Source: Société Générale.

and discretion on the remuneration. These three essential features have an impact on the issued securities from a rating, tax and accounting perspective.

- *Maturity/permanency of the funds within the balance sheet of the issuer*. In order to replicate the absence of maturity of an equity security, a typical hybrid instrument targeting the euro institutional investor market has no maturity, a first call option for the issuer in year 10 (or longer) and a coupon step-up in order to create an incentive for the issuer to exercise the call. A replacement provision by which the issuer declares his intention to replace the qualifying hybrid by a new instrument with at least the same equity features before any redemption, is also needed to mitigate the negative impact of the coupon step-up for rating agencies. No legal maturity or event that triggers an early redemption are key to attaining an equity accounting treatment while rating agencies grant equity content to long-dated maturity issues (at least 50 years over the first call date).
- *Ranking*. To optimise the 'equity content' from rating agencies, the instrument needs to be junior to every other obligation of the issuer except common shareholders. At the same time, the choice of an instrument or another (deeply subordinated bond versus preference shares, for example) will mainly be driven by the necessity to ensure tax deductibility on interest payment and avoid any withholding tax. For each jurisdiction, various legal forms are used to comply with the local tax and legal system.
- *Interest payment mechanism*. This is the area where we have seen, and should see, the most diversity. Various interest payment mechanisms have been put in place to replicate the discretionary payment of the dividend on a common share, but the idea is always the same: to offer the issuer the possibility to defer coupon payments (on a cumulative or non-cumulative basis) and at the same time not alter the treatment of hybrid holders versus shareholders through dividend pusher or stopper mechanisms. 'Dividend pusher' is the structure when the coupon is mandatory if a remuneration is given to the shareholders whereas 'dividend stopper' states that the issuer undertakes not to pay any dividend if he does not pay any remuneration on the hybrid structure. To date, two main interest payment mechanisms have been used:
  - Non cash-cumulative optional coupon payment in case of no dividend (which qualified for a 50 per cent equity content from rating agencies); and
  - in order to boost equity content (up to 75 per cent for Moody's) a mandatory trigger deferral, a legally binding replacement language can be included and set at a level that usually corresponds to a downgrade of the issuer below investment grade. Alternatively the same goal can be achieved through the inclusion of a legally binding replacement language.

The trade-off when using, or not, a mandatory trigger deferral is that in this case S&P's rating for the hybrid will be three notches below the corporate credit rating instead of two for the first option. Some recent transactions have circumvented this issue thanks to an obligation for the issuer to make an equity increase in advance of the mandatory deferral.

Why use a hybrid instrument and when does it makes sense?

Hybrid instruments allow corporates to raise funds which can be seen as quasi-equity by ratings agencies and equity from an accounting perspective. At the same time, these instruments have many merits from the shareholder perspective as they are non-dilutive and have positive impacts on cost of capital and are, therefore, a valid substitute to common equity. Some of these merits are listed here.

- *Strengthen the capital structure*. Most hybrids issued over the past 12 months have achieved an equity balance sheet accounting treatment under International Financial Reporting Standards (IFRS) thanks to IAS 32 which requires no defined maturity and an optional payment for all coupons. Nevertheless, some issues have received a debt treatment due to a fixed tenor. Here, the main trade-off is to have an equity treatment or the hedge accounting benefit for the associated swap as any hedge of an equity treated instrument will result in a mark-to-market (MTM) valuation of the swap in the P&L.
- *Increase the financial flexibility*. Rating agencies have disclosed and clarified their methodologies about the benefits of hybrid instruments. Moody's opened the ball in 2004 and Standard and Poor's (S&P) and Fitch followed suit in 2005. All recently issued hybrids have received a 50 per cent to 75 per cent equity credit by Moody's and an intermediate equity treatment from S&P. Greater transparency from the rating agencies has been an important driver of the increasing volume of issuance as market participants know the level of equity replication that can be achieved with a specific instrument. Higher equity value can theoretically be achieved but has not been tested yet as the additional constraints imposed on issuers or investors, such as legally binding replacement language or mandatory interest deferral triggers with a higher probability of occurrence have raised questions about the marketability of such structures.
- *Shareholder value*. Hybrids strengthen the capital base by adding a 'buffer' between senior creditors and shareholders. At the same time, they are tax deductible equity-like products, and therefore enhance the cost of equity of the issuer. Last but not least, coupons on hybrids treated as equity for balance sheet purposes are not accounted as a financial charge and, therefore, have a positive impact in the net income when used instead of, or to replace, senior debt instruments while it remains non dilutive, under IFRS.

When does it make sense?

As long as investor appetite remains strong, hybrids are in the financing tool box of every treasurer. There is a large consensus in the market to consider hybrids as a form of capital with many merits, and when talking to potential issuers one often hears the question: 'What rationale can I sell internally and externally which justifies the issuance of a hybrid instrument?'

The merits listed above theoretically justify an issue in themselves. Nevertheless, such instruments should not be seen as purely opportunistic funding as a strong rationale has to exist to justify the premium paid over senior debt and convince investors of this choice.

Among these specific situations, acquisition-related funding, a strengthening of rating credit metrics (and, therefore, an increase in the financial flexibility within a rating category) for an issuer with a stable business profile and pre-funding pension deficits seem to be the most appropriate and these have also been well perceived by investors (see Exhibit 14.4).

Exhibit 14.4

Rationale for issuance of a hybrid instrument

Issuer	Rationale for issuance	Issue size
Solvay	Strengthen its financial structure and consolidate its long-term debt	€500m
Lottomatica	Part of the financing package of the US-based GTECH (leading provider of gaming technology	€750m
Vinci	Refinance their recent acquisitions, consolidate the financial structure and improve the financial flexibility, and to increase the average debt maturity	€500m
Porsche	Refinance the strategic liquidity reserves and repayment of maturing bonds	US$1,000m
TUI	Refinance the acquisition of CP Ships	€300m
Henkel	Fund the pension obligations using a long-dated maturity instrument	€1,300m
Thomson	Refinance a convertible bond using another instrument with an equity content	€500m
Bayer	Repay its bond maturing in April 2007 (€860m refunded for a total of €3bn) and increase financial flexibility	€1,300m
Otto	Repayment of existing debt and raise quasi-capital through a non-dilutive instrument	€150m
Dong	Acquisition financing	€1,100m
Vattenfall	Retain financial capacities for acquisitions and overcome the fact that they do not have access to the equity markets (100 per cent state owned)	€1,000m
Sudzucker	Increase financial flexibility and consolidate the balance sheet structure	€700m
Union Fenosa	Consolidate the company's financial structure and neutralise the reclassification of 'old' preference shares from equity to financial liability under IFRS	€750m
Casino	Consolidate the financial structure and improve debt ratios	€600m
Class	Refinance existing senior and strengthen the capital structure	€80m
Michelin	Reinforce the company's financial structure by refinancing senior debt using a lower ranking instrument to optimise the weighted average cost of capital and to extend debt maturity profile	€500m
Linde	Refinance existing senior and strengthen the capital structure	€400m

Source: Société Générale.

Investors: what's in it for fund managers?

Fund managers are in a low-yield environment and are yield-hungry. In addition, many of them have guidelines for their investments, preventing them from buying notes issued by non-investment-grade companies and, therefore, in the investment-grade category, hybrids are the bonds offering the most attractive yield they can buy.

The subordination in hybrid bonds and other embedded risks (such as extension risk, interest deferral risk, and so on) implies a pick-up in the spread of the issue, reflecting the additional risk for the investor.

Various types of structures are available (up to now, each new issue has brought a new feature) and offer investors different types of risk. Some of them, with non-cash cumulative coupon encourage more responsible issuer behaviour (as the issuing company would have to pay for deferred coupons in the future) when others implied a strong view on the shareholders policy and management intention from investors. Nevertheless, buyers of hybrids agree that the key decision for them is on the underlying credit of the issuer, and not on the hybrid itself. Therefore, investors would favour buying subordinated debt of a stronger credit than the senior debt of a weaker credit.

Methodology for pricing

Issuers and investors face a relatively new asset class with different and complex structures and not enough outstanding issues yet to conduct a pure relative value analysis. Therefore, after choosing the right instrument, the next question is: what is the fair value of this instrument?

Even if at the end of the day the credit spread at launch remains a bargaining between investors and issuers, bankers have developed sophisticated pricing methodologies. Société Générale has an innovative methodology for pricing subordinated bonds. It computes a fair price for a hybrid issue based on the senior spreads of the company. This fair price calculation depends on the specific characteristics of the hybrid issue in terms of coupon deferral and extension mechanisms.

Société Générale's hybrid model uses a three-step approach to compute a fair price for a new structure:

- *Simulate all possible scenarios on future spreads financial ratios of the company.* This first step heavily depends on the spread curve of the company as this curve gives information about the market's perception of future spread dynamics.
- *Determine the company's decision regarding coupon deferral and extension in each scenario and compute the price of the security in each case.* This step takes into account the specificities of each structure, and differentiates between cumulative and non-cumulative mechanisms and between mandatory and optional deferral languages.
- *Assign a probability to each scenario*, and then compute the fair price of the structure by making a net present value of all scenarios weighted by their probability.

This three-step approach is a mathematically consistent way to price hybrid issues which takes into account all the options embedded in hybrid securities. Investors increasingly rely on this kind of pricing approach before making any investment decision. Having this kind of model is therefore key to ensure an accurate pricing and a successful distribution of these products. The model enables a comparison of the fair value of each element of the structure, therefore enabling investors to optimise structures to minimise the cost of funding.

Vinci

Last February, Vinci, one of the world leaders in concessions, construction and related services businesses issued a €500m 6.25 per cent perpetual hybrid transaction with a first call date in year 10. Société Générale has acted as structuring adviser and bookrunner on this transaction.

Rationale

The aim of the transaction was to initiate at a very early stage the refinancing of the ASF acquisition, increase the average maturity of its debt and optimise the financial structure of the group by using a cheap source of quasi-equity funding at present market conditions.

Structuring considerations

The structure of the instrument has been driven by a number of constraints. In particular, it should:

- be treated as equity for accounting purposes by Vinci auditors;
- receive at least equity treatment Intermediate by S&P and Basket C that is, 50 per cent equity credit) by Moody's;

Exhibit 14.5

Vinci allocations

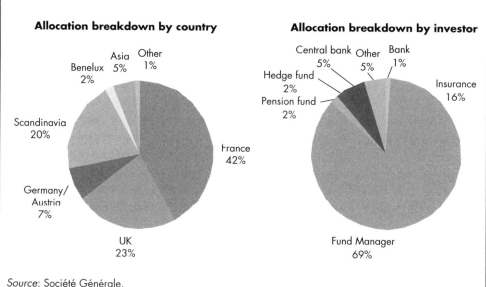

Allocation breakdown by country

Asia 5%
Other 1%
Benelux 2%
Scandinavia 20%
Germany/Austria 7%
UK 23%
France 42%

Allocation breakdown by investor

Central bank 5%
Other 5%
Bank 1%
Hedge fund 2%
Pension fund 2%
Insurance 16%
Fund Manager 69%

Source: Société Générale.

- be rated in the investment-grade category;
- be tax deductible according to French tax rules.

Therefore, in order to combine all these requirements the hybrid instrument has been designed as follows:

- perpetual;
- junior to all obligations of the issuer and senior to all classes of shares;
- early redemption possible for Vinci starting November 2015 and at each interest payment date thereafter;
- early redemption possible in case of tax changes or equity accounting disqualification;
- coupon fixed annual until November 2015 and floating thereafter; and
- interest payment is compulsory in case of dividend payment or share buyback (dividends pusher). Otherwise interest payment is optional and non-cumulative.

Execution

The company completed a five-day roadshow in Paris, London, Germany and the Netherlands. The initial spread guidance of mid-swap + 275 basis points (bp) was released on Tuesday 7 February at noon. The order book was opened immediately after the spread guidance was announced and closed three hours later with orders from high-quality accounts. The final re-offer spread was mid-swap + 275 bp. This innovative marketing procedure on the hybrid debt market permitted, through accelerated book building, to favour quality of the placement and to limit the risk of arbitrage exposure and the bond immediately performed in the grey market (–6 bp).

Chapter 15

Bank capital
Tier 1, Upper Tier 2 and Lower Tier 2

Jackie Ineke and Christine Miyagishima*
Morgan Stanley

Introduction

A bank's capital comprises share capital, reserves and a series of dated and hybrid capital instruments, which are split into the categories of Lower Tier 2, Upper Tier 2 and Tier 1, depending on their characteristics. Capital in the form of debt instruments is always subordinated – senior debt does not count as bank capital. This debt has to adhere to supervisory guidelines concerning its characteristics in order to count as capital. In setting these guidelines, bank supervisors are first and foremost concerned with the protection of the depositor. Bank capital can be regarded as a safety net that absorbs a certain level of unexpected losses without the interests of depositors being adversely affected.

Capital provides a buffer for depositors in two major ways. First, the strongest type of capital is flexible, in that banks can defer or even cancel dividends or interest payments to holders of this kind of capital. This can relieve pressure on the bank in times of financial stress so that it can continue servicing its depositors. Second, in liquidation, bank capital ranks behind the claims of depositors. This again allows the bank to repay depositors ahead of reimbursing any subordinated debt or equity holders, for example.

Requiring banks to issue a certain level and type of capital is only one part of a bank supervisor's remit. As discussed above, capital is considered a safety net but banks must also manage their risks correctly so that the probability of requiring this safety net is minimised. We concern ourselves here just with the regulations that require banks to hold capital (capital adequacy guidelines) and with no other part of bank supervision – for example, adequate provisioning.

Setting the guidelines

Regulators across the world tend to look toward the Bank for International Settlements (BIS) for guidance in setting the capital adequacy framework for banks. The BIS (also frequently used to refer to the Basel Committee on Banking Supervision) is made up of central bankers from around the world and pursues a common policy on capital adequacy. The most famous BIS Accord is known as Basel I (1988), which provides guidelines as to how banks ought to calculate their capital requirements (subsequently, Basel II was created in 2004). In order to become law in the EU, BIS guidelines have been incorporated into Directives, which lay

Exhibit 15.1

Size of the institutional capital markets

	£	€	US$
Tier 1	£19.4bn (US$32.9bn); 73 deals	€84.8bn (US$98.0bn); 194 deals	US$79.7bn; 59 deals
UT2	£22.1bn (US$36.0bn); 64 deals	€26.4bn (US$30.4bn); 49 deals	US$16.9bn; 12 deals
LT2	£18.7bn (US$31.4bn); 82 deals	€173.9bn (US$191.8bn); 531 deals	US$75.0bn; 92 deals

Source: Bondware/Dealogic; as at 26 May 2006.

down the minimum EU standards. National legislators are then required to incorporate Directives within their own banking regulations.

National capital guidelines in the EU are derived from the following Directives, which are closely aligned to BIS papers on capital adequacy.

- the Own Funds Directive (OFD, 89/299/EEC);
- the Solvency Ratio Directive (SRD, 89/647/EEC); and
- the Capital Adequacy Directive (CAD, 93/6/EC).

As Directives set down only minimum criteria, there can be significant variations in capital guidelines across EU countries. In this chapter, we follow closely the guidelines as laid down by the UK's financial regulator, the Financial Services Authority (FSA). The FSA has tended to take the most conservative view (that is, the strictest interpretation) of EU Directives.

The different tiers of capital

Tier 1

Main components

- Ordinary shareholders' equity (net of any own shares held);
- retained earnings, that is, internally generated capital from accruing profit to reserves;
- perpetual non-cumulative preferred stock (what is known in the market as 'Tier 1 preferred', see below);
- reserves created by appropriations of retained earnings, share premia and other surpluses;
- minority interests. These arise when a bank has a subsidiary that it does not wholly own. The bank's consolidated balance sheet includes all the assets of that subsidiary, so all its share capital and reserves are also consolidated.

Main Tier 1 preferred characteristics

- Perpetual and senior only to equity;
- coupons are deferrable and non-cumulative;
- interest and principal can be written down.

Characteristics

- *No fixed costs*. Tier 1 capital is also known as 'core' capital. It should have no fixed costs, which means that there should be no contractual obligation to pay dividends or interest to Tier 1 holders. The deferral of dividend or interest is normally at the option of the issuer. When capital ratios are threatened, deferral can be at the option of the regulator.
- *Non-cumulative coupons*. Deferred coupons or dividends are non-cumulative. This essentially means that coupons can be cancelled and not repaid at a later date, which ensures that core capital has no fixed costs.
- *Loss-absorbing*. Tier 1 should be able to absorb losses before, or instead of, general creditors. It is, therefore, subordinated to all debt and senior only to common equity. Principal and interest may be written down to allow the issuer to remain solvent.
- *Perpetual*. Tier 1 preferred must be perpetual, but the FSA allows a limited step-up associated with a call after the tenth anniversary of the issue. Equity is considered the strongest form of capital by the FSA as there is statutory subordination through the Companies Act and the Insolvency Act in the UK. This means that shareholders are the last to be paid in the event of liquidation.

Upper Tier 2

Main components

- Perpetual deferrable subordinated debt (including such debt convertible into equity);
- revaluation reserves from fixed assets and fixed-asset investments;
- general provisions, up to a maximum of 1.25 per cent of risk-weighted assets. Specific provisions are not included in Upper Tier 2 capital.

Upper Tier 2 debt characteristics

- Perpetual, senior to Tier 1 preferred and equity;
- coupons are deferrable and cumulative;
- interest and principal can be written down.

Characteristics

- *Perpetual*. The FSA requires that UT2 is perpetual, but this is not a requirement in the Own Funds Directive, and certain European banks (that is, the Italian and Danish banks) are allowed by their regulators to issue dated UT2. No repayment can be made without prior consent of the regulator.

- *Deferrable coupons*. Coupons can be deferred at the option of the issuer but they are cumulative, so the issuer has to pay deferred coupons in the future. This can include interest on interest.
- *Loss-absorbing*. Principal and interest can be written down to allow the issuer to remain solvent. UT2 is subordinated to all other debt and senior only to Tier 1 preferred and common equity.

Lower Tier 2

Main components

- Dated subordinated debt with a minimum maturity of five years;
- any perpetual debt with no loss absorbency features or interest deferral provision (rare).

Lower Tier 2 characteristics

- Subordinated only to senior debt;
- no deferral of coupons and no write-down of principal or interest;
- dated with minimum maturity of five years.

Characteristics

- *No deferral*. LT2 capital is classified by the regulator as of lower quality because its loss absorption features are only relevant in the event of insolvency. Further, it has less flexibility than UT2 or Tier 1 preferred as deferral is normally an event of default. LT2 is subordinated only to senior debt.
- *Amortisation*. In order to avoid a sudden diminution in capital base, LT2 is normally amortised on a straight-line basis in its final five years to maturity. This explains why a number of banks have issued 10-year LT2 debt with a step and call at year five. The incentive is to call the bonds at year five to avoid the amortisation. For bullet structures, banks are only allowed early repayment with prior written consent from the FSA. The bank must be able to satisfy the FSA that the bank's capital is adequate after repayment and that it will remain so for the next two years.

Regulatory limits and calculating ratios

Capital requirements are calculated according to the size and type of risk associated with a bank's assets. We are currently under 'Basel I' rules, whereby each asset on a bank's balance sheet is assigned a risk-weight. These are aggregated to give a risk-weighted assets total. A bank's capital is divided by its risk-weighted assets to give a capital adequacy ratio. At all times, a bank's Tier 1 ratio must be greater than 4 per cent and its total capital ratio greater than 8 per cent. National regulators set bank-specific guidelines higher than this. 'Basel II' will be introduced from 1 January 2007, and it aims to bring regulatory capital requirements more into line with actual economic capital needs. This is fully discussed in *Basel II A–Z*[1] and is beyond the scope of this short chapter. The minimum capital ratios noted above will remain in place under Basel II; it is the way capital requirements themselves are calculated, that will change.

Capital limits

Bank regulators regard Tier 1 as the strongest form of capital. In order to ensure banks maintain a strong capital base, regulators place limits on the amount of weaker forms of capital a bank can use to calculate its capital adequacy ratio. Restrictions are not only placed on the amount of Tier 2 and Tier 3 capital that can be issued in proportion to Tier 1, but also on the types of activity it can support. Prior to calculating capital limits, a bank splits its business into two – banking book and trading book. These are purely regulatory terms, with a trading book being very broadly defined as any proprietary positions held to benefit from short-term price or interest rate movements. The banking book is whatever does not fall into the trading book. In general:

- There is no limit on the amount of Tier 1 capital a bank can hold, with the exception of 'redeemable' Tier 1 preferred. This limit is discussed below.
- Tier 2 subordinated term debt (Lower Tier 2) cannot exceed 50 per cent of total Tier 1 capital.
- Tier 2 capital used to meet banking book capital requirements must not exceed 100 per cent of the Tier 1 capital used to meet those requirements.
- Tier 3 capital (not defined above as is extremely rare, but effectively short-dated subordinated debt) can only cover trading book requirements.
- Tier 2 and Tier 3 debt used to meet the trading book capital requirements must not exceed 200 per cent of the Tier 1 capital used to meet those requirements.
- Tier 2 and Tier 3 capital cannot exceed Tier 1 overall.

Any capital that exceeds these limits cannot be used in the bank's calculation of its Tier 1 and total capital ratio. Once these limits have been taken into account, a bank is left with a figure for its 'eligible' capital.

Not all capital is created equal . . .

While all forms of debt capital (including the most equity-like Tier 1) are traded in the fixed-income markets, not all structures are quite the same, and they pose different risks to investors. Lower Tier 2 debt is extremely similar for all European banks – it is dated, and non-payment of coupons is an event of default. We've already mentioned above the slight differences in Upper Tier 2, whereby Italian and Danish banks can issue dated Upper Tier 2. These rank *pari passu* with Lower Tier 2 (indeed, Danish banks do not issue what we've described as Lower Tier 2 above), but they do have deferral of coupons, which are cumulative (like regular perpetual Upper Tier 2).

Tier 1 is quite different – here, we have a very wide variety of different structures. These range from what we would regard as the most risky form for investors – perpetual preference shares with no step-up at the call date (the risk here being perpetuity) to the least risky – the German dated Tier 1 structure, which has a clear maturity. This wealth of structures has arisen from slightly different guidelines between EU countries, the problem relating to step-up Tier 1 and the quest to create structures that are tax-efficient, yet meet all regulatory requirements. We will not touch on tax efficiency, but focus here on the step-up limit. Banks are only allowed to issue up to 15 per cent of their Tier 1 in a 'redeemable' format, which generally means a structure that has an explicit or implicit step-up feature that might induce the bank to call it at the call date.

The typical form of Tier 1 capital that trades in the fixed-income market is this step-up Tier 1 structure. It is perpetual, with a fixed coupon until the call date. If it is not called, then it steps-up to a floating coupon for the rest of its life. Investors are happy to buy these structures, as they believe the banks have a strong incentive to call them, to avoid the higher financing costs. The 15 per cent limit does not apply to Tier 1 with a pure call option and no step-up, and banks have tried to manipulate structures to get around this 15 per cent rule, while still having some kind of implicit step-up. These have been successful in the past, but generally the regulator has ultimately grandfathered these types of structures, and any future ones will fall under the 15 per cent limit. Please see Chapter 5 of our *Bank Capital A–Z*[2] book for further details.

In brief, there are many ways to place Tier 1 issues in distinct classes, but our favourite is to group them in terms of the risks/comforts they provide to investors. Essentially, we'd count six main categories of institutional Tier 1 preferred. Ignoring the bells and whistles on certain issues within a class, we'd place them in the following order, in terms of decreasing risk to the investor (you'll see that dated Tier 1s are the least risky, in our view).

- *Non Steps.* These are Tier 1 issues that are perpetual with a call date, but no step-up. These have been sold into the retail market (with a call in year five) and, more recently, into the institutional market (with calls in year ten or later) after Barclays' first non-step institutional Tier 1 was launched in December 2004. Of all the structures listed here, these do not fall into the 15 per cent limit, as there is no step-up feature. They tend to trade wide to all other structures, due to the increased likelihood of perpetuity.
- *Vanilla.* These issues are perpetual and have a step-up and call. They are normally issued via a special purpose vehicle (SPV), and guaranteed by the bank or the bank holding company. They are also tax-deductible when issued via an SPV, although can be directly issued and non-tax deductible.
- *Cumulative issues.* These have been branded both Reserve Capital Instruments (RCIs) and Perpetual Regulatory Tier One instruments (PROs) to name a few variations. Cumulative issues are perpetual and usually have a step-up and call. They are issued directly from the bank or bank holding company and are tax-deductible. Coupons can be deferred but are effectively cumulative, due to a mechanism whereby any deferred coupons can be paid for by the bank issuing fresh equity to raise the cash coupon amount.
- *Non-innovative.* These issues are perpetual, have a call, and, like all other Tier 1s mentioned here, are senior only to equity in a liquidation of the issuer. They are normally

directly issued and are tax-deductible. The key difference between these and vanilla Tier 1s is that non-innovative Tier 1 has no explicit step-up at the call date. Instead, there is a mechanism whereby any coupons made after the call dates have to be financed from equity sales. This is, in effect, a very large step-up in financing cost to the issuer. These were initially allowed to fall outside the 15 per cent limit, but have since been grand-fathered and any future issues will fall within the limit. Compared to cumulative issues above, we prefer non-innovative in terms of risk to the investor – we'd prefer to have greater certainty of maturity (non-innovative step-ups are extremely high) than cumula-tive coupons.

- *Equity settlement*. These issues are perpetual and have a step-up and call. They are normally issued via an SPV, and guaranteed by the bank or the bank holding company. If these issues are not called at the call date, the investor can effectively 'put' bonds back to the bank, which has to sell fresh equity in order to repay the bonds at par. Barring any problems in selling equity, this arguably gives investors an effective matu-rity date for the Tier 1s.
- *Dated Tier 1*. These issues are dated, can have a step-up and call, and are normally senior only to equity in a liquidation of the issuer. They are only issued by German banks.

The view from the ratings agencies

The three main ratings agencies approach bank capital ratings in slightly different ways. The agencies often stress that they rate bank capital on a case-by-case basis, but it is possible to draw very general guidelines.

The senior rating of a bank is the agency's current opinion of its overall capacity to meet its financial obligations – essentially its fundamental creditworthiness. Ratings for other forms of debt take into account the nature and provisions of the debt, the probability of default and the expected loss should default occur. Subordinated debt is accordingly rated

---

Exhibit 15.2

Rating agencies' treatment of bank capital – notching from senior debt levels

Senior rating	Lower Tier 2	Upper Tier 2	Tier 1	Tier 3
S&P				
Senior debt above BBB–	+1 notch	+2 notches	+2 notches	+3 notches
Moody's				
FSR C and above	+1 notch	+1 notch	+2 notches	+2 notches
Fitch				
Senior above A–	+1 notch	+1 notch	+1 notch	+1–2 notches
BBB– to BBB+	+1 notch	+2 notches	+2 notches	+2 notches
Source: Moody's, S&P, Fitch.				

below the senior rating. Tier 1 preferred will have even lower ratings due to its more equity-like characteristics. The degree to which a specific issue is notched below senior debt will also depend on a bank's overall credit quality.

In Exhibit 15.2 we detail how the agencies have generally approached traditional 'vanilla' tiers of bank capital in the past, but note again their flexibility to notch on a case-by-case basis.

---

* The authors are research analysts at Morgan Stanley & Co. International Limited. This material does not constitute a research recommendation or investment advice. Morgan Stanley is involved in many businesses that may relate to issuers or securities mentioned in this material, including market-making, proprietary trading and investment banking, and may have a position in the securities.

[1] *Basel II A–Z*, written by Jackie Ineke of Morgan Stanley, published November 2004.

[2] *Bank Capital A–Z*, written by Jackie Ineke of Morgan Stanley, published January 2003.

Chapter 16

The Italian state securitisations

Sriram Soundararajan and Silvio Angius
Lehman Brothers

Introduction

Complex financial instruments, including structured products, have often originated as solutions to problems faced by the corporate sector or by financial institutions. In times of need, however, governments also take to financial innovation to help manage their accounts. Securitisation has proven to be one such innovation that has come to the aid of European governments that are working towards meeting the Maastricht convergence criteria. In 1997, the EU member states adopted the Stability and Growth Pact, agreeing to maintain fiscal discipline in order to meet the convergence criteria, which included keeping the budget deficit below 3 per cent of GDP and taking the debt-to-GDP ratio closer towards 60 per cent. With many countries, including Italy, Greece and Belgium, running debt-to-GDP ratios that were well above 100 per cent, there was a need for reform in the longer run and some financial engineering in the short term (see Exhibit 16.1). This is where securitisation has played an important role, as it has allowed governments to raise money by moving assets off their balance sheet rather than issuing more debt. In this chapter, we will have a closer look at how Italy has used securitisation to help them move closer towards meeting the Stability and Growth Pact criteria, and, in the process, have improved the efficiency of the state machinery involved in these transactions. We will also see how these transactions have had a beneficial impact on the credit management processes and have improved overall return on state-owned assets.

Why is securitisation a valuable tool for governments?

The Italian Government, not unlike many others, has a fairly bulky balance sheet with several assets including, among others, property, utilities and certain claims such as taxes and social security payments. One of the ways in which the state can raise cash without issuing debt is to sell the non-strategic and less essential assets to the private sector. Certain assets, such as the government's stake in firms and in utilities can be sold directly to the private sector as has been done in France with EDF and GDF and in Italy with Poste and Enel. However, for many other assets, such as tax and social security claims or large property portfolios, the disposal procedure can prove more complex as potential investors may be more difficult to identify. Such assets require time and effort to be worked through and cash proceeds are likely to flow in over time. In such circumstances, capital markets may

Exhibit 16.1

State of government finances in Europe 2005

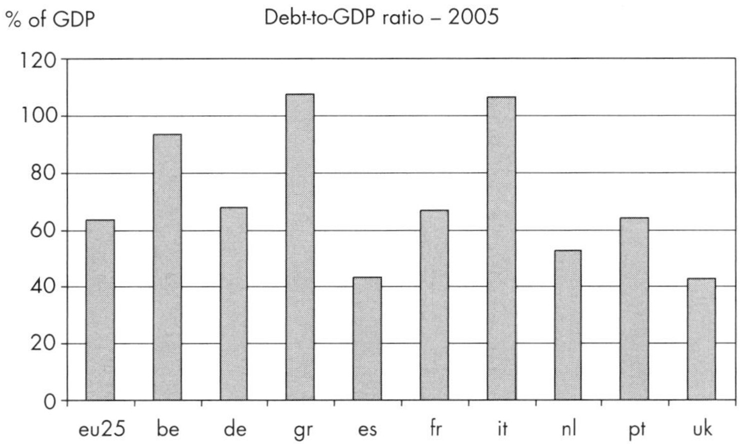

% of GDP
Debt-to-GDP ratio – 2005
120
100
80
60
40
20
0
eu25
be
de
gr
es
fr
it
nl
pt
uk

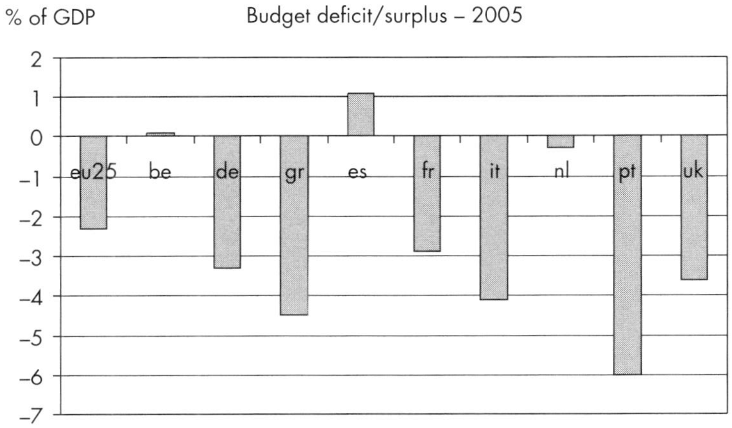

% of GDP
Budget deficit/surplus – 2005
2
1
0
–1
–2
–3
–4
–5
–6
–7
eu25
be
de
gr
es
fr
it
nl
pt
uk

Source: Eurostat.

represent an interesting option, and it is precisely in such situations that securitisation has proved most beneficial.

Through using a typical securitisation structure (see Chapter 5), the government can sell these assets into a special purpose vehicle (SPV) thereby realising cash upfront. The SPV, in turn, sells bonds that are backed by these assets to institutional investors. Over time, as the government agencies service these assets and generate cash revenues, the bondholders are paid back. The government is thus able to realise the cash flows from these assets upfront. Given that the bonds in a securitisation are not the obligation of the government, they do not count towards public debt, but they are obviously more expensive to issue than straight government debt. Even so, the interest costs tend to be fairly low for securitisations given the fact that the bonds are secured and that structural protection can be built in. For instance, the average coupon on the latest Società di Cartolarizzazione dei Crediti INPS (SCCI) transaction from the Italian state was just around 23 basis points (bp) over where the government can issue debt.

Apart from the benefits listed above, securitisation has proved to be a significantly useful tool in one other way. A securitisation effectively exposes the government machinery that is servicing the assets to investors and thereby to the external world in general. Their performance ends up being measured in fairly objective terms against a certain minimum level of performance that is expected of them. The fact that the performance of the bureaucracy is being measured in objective terms plus the focus from the investment community has meant that several government agencies have been forced to reassess their processes and procedures in order to increase efficiencies. Such benefits are now being recognised and cited as one of the main reasons for the governments' choice of securitisation as a funding tool.

Italy's experience with securitisation

The Italian Government was among the first in Europe to use securitisation as a funding tool and, to date, remains a significant originator of such transactions. The first securitisation executed by the Italian state was the SCCI transaction, issued in 1999. The transaction securitised delinquent social security payments owed to the INPS (Istituto Nazionale per la Previdenza Sociale), the state agency, by firms and individuals. Since then the Italian Government has issued, on average, around €5.5bn of bonds each year through securitisations (a total of €38bn of issuance between 1999 and 2005) (see Exhibit 16.2). This meant that the government raised enough cash through securitisation to reduce its budget deficit by about 0.4 per cent of GDP per year on average. Also, as mentioned earlier, the bonds, for most part, were not counted towards public debt.

The Italian Government has securitised a variety of assets including real estate assets both commercial and residential, delinquent social security payments, research loans provided to firms, loans made to public sector companies and even lottery receivables, and in the process of securitising these assets the government has benefited from the improvements in the workings of the government agencies involved in generating and servicing these assets. In fact, the benefits of securitisation have been apparent to different political fronts in Italy. The first securitisation was issued in 1999, when the centre-left government was in power,

Exhibit 16.2

Treasury securitisations from Italy – issuance volumes

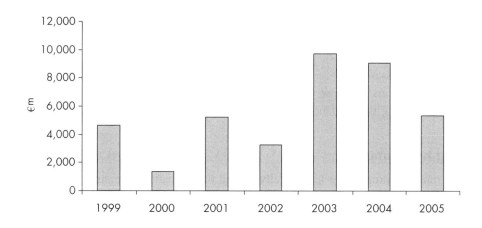

Source: Lehman Brothers.

and the programme has been continued by the centre-right coalition government. It is expected that the next government will also take advantage of this successful programme.

The Italian Treasury's securitisation programme has not been without its hiccups. The SCCI transaction suffered from lower than expected performance in the first year after it was issued. Collections from the securitised delinquent claims were well below initial projections. However, after a brief period, performance improved to match and even surpass expectation. Another transaction that suffered from negative performance was the Società Cartolarizzazione Immobili Pubblici 2 (SCIP 2) transaction. This was the state's second securitisation of real estate assets and the transaction depended on a steady disposal of these assets to generate cash to pay back the bonds. Right from the start, the performance of the agencies handling the asset sales was below expectations. Even though the value of the assets was not a major concern given that property prices were appreciating in Italy, the transaction suffered from the fact that cash inflows were not sufficient to meet the schedule of payments promised to the bondholders. Consequently, in 2005, the Italian Treasury stepped in and refinanced the transaction with a slower plan for collections. Apart from these two situations, which have since seen improvements, the Treasury securitisations have been performing well to date.

The programme also suffered some setbacks when the Eurostat came out with rules for state securitisations in 2002 (see later in this chapter). Under these clarified rules, the Eurostat disallowed some state securitisations for qualifying as off-balance sheet debt. In other words the transactions were subsequently counted as public debt according to Eurostat and therefore deficit and debt numbers were restated for the years in which the transactions were

done. Since then, the Italian state has been in close dialogue with Eurostat and most transactions are issued only when it is sure to get off-balance sheet status.

The programme has served the government quite well, especially at a time when the
economic performance of the region has been quite weak. The lacklustre economic growth
over the past several years has meant that Italy is still in breach of the convergence criteria.
While the budget deficit has been increasing over the past few years, the programme has
helped keep it from getting out of hand as well as helped them slowly grind down their
debt burden (see Exhibit 16.3). In the longer term, the country needs structural reform in
order to achieve sustained economic growth, but in the current political and social environment such reforms are slow in taking place. In the meantime, securitisation will help
them with managing their balance sheet and improving their bureaucratic efficiencies.

Leading by example

The government's programme has actually helped the formation of a strong securitisation
market in Italy. The first securitisation laws to be passed in the country were put together
at the time the state was implementing its securitisation programme and they were then
widely used by other issuers, primarily banks and other specialised finance companies. As
a matter of fact, the Italian securitisation market has been a fairly large player in the European
market issuing several billion of bonds backed by residential mortgages, small business

Exhibit 16.3

Deficit and debt numbers – Italy

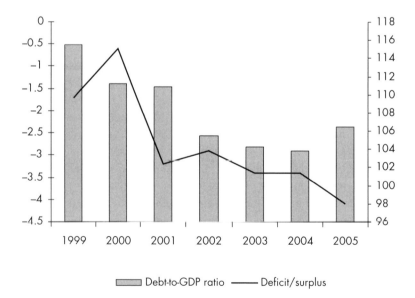

Debt-to-GDP ratio ——— Deficit/surplus

Source: Eurostat.

loans and leases and recently even commercial property (see Exhibit 16.4). To some extent this has been possible due to the legislative framework that was put together in a fairly short period of time by a government that was keen to use this financial tool for its own benefit as well.

The various Italian regional governments and local authorities, not wanting to be left behind, have also used securitisation as a funding tool, though for different reasons. In their case, securitisation offered two benefits. First, securitisation can help the regions achieve lower interest costs as they can be structured to have bonds with ratings higher than the region's own. Secondly, the local governments cannot borrow except to invest and securitisation offers them a way of raising revenue without breaking this rule. One of the areas where securitisation has been used is, for example, in the case of the regional healthcare agencies.

Of course, securitisations by the central government usually tend to be much larger than those from the regional governments or the private sector. The Italian Treasury securitisations average about €2–5bn in size compared to private sector or regional deals which usually are sized at €0.5–2bn. Investors usually prefer larger deals since larger deal size usually means a broader investor base and hence potentially better liquidity in the secondary markets. Additionally the treasury securitisations are traded on the MTS electronic market where government bonds are usually traded and this provides additional liquidity for this sector.

Exhibit 16.4

Issuance volumes of Italian securitisation

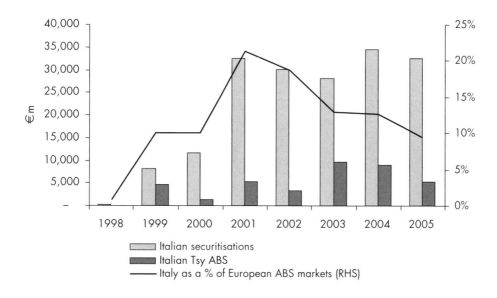

Source: Lehman Brothers.

The SCCI transaction – a case study in state securitisation

No transaction can better highlight the various issues that the Italian state securitisation programme has gone through than the SCCI securitisation, the first of such deals. We will take a closer look at this transaction in order to illustrate the use of securitisation techniques in a sovereign context.

The assets

The Italian government, and in particular the INPS, the state social security agency, collects social security contributions from firms as well as from self-employed individuals. Each year a portion of such claims falls into arrears and starts accumulating interest and penalties. Subsequently, the agency starts collection proceedings against such delinquent firms and individuals, resulting in either outright recoveries or in some form of work-out plan where the debtor makes regular payments. INPS accumulates such delinquent claims every year from which they realise cash gradually over the years. It is these claims that form the collateral pool for the SCCI transaction. Through a securitisation, the government can realise the value of these assets upfront and transfer the risks of recoveries to the capital markets. The trend in total outstanding gross book value of the claims that have been securitised is given in Exhibit 16.5.

The structure

The transaction takes the form of a 'master trust' where a common pool of collateral supports different series of bonds issued at different points in time. Each year INPS can add further

Exhibit 16.5

Outstanding gross book value of delinquent claims securitised

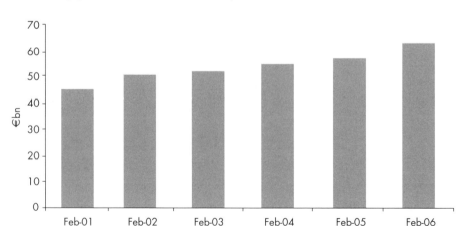

Source: Author's own

collateral to the pool and issue a new series of bonds as long as there is sufficient collateral to support the ratings on the new bonds. The credit enhancement is obtained through over-collateralisation, that is, through having collateral that is higher in value (net recoverable value and not the book value of the assets) than the amount of bonds outstanding. In addition the structure incorporates a debt service reserve that will be used to support bonds in case recoveries on the assets fall short of expectations. In each period, collections from the collateral are pooled and, after paying servicing and hedging fees, are first used to pay interest on the bonds on a pro-rata and *pari passu* basis. The bonds are then paid principal based on a pre-decided schedule. The bonds are either paid out as soft-bullets in one single payment on the expected maturity or have a schedule of payments over time. There are triggers in place that ensure that if the performance of the transaction deteriorates or, in other words, if collections fall well short of expectation, the bonds will be paid out on a pro-rata and pass through basis. That is, the collections will be passed onto the bonds as and when they come through and all the bonds will receive a share of the principal based on their relative sizes in each period. The triggers are in place to ensure that all the bonds share the risks of the pool performance, especially if it deteriorates, since they all share the same triple-A rating.

The liabilities

The transaction has to date only issued bonds that are rated triple-A, the highest rating achievable. This has been possible through the amount of overcollateralisation and the level of reserves that have been added to the structure. To date, 13 bonds have been issued from six transactions. The expected maturity of the bonds do not follow the same order in which they were issued with some bonds issued through later transactions having a shorter expected maturity than those issued earlier. This has been possible due to the better than expected collections in the initial years which meant that the transaction was generating cash in excess of what is required to meet the expected maturity on the bonds. The government was thus able to issue bonds with short maturities which are paid back utilising such excess collections. The master-trust structure has thus given the government the flexibility to adjust the structure of the liabilities based on the past performance of the transaction.

Legal issues

There were a few legal changes that were made in order to make this transaction possible. In 1998, the government passed the Law Decree 448/1993, one of the articles of which enabled INPS to securitise delinquent assets. Furthermore, in 1999, a few months before mandating the transaction, the government made changes to the legislation that regulates the collection process of INPS in order to allow certain claims to be collected by the private sector. Thus, instead of the collection and recovery procedures being administered by the local offices of the INPS, it would now be done by a group of *concessionaris* – private companies who are experienced in the area of debt collection. This move was expected to improve the recovery rates on the assets since the private sector is, in general, more efficient and flexible than government departments.

Rating agency methodology

As with any securitisation of delinquent claims, the rating agencies base their analysis on historical recovery rates that have been achieved by the servicing agencies. INPS provided a history of recoveries achieved from each type of claim in the portfolio which indicated that most recoveries occur within the first year of a claim falling into arrears. The rating agency then base their 'stress' scenarios for a triple-A rating on the historical recovery rates and arrive at the level of overcollateralisation and debt service reserve that is required to ensure that the bonds are safe enough to qualify for a triple-A rating.

Servicing of the portfolio

Each claim in the portfolio falls into one of three phases in the collection process. A claim can either be in the administrative phase, a legal phase (when judicial procedures are commenced against the debtor) or an amnesty phase (when the debtor has agreed to, and is making, repayments over time). INPS is responsible for collections on claims that are either in legal proceedings or have been granted amnesty. Collections on all other claims are the responsibility of the *concessionari* as described earlier.

Pricing

One of the debates that has continued in the ABS markets among investors and analysts is the level of pricing that is appropriate for state securitisations. Often, the pricing on government securitisations tends to be much closer to the treasury markets than any other sector in the ABS markets. In other words, the pricing on such bonds seems to indicate that investors are associating a lower risk of default on the bonds than would be suggested by the nature of the underlying collateral. To some degree, this might be explained by the association of a central government with such transactions. Investors could be betting on the government having sufficient power to prevent or rectify any serious deterioration in the transaction. The SCCI deals are no exception and price fairly tight given the fact that the collateral is essentially delinquent claims. For comparison, one of the first bonds from the programme paid a coupon of London interbank offered rate (Libor) minus 2 bp for a two-year bond, at a time when deals backed by prime residential mortgages (RMBS) were paying Libor plus 15 bp for a similar bond. Typically deals backed by granular performing mortgages, which are backed by the security of the borrowers residences are considered among the safest asset classes in the securitisation markets. Hence, the SCCI transaction should have priced wider (or in other words, should pay a higher coupon rate) than where RMBS bonds were pricing since it was backed by higher-risk delinquent collateral. The first few investor reports for the transaction helped to correct the pricing differential, when collections fell short of expectation. The *concessionari* system was slow to get off the ground and caused collections to falter. The second transaction from the programme priced slightly wider than RMBS bonds as a result, indicating that investors became more wary of the true risks in the transaction.

Performance

In most asset classes in the securitisation world, the measures of performance include the level of arrears and defaults on the assets. Such measures obviously hold little relevance in securitisations of already delinquent claims. In such cases, the main measure of performance is the recovery rate on the assets and the speed of collections. In the initial few periods of the SCCI deal, collections fell short of expectation mainly due to the *concessionari* process not taking off. When the first investor report was released and showed low collections, investors and rating agencies were concerned. However, the Italian Treasury came out with a statement to reassure investors and they also met with rating agencies to explain the deal's performance. This experience was to prove useful in subsequent years when the SCIP 2 transaction would underperform and these events also helped investors form a positive opinion on the response of the Italian state as a securitisation originator. Since then the *concessionaris* have picked up the pace and currently contribute to 25 per cent of collections in each period. In fact, collection rates have been better than expected over the past few years allowing the Treasury to issue additional bonds to remove the excess cash accumulated in the structure. This better than expected performance has been achieved during a period when the Italian economy has been fairly weak. Hence, looking forward, it is expected that current performance levels will be maintained and maybe even improved upon.

The SCCI programme has proved to be quite successful despite the initial worries on performance. The Treasury has issued bonds from this programme at least once a year for the past few years and is expected to continue to tap it in the future as well. The Italian Treasury and INPS also realised the importance of improving the efficiency of the servicing systems and of keeping investors informed on the reasons and remedies for any underperformance. The success and lessons of this programme clearly helped the Italian Government in planning and executing its relatively successful securitisation strategy.

Are there only benefits from securitisations?

The discussions above clearly highlight the benefits of securitisation as a funding tool for governments. It has, however, not been without its downsides. The basic idea of a securitisation involves the sale of assets by the originator to an SPV. In the case of state securitisations, the government is essentially selling some of its assets to realise revenue. If these are real assets, there are few arguments against the use of securitisation techniques to achieve the sale. While the rationale for the sale of such assets might be questioned, the choice of securitisation as a tool is not particularly controversial. However, the questions have mainly been raised against the sale of certain future flows and against transactions where the government had extended its guarantee to the transaction either directly or indirectly.

The Eurostat, the central statistics agency for the EU, has been concerned about the use of 'creative accounting' surrounding some securitisation transactions. For instance, in some cases, governments have extended either a direct or indirect guarantee towards the securitisation bonds. This effectively meant that the bonds in the securitisation were a liability of the government if the assets failed to generate sufficient revenues. In a few other cases, the securitisation involved 'future flows'. These are securitisation of assets that do not exist currently but will only be created in the future. An example would be the securitisation of lottery receivables completed by the Italian state in 2000. In this transaction the government had essentially sold future revenues that were to arise from the state lottery. These were not currently assets on the government's balance sheet since they were neither real assets nor were they existing claims. Such transactions obviously did little to improve the quality of the state's balance sheet and hence were reclassified by the Eurostat in 2002.

Also, as with any balance sheet, be it corporate or sovereign, the sale of assets always raises some concerns for the existing bondholders. In the case of Italy, the rating agencies have been keeping a watchful eye on the securitisations since substantial asset sales without a corresponding paydown of debt would increase the credit risk of the government.

Clearly, the use of securitisation has caused some concern in some quarters. However, the main worry is not on the use of securitisation itself but, rather, in the way it is used by the governments.

Eurostat's view on state securitisations

With a view to clarifying its position on securitisation and to block some of these loopholes, the Eurostat, in 2002, came out with certain guidelines for what would constitute a true off-balance sheet securitisation. Briefly, the main ones included:

- *un-attached future cash flows:* securitisations of future cash flows not attached to a pre-existing asset are always to be treated as government borrowing;
- *guarantees:* securitisations where the government grants a guarantee to the SPV imply an incomplete risk transfer and should be treated as government borrowing; and
- *discounts:* if a securitisation includes future payments beyond the initial payment by the SPV to the government, specific provisions apply: the transaction has to be treated as government borrowing if the discount (excess of collateral value over initial payment) exceeds 15 per cent.

Since then governments have tried to ensure that most transactions fall within these guidelines. There still continue to be a few grey areas and some transactions that are being reviewed by Eurostat more closely. Still, to a large extent, recent transactions have met the requirements of the Eurostat while helping the state achieve its funding needs. Furthermore, to reduce uncertainties surrounding its decisions, Eurostat has promised to come out with more detailed guidelines in the near future.

The future looks bright

Greece and Italy were among the first governments to originate securitisations in Europe. More recently, as lacklustre economic growth continued to hamper state balance sheets, other countries have followed suit. Germany, Portugal and Belgium have issued a securitisation each and more such transactions can be expected to follow suit. Greece is also reported to be considering restarting its securitisation programme. In the near term, the slow pace of economic recovery and the continued difficulty that governments face in making structural reforms mean that the use of tools such as securitisation will remain popular. At the same time, as the Italian Government has discovered, securitisation offers other long-lasting benefits and has proven itself as an efficient means of realising revenues. It is thus likely that European governments both at the national and regional level will continue to tap the securitisation markets in the near future.

Chapter 17

Back to the future

Aircraft portfolio securitisations

Cecilia Park
UBS Investment Bank
Zarrar Sehgal
Milbank, Tweed, Hadley & McCloy LLP

Introduction

The year 2005 marked a watershed for aircraft finance in general and pooled aircraft securitisations in particular. The 9/11 attacks combined with the general cyclical downturn in the aviation industry resulted in a relatively dormant securitisation market. Fear of additional outbreaks of SARS (severe acute respiratory syndrome) and other epidemic disease further contributed to the unwillingness of the capital markets to participate in such transactions. Activity levels in the pooled aircraft securitisation market returned in 2005 to those consistent with the end of the 1990s, 2000 and the first half of 2001. The year was marked by a number of large transactions such as the US$1.0bn Aircraft Lease Securitisation Limited, or ALS, transaction that closed in September and the US$1.86bn ACG Trust III securitisation that was completed just before the end of the year. Recently, the industry witnessed the consummation of the Aircastle 2006–7 transaction (also known as ACS). This chapter examines a brief history of pooled aircraft securitisations and the challenges that sponsors and underwriters face in bringing such transactions to the market. This chapter also focuses on the use of pooled aircraft securitisations as a means of obtaining permanent financing for large-scale acquisitions and discusses some of the challenges facing new entrants to the market.

In the beginning

Various forms of aircraft financing in the capital markets have existed for approximately two decades or more, beginning with equipment trust certificates, also known as ETCs, pass-through trust certificates, also known as PTCs, and enhanced equipment trust certificates, typically referred to as EETCs. ETCs were used to fund a single aircraft in use by a single airline with the PTCs and EETCs being used later to finance multiple aircraft in use by a single airline. Each of these forms of financings essentially represented a corporate obligation of the issuing airline secured by the related aircraft and enhanced, in certain structures, by the use of features such as a liquidity facility dedicated to making timely payments of interest on the related certificates. In contrast to PTCs and EETCs, pooled aircraft securitisations developed as a technique to finance multiple aircraft in use by numerous airlines around the world. Aircraft operating lessors have historically been the primary sponsors of pooled aircraft securitisations. The technique has been utilised by the sponsors to either obtain long-term financing or create balance sheet capacity. As the owner of the aircraft, the operating lessors are responsible for managing the residual risk of the aircraft, which includes remarketing the aircraft to a new lessee after the expiry of the existing lease term. As the leases entered into by the operating lessors with lessees (typically airlines) are often on a short-term basis, the remarketing function is critical in maximising value from the portfolio. Pooled aircraft securitisations, therefore, heavily rely on the ability of the servicer to maximise cash flows for the bondholders by remarketing the aircraft as each lease expires. In addition, the servicer in such transactions is responsible for identifying opportunities to sell the aircraft subject to certain parameters set forth in the transaction documents. In the past, the sponsor has typically acted as the servicer, earning servicing fees in return which are often a percentage of the lease rental receipts.

The utilisation of securitisations as a means to finance aircraft portfolios is not a novel financing mechanism. In 1992, former Irish lessor Guinness Peat Aviation, or GPA, brought the first pooled aircraft securitisation to the market with the Aircraft Lease Portfolio Securitisation, also known as ALPS, offering over US$350m of bonds secured by the resale value of the aircraft in the portfolio. Following ALPS, the pooled aircraft securitisation model continued to evolve over the course of the 1990s, eventually securing offered bonds by the expected cash flow generated by lease payment streams in addition to the resale value of the subject aircraft. The modern form of pooled aircraft securitisations really took flight with the US$4.1bn Airplanes Pass Through Trust issued in 1996, the US$1.2bn Aircraft Finance Trust offering in 1999 and the US$1.0bn Morgan Stanley Aircraft Finance offering in 2000. Each of the subsequent transactions in this sector has followed essentially the same underlying principle: to securitise the expected cash flow of aircraft leases from existing contractual cash flows as well as future re-leasing cash flows for the full term of the useful life of the assets. The typical useful life of an aircraft is assumed to be 25 years.

Offerings

As Exhibit 17.1 demonstrates, between 1996 and 2001, there were over US$26bn in issuances in the 'modern' pooled aircraft securitisation market. Enthusiasm for such financings understandably drastically declined after 9/11 and the pooled aircraft securitisation sector, like other areas of the industry, became distressed, effectively closing the door to new issuances. Aircraft portfolios otherwise ready to be securitised, such as the AWAS (Ansett Worldwide Aviation Services) portfolio owned by Morgan Stanley, failed to be brought to market notwithstanding that transactions in respect of such asset portfolios had previously been planned and, in some cases, were in advanced stages of the documentation process. As the aviation sector commenced its recovery, the pooled aircraft securitisation market became more feasible. Prospective bondholders and rating agencies, though, required some drastic changes to the traditional methodology of aircraft portfolio valuation and demanded less aggressive levels of leverage than previously offered. By every measure, current aircraft finance deals are structured more conservatively than the deals of the 1990s and are designed to better withstand the cyclicality inherent in the industry. Most of the US$7bn issued in the pooled aircraft

Exhibit 17.1

Issuance volume by year

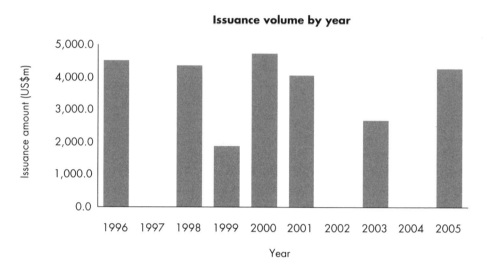

Issuance volume by year

Source: Bloomberg and UBS Investment Bank.

securitisation market since 9/11 occurred in 2005 (see Exhibit 17.1) seemingly signalling a revival of this sector. Further, while the pooled aircraft securitisation market has traditionally been dominated by passenger commercial aircraft, other aviation assets, such as spare engines and spare parts, were introduced to this market in the last five years and one can expect to see more activity in the capital markets for these asset types as well.

Acquisition financing

One method of financing acquisitions in the aircraft industry that gained momentum in 2005 included a two-phase structure consisting of a first phase bridge loan to facilitate the acqui- sition of certain aircraft assets followed by a pooled aircraft securitisation to provide permanent financing for the portfolio of assets. In the third quarter of 2005, Cerberus Capital Management brought ALS to market to retire the interim or bridge financing used to finance the acquisition of debis AirFinance (since renamed as AerCap). Cerberus used the proceeds of the bridge financing to acquire debis AirFinance and its aircraft portfolio. The proceeds of the subsequent ALS offering were applied to repay in part the bridge financing and, hence, provide a permanent financing for the acquisition.

Aviation Capital Group announced its plans to purchase Boullioun Aviation Services, also known as Boullioun, from WestLB AG in the first half of 2005. The purchase of Boullioun allowed Aviation Capital Group to acquire over 110 aircraft making them one of the largest aircraft operating lessors in the world. Aviation Capital Group, like Cerberus, facilitated the purchase of Boullioun through the use of interim bank financing. Aviation

Capital Group effected the ACG Trust III securitisation, their third securitisation in five years, to replace the bridge financing used to acquire Boullioun under great time pressure, bringing the offering to market in only a few months and closing the transaction prior to the new year. The proceeds of interim loans in both transactions essentially functioned to provide parties with the immediate liquidity necessary to consummate the initial acquisition. Most interim financings are subject to time pressure to repay the associated bridge loan without incurring increased interest rates and/or other penalties. In addition to financing that include a two-phase structure, other new features are being introduced in the securitisation market. The AOS transaction, for example, was structured to allow, for the first time, regular equity payments. This payment was subject to the satisfaction of debt service coverage ratio.

The securitisation market can be an attractive source of financing for aircraft assets as compared to the traditional bank loan market. The pooled aircraft securitisation market offers greater liquidity and significantly diminishes refinancing risk by allowing for longer-term financing. The chief limitation of this market, however, is that the securitisation structure in connection with aircraft financing tends to be somewhat inflexible in accommodating the inevitable changes in the characteristics of an aircraft portfolio as it ages, goes through industry cycles and weathers the new developments of the aircraft industry, such as the introduction of new aircraft models and new technology.

Characteristics of recent transactions

In aircraft financing transactions in the 1990s, a portfolio of aircraft could include a broad range of aircraft types and ages. In aircraft acquisition financings that have occurred in the last two or three years, the types of aircraft in the portfolio intended to be financed have become increasingly important and more recent pooled aircraft securitisations have focused on a younger average portfolio age and more current aircraft models. This concern for the quality of the aircraft in a portfolio is reflected in the many conditions that must be satisfied before the initial lending in respect of a bridge financing can take place, including the prerequisite that a certain number of the aircraft in the subject portfolio be novated prior to, or concurrently with, the initial lending. Similarly, in the context of pooled aircraft securitisations, rating agencies and monoline insurers have required a certain number of aircraft, or even particular aircraft in the portfolio, actually be delivered into the transaction no later than the bond issuance date. In addition, the balance of the undelivered assets must be novated or delivered within a certain period of time following the closing. In most transactions, funds for the undelivered assets are held in separate accounts to be applied in connection with the delivery of such assets. In the event that a particular aircraft is not novated or delivered within the established timeframe, funds in the related segregated account will be utilised to repay an allocable portion of the debt. These novation and delivery requirements, present in both the ALS and ACG Trust III transactions, stem from the importance of a young, diversified pool of aircraft and are critical in order to assure that the funds advanced and bonds issued have the benefit of an acceptable mix of aircraft assets. The emphasis on increasing the quality and decreasing the age of the aircraft in an asset pool, while still maintaining a degree of diversity among the aircraft, is also an attempt to minimise the risks of volatility in lease rates and defaulting lessees. Recent transactions, including ALS, ACG Trust III and ACS have incorporated a liquidity facility available to counteract such risks if realised. Credit facilities provide increased liquidity and can be drawn on to cover certain expenses, senior swap payments and interest on the senior class or subclass of bonds.

Pooled aircraft securitisations also include specific regional concentration limits as to the location of the lessees as well as requirements in respect of the target sale price of each aircraft in the portfolio before such aircraft can be sold. These criteria are established at the outset of the transaction and can be very cumbersome to later modify as such changes typically require a bondholder vote. Concentration limits attempt to provide comfort to the bondholder by limiting the political risk at the expense of the bondholder. The concentration limits restrict the ability of the securitisation vehicle to act as compared to other operating lessors who, free of such restrictions, are able to make more productive use of their aircraft by deploying such aircraft in regions or countries with the greatest demand for them. In addition, operating lessors that have financing arms can use such leverage to ensure that their aircraft remain in revenue service. By establishing fixed criteria at the outset of the transaction, the deal structure can greatly constrain the ability of the servicer to effectively place aircraft in revenue service and, as a result, can act as a detriment to bondholders. In order to make these structures more viable, these concentration limits need to incorporate an element of dynamism to provide the securitisation vehicle with increased flexibility to manage specific regional downturns.

Monoline insurers and bondholders recognised that pooled aircraft securitisations in the 1990s were based on financial models that assumed insufficient expenditures in respect of the aircraft. In transactions that have occurred post-9/11, the methodologies for stress case scenarios with respect to pooled aircraft securitisations have been more conservative and assume a greater level of expenses, including maintenance and capital expenditures. One of the lessons learned from pooled aircraft securitisations completed in the 1990s is the need for better monitoring of periodic expenses which may be accomplished through more extensive reporting requirements and detailed information in respect of the aircraft and the related lessees. The more transparent information requirements in recent transactions have helped to provide the monolines and junior bondholders with the ability to monitor and better determine the reasons behind cash flow volatility.

Role of monolines in the revival of the market

It is important to note that the recent revival of the pooled aircraft securitisation market has been largely aided by the participation of monoline insurers. Aviation Capital Group's second securitisation, ACG II, is credited with returning pooled aircraft securitisations to the market. The ACG II transaction was made possible through support from MBIA Insurance Corporation, a monoline insurer. In ACG II, MBIA wrapped two senior tranches of bonds, while a single junior tranche was offered without monoline support. ACG II also made use of a supplemental rental facility designed to amortise the bonds on an assumed base case scenario. The supplemental rental facility provided extra liquidity in the event that cash flow from rental payments fell below an assumed threshold triggering the securitisation vehicle's ability to draw on such facility.

In transactions such as ACG II, ALS and ACS, a single monoline insurer issued a financial guaranty insurance policy in favour of senior classes or subclasses of bonds to secure specific payment terms, including, among other things, the payment of timely interest on such insured class of bonds and the repayment of outstanding principal on the final maturity date of the bonds. As one may anticipate, monoline insurers have required a fair amount of control over the transactions in which they have been involved. Monoline insurers have rights to consent to, among other things, the sale of any aircraft in the portfolio, as well as the acquisition of future aircraft, the issuance of any bonds offered in a refinancing and the securitisation vehicle's hedging policies. In addition, monoline insurers have obtained independent rights to terminate the servicer. This could be perceived as a disadvantage to junior bondholders who purchased bonds in reliance on the strength of the servicer, as such servicer may now be terminated for reasons unrelated to the performance of the aircraft portfolio. A potential check on the monoline's ability to unilaterally terminate a servicer is that each securitisation vehicle is required to have an approved servicer in all instances; therefore, even if the initial servicer is terminated, a replacement servicer must be in place. This may be cold comfort to those who entered the transaction on the basis of a recognised servicer. Further, monoline insurers have obtained extensive transaction approval requirements. This raises the concern in a multiple monoline deal, such as ACG Trust III, that there may be circumstances in which the servicer determines that a certain course of action will maximise value for the bondholders but a single monoline has the right to veto such action. Expanded junior bondholder buyout rights in pooled aircraft securitisations such as ACG Trust III that are more consistent with those in EETCs, such as the jetBlue EETC transaction, provide some protection. In such transactions, following an event of default under the debt documents the junior bondholders have the right to buy out the senior class of bonds and, if such bonds are subject to a monoline policy, concurrently cancel such policy and act as controlling party. These rights obviously only make sense if the junior bondholders view the collateral as having sufficient value to justify the additional outlay of funds.

In 2005, the ACG Trust III securitisation departed from the norm of having a single monoline insurer in order to securitise the largest portfolio of aircraft since the 1996 Airplanes transaction. In ACG Trust III, the securitisation vehicle issued three classes of bonds. Three separate policies offered by three different monoline insurers wrapped the most senior class of bonds on a rateable and several basis. This was the first time in pooled aircraft securitisations that three monoline insurers, each offering an individual policy, wrapped the same subclass of bonds. The presence of multiple monoline insurers in ACG Trust III acted as an additional challenge in the transaction. The rating agencies expressed concern about the decreased flexibility of the securitisation vehicle resulting from accommodating the varying concerns of three monoline insurers with separate institutional policies. The concept of several and rateable draws on the three monoline policies presents the theoretical notion that one monoline insurer may default on its payment while the other monoline insurers advance their respective rateable portion of the required amount in full. The result would be that the bondholders could receive less than the total insured payment. Multiple monolines also constrained the perceived benefit of a single entity acting as the controlling party in the transaction. In typical single monoline transactions, absent a default by such monoline insurer, the monoline insurer has the sole right to act as the controlling party, providing such monoline insurer with the right to direct the exercise of the available remedies following an event of default with respect to the securitisation vehicle. With multiple monoline insurers in ACG Trust III, the right to act as controlling party becomes more complicated as it requires the monoline insurers to, in effect, act as a cohesive unit. Consent requirements are further complicated by the possibility of a single monoline insurer dissenting from the actions of the other monoline insurers. The majority vote in ACG Trust III was designed to ameliorate some of these perceived concerns with respect to the requirement of unanimous consent.

In pooled aircraft securitisations structured in the last three years, incorporating monoline support has become crucial to the feasibility of a transaction, as well as the pricing, and to ultimately attract investors. However, as the underlying fundamentals of the aviation industry and the capital markets' receptivity of aircraft transactions improves, one can expect stand-alone, non-wrapped transactions to become more viable from an execution as well as an economic standpoint. In the meantime, one can anticipate that most transactions will be effected with some involvement by the monoline insurers.

Aircraft finance players

Most of the major aircraft operating lessors have accessed the pooled aircraft securitisation market at one time or another, including, among others, International Lease Finance Company, GE Capital Aviation Services, AerCap (along with its predecessor, AerFi) and Pegasus Aviation Finance Company. Not all lessors, however, have the same motivation or the same amount of resources to access the pooled aircraft securitisation market. Some lessors are searching for more effective permanent debt financing by matching the assumed useful lives of the assets to the long tenor of debt. Others aim to utilise the securitisation market as a portfolio management tool in order to generate aircraft sales without having to lose customer interface. In terms of the arrangers who have been active in this sector, the summary league table of the transactions in 2005, the most active year post-9/11, is shown in Exhibit 17.2.

It should be noted that pooled aircraft securitisations have been attracting many new and varied sources of capital. The current aircraft market is considered by many institutions one of high risk and a corresponding high return. Due to this perception, many of the veteran players in the aircraft finance market are systematically reducing their exposure in the aviation industry, or exiting the sector altogether. Meanwhile, private equity funds and hedge

Exhibit 17.2

Aviation securitisation league tables for 2005

Rank	Arranger	Volume (US$m)
1	UBS	2,201.9
2	Wachovia	1,390.0
3	Lehman Brothers	1,000.0

Source: Bloomberg and UBS Investment Bank.

funds have been participating in greater numbers recently in all aspects of the aviation industry. These new industry participants are offering a range of aircraft financing options, including by making debt investments and providing equity capital to new aircraft operating lessors, either by acquiring an existing operating lessor or by creating an operating lessor company through an initial acquisition of aircraft. Recent examples include the acquisition of AerCap by Cerberus in 2005, the acquisition of Pegasus Aviation by OakTree Capital Management and the acquisition of Morgan Stanley's AWAS by Terra Firma, among others. In various asset classes, many private equity and hedge funds are attracted to the whole business securitisation model as their first entry into the securitisation market pursuant to which an entire operating business is securitised with established cash flows generating liquidity for growth, among other things. This whole business type of securitisations has attracted greater scrutiny from the rating agencies because of the potential and unpredictable impact of the Days Inn deal. Briefly, in the Days Inn bankruptcy in the early 1990s the bankruptcy court ordered the substantive consolidation of the parent company, as debtor, and the special purpose vehicle (SPV) formed in the Days Inn deal that held the securitised assets because, among other things, the assets were deemed to be 'core operating assets' of the debtor or assets that are sufficiently distinct and vital to the debtor's business. In essence, the bankruptcy court found that the core operating assets were too intertwined with the debtor's operations to truly be isolated in a bankruptcy-remote entity and the securitised vehicle was hence disregarded as a separate entity. In attempting to utilise the whole business securitisation model, one will have to carefully distinguish the facts of the proposed securitisations from the facts in the Days Inn transaction and demonstrate that the assets to be securitised do not constitute 'core assets' of the sponsor.

It will be interesting to determine if the new entrants will have a major impact in the area of pooled aircraft securitisations as generally rating agencies and investors have preferred servicers with an established operating history. Nevertheless, these new sources of financing have established themselves as key players in the aircraft finance market and one can expect that they will play a critical role in the continued revival of the pooled securitisation market. Whether these new entrants anticipate aircraft leasing to be a long-term investment remains to be seen. In 2006 and 2007, however, market participants can expect to see a greater variety in the capital structures used as well as the sources of funds in the pooled aircraft securitisation market.

Return to the future

Currently, the aircraft operating leasing industry supplies over one-third of the worldwide commercial aircraft fleet. This industry is expected to take on even greater market share as the aviation industry continues to recover, as airlines grow and adjust to meet expected increased traffic and as airlines continue to be conservative on larger capital expenditures. As a result, anticipation is high for the year 2006 in aircraft finance and we can expect to see continued expansion in the pooled aircraft securitisation market. As the aircraft operating lessors take on a bigger role, they will have great interest in ensuring that access to the capital markets is preserved. Many of the deals in 2005 were effected to provide permanent financing for aircraft asset pools. Some of the more established aircraft operating lessors may not be attracted to such structures because, among other reasons, they place greater emphasis on the ability to sell and acquire aircraft on a less constrained basis than current securitisation models currently offer. ALS and ACG Trust III represented marked improvements in the older securitisation structures and have revitalised the market for pooled aircraft securitisations. Still, further opportunities to improve the model remain. As the uninitiated always discover, the aircraft finance market, in contrast to other structured finance markets, appears to operate under its own unique set of assumptions and considerations. The challenge that lies ahead is the development of more innovative financing techniques in order to meet the varied and complex goals of the sponsors, whether by adapting solutions used in other asset classes or otherwise.

Cecilia Park is Executive Director, Transportation Asset-Backed Finance Group, UBS Investment Bank. Zarrar Sehgal is Senior Associate, Global Transportation Finance Group, Milbank, Tweed, Hadley & McCloy LLP. The authors would like to thank Alexandra Johnson, Associate, Global Transportation Finance Group, Milbank, Tweed, Hadley & McCloy LLP, for her help with this chapter.

Chapter 18

Development and structure of the jumbo covered bond market in Europe

Heiko Langer
BNP Paribas

Market development

Driven by the success of the German jumbo Pfandbrief market in the second half of the 1990s, several other European countries implemented new covered bond frameworks or amended existing frameworks. With the jumbo market German issuers created a liquid segment of the Pfandbrief market by agreeing on a minimum size per issue and a market-making facility from the underwriting banks. While in the beginning the minimum issue size was equal to €250m it is now €1bn per issue. At the same time more and more issuers had their Pfandbriefe rated by one or two of the major rating agencies. The main aim of these measures was to increase international investor acceptance for the Pfandbrief. Within the first years of the jumbo market, the growth development was driven by the issuance of public sector covered bonds, mainly Public Pfandbriefe. But also Luxembourg Lettres de Gage and at an initial stage French Obligations Foncières and Irish Asset Covered Securities were focusing on public sector issuance. Within the last five years the focus of covered bond issuance shifted notably towards mortgage covered bonds. An increasing number of mortgage covered bond issuers, especially from Spain and the UK, but also from established markets such as Germany and Ireland, were the main driving forces of this development (see Exhibit 18.1).

At the same time, the issuance of public sector covered bonds dropped significantly. On the one hand, several German mortgage banks withdrew from the public sector lending business due to reduced profitability, while, on the other hand, many public sector entities decided to tap the capital markets directly with public bond issues. When German public sector banks (Landesbanken and Sparkassen (savings banks)) lost their public guarantees in 2005, a further source of collateral for Public covered bonds dried up.

As a result, the share of outstanding public covered bonds has been shrinking for several years now. With the increased focus on mortgage covered bonds, the market is actually returning to its roots. Long before the creation of the jumbo market, covered bonds were mainly used to fund mortgage loans while public sector covered bonds are a relatively new phenomenon.

Exhibit 18.1

Outstanding jumbo covered bonds by collateral

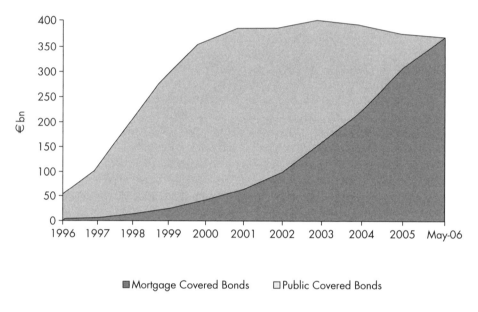

■ Mortgage Covered Bonds   □ Public Covered Bonds

Source: BNP Paribas.

The main jumbo markets

German Pfandbriefe

The largest jumbo market in terms of outstanding volume and number of active issuers is still the German Pfandbrief market, although its market share has been decreasing notably within the last five years (see Exhibit 18.2). Reduced issuance activity and a high volume in redemption fuelled this development. There are two types of Pfandbriefe, Public and Mortgage Pfandbriefe. While Public Pfandbriefe still account for 40 per cent of the jumbo market, Mortgage Pfandbriefe have managed to gain a greater market share in the last four years. Until July 2005 Pfandbriefe could only be issued either by specialised mortgage banks or public sector banks. With the introduction of a new Pfandbrief Act, the special banking principle was dropped enabling every German bank to apply for a Pfandbrief issuing licence. At the same time existing issuers were no longer limited in their business activities to public sector and mortgage lending. So far, the drop of the special bank principle has not led to a notable increase in issuance activity. However, several mortgage banks were integrated into their respective parent companies, mainly to reduce operational cost.

Exhibit 18.2

Overview of European jumbo covered bond markets (May 2006)

Market name	Outstanding jumbo volume (€bn)	Net issuance in 2005 (€bn)	Number of jumbo issuers
Pfandbriefe	366	–19	28
Cédulas	185	54	15
Obligations Foncières	56	1	3
ACS	34	5	4
UK covered bonds	32	9	5

Source: BNP Paribas.

Spanish Cédulas

Since 2001 the Spanish Cédulas market has been one of the fastest growing markets, mainly driven by unprecedented expansion of the Spanish mortgage market. It is now the second largest jumbo covered bond market and has the second largest number of active issuers. In addition, the market currently only shows very limited redemptions due to its relatively young age and strong focus on longer maturities. There are Cédulas Hipotecarias (covered by mortgage loans) and Cédulas Territoreales (covered by public sector loans). With a market share of 96 per cent, Cédulas Hipotecarias are dominating the Spanish covered bond market. As a specialty of the Spanish market, covered bondholders have a preferential claim against all mortgage loans or public sector loans, respectively, which are held by the issuing bank. This means that the preferential claim is not limited to an earmarked selection of assets within a defined cover pool.

Cédulas can be issued by any Spanish bank. The issuers are large commercial banks as well as smaller savings banks. Besides direct bank issues there are also pooled multi-issuer tranches. Within these issues a special fund holds a number of Cédulas issued by a group of individual banks. The fund itself issues one large bond which is backed by the underlying Cédulas. Cash flows from the Cédulas are passed through to the holders of the large bond. These pooled Cédulas issues had a jumbo market share of 37 per cent as of April 2006 within the Cédulas market (see Exhibit 18.3).

French Obligations Foncières

Compared to Spanish Cédulas, the French Obligations Foncières market developed at a much more moderate speed. Growth of the jumbo market is hampered by the trend of French issuers focusing to an increasing extent on non-jumbo issuance. Similar to the German market, the French market is now in a phase where larger amounts of outstanding jumbo issues become due. The three existing issuers in the market (Dexia MA, CFF and CIF Euromortgage) are highly specialised, acting virtually as funding vehicles of their parent companies. Origination of cover assets and management of the issuing entities is conducted

Exhibit 18.3

Development of outstanding jumbo covered bonds

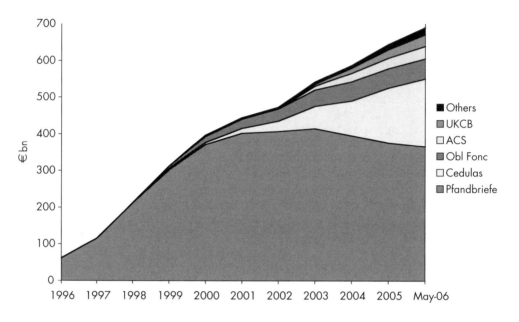

Source: BNP Paribas.

by the parent companies. Obligations Foncières are basically backed by all assets on the balance sheet of the issuer, which, due to the high degree of specialisation, is only allowed to hold eligible cover assets. There is no distinction between public and mortgage Obligations Foncières, that is, the collateral can consist of a combination of both.

Irish asset covered securities

The Irish asset covered securities (ACS) market started in 2001 with a strong focus on public sector covered bonds. It was only in 2004 that the first mortgage covered bond was issued under the ACS law. Today, the majority (79 per cent) of outstanding ACS are still covered by public sector debt, however, the share of mortgage ACS should rise in the future. The structure of ACS is comparable to German Pfandbriefe where mortgage and public sector collateral are held in separate pools on the balance sheet of the issuer.

UK covered bonds

The UK covered bond (UKCB) market was the first jumbo market based not on a covered bond law but purely on contractual agreements. The covered bond structures use several securitisation techniques which are similar to those known in the MBS market. So far, covered bonds have been issued by commercial banks and building societies. Although each of the existing five issuers uses individual covered bond structures, which differ in some details, all UKCB so far have been collateralised by UK residential mortgages only. The lack of a covered bond law resulted in a higher risk weighting (20 per cent instead of 10 per cent) of UKCB in Europe. In February 2006 the Financial Services Authority (FSA) announced the introduction of a covered bond regime in the UK which would reduce the risk weighting of UKCB to the same level as its continental peers.

Other markets

Besides the markets described above, there are a number of other European covered bond markets that have issued covered bonds in jumbo format, including Luxembourg, Finland, the Netherlands and Italy. The largest non-euro market is the Danish covered bond market with a total equivalent outstanding amount of well over €200bn, making it the second largest covered bond market in the world. A number of Central European countries have also established covered bond frameworks since 1996, however, issuance volumes in euros have so far been limited.

Spread drivers and differentiation

Covered bond rating

Although covered bonds are generally perceived as a triple-A product, there can be rating differences that have an impact on the spread level of the covered bond in question. Where a covered bond is rated differently by two or more rating agencies, usually the lower rating will impact the spread level. While all S&P rated jumbo covered bonds currently achieve a AAA rating, the ratings range from Aaa to Aa3 in the case of Moody's and from AAA to AA– in the case of Fitch. The absolute spread difference per rating notch depends to a large part on the overall swap spread environment, credit differentiation in the whole bond market and the maturity of each bond. Within the jumbo market spread differentiation between rating classes has so far varied from 0.5 basis points (bp) to 3.5 bp per rating notch. Exhibit 18.4 shows the rating differentiation within the Spanish Cédulas market as of April 2006 which represents a relatively low level of differentiation.

Besides the impact of the covered bond rating, the issuer rating can have a pricing impact as well, even when there is no difference in the covered bond rating. Although the impact of different issuer ratings is less visible than that of different covered bond ratings there are several factors that can explain such a differentiation.

Many investors have the same credit line for secured and unsecured debt of the same issuer. A lower issuer rating can thus impact the ability of an investor to buy the covered bond even if the secured rating is at an AAA level.

Within the rating methodologies of Moody's and Fitch the issuer rating can at some point impact the covered bond rating. Although the issuer rating does not directly influence the covered bond rating, it can give a certain indication about the future stability of the covered bond rating.

Exhibit 18.4

Jumbo swap spreads of Spanish Cédulas

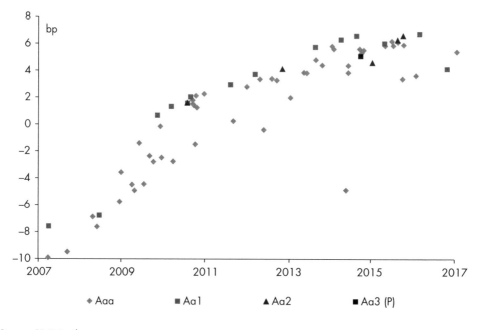

Source: BNP Paribas.

It is possible that the issuer rating will get a greater pricing influence with the introduction of Basel II, where the risk weighting of the covered bond can be influenced by the unsecured rating of the issuer.

Type of collateral

Another factor of differentiation is the type of collateral used to back the covered bonds. Most covered bond frameworks distinguish between public sector and mortgage collateral, with public sector collateral usually being regarded as the safer type. In some cases this has resulted in lower ratings for mortgage covered bonds than for public covered bonds of the same issuer. Consequently, the general distinction between public sector and mortgage collateral can have a relatively strong pricing impact, especially when it results in a different covered bond rating.

Within the two collateral classes further distinction can be made by the geographical range of eligible assets which stretches from single market pools (Spain, UK) to the whole OECD area (Luxembourg). Within the mortgage segment there is a distinction between residential and commercial mortgages used as collateral. While most frameworks allow mixed mortgage pools, UKCB and Irish ACS concentrate on residential mortgages or limit commercial mortgages to 10 per cent, respectively. Due to the dynamic nature of the cover pools, which can change the geographical diversification (within the legal limits) or the type of mortgages used, it is difficult to observe a significant price impact of these factors.

The rapid growth of the covered bond market, and the correlated product innovation, has significantly increased the complexity within the covered bond market. An important step was the occurrence of structured covered bonds with their relatively complex documentation, which also vary from issuer to issuer. Usual points of differentiation are eligibility criteria for the cover assets, different levels of overcollateralisation and potential maturity extension. In order to compensate investors for the required research effort, new market participants usually pay a certain pick-up over other, established markets. Ideally this entrance fee reduces or vanishes over time as the market becomes established and regarded to be of similar quality as the other markets.

Pricing and funding advantages

High liquidity and top ratings in the jumbo market make covered bonds an attractive tool to complement a bank's funding mix. Reduced funding costs, access to liquid institutional investors and the potential to extend the maturity base are the main advantages covered bonds offer to issuers.

Exhibit 18.5

Jumbo swap spreads of Spanish Cédulas

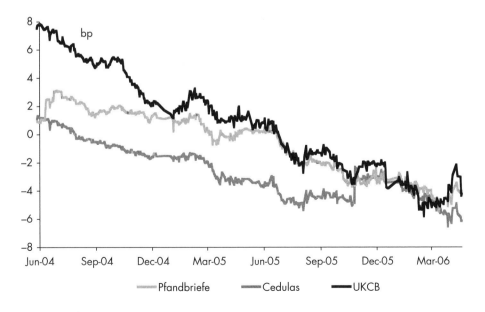

Source: BNP Paribas.

The reduction of the funding cost often is one of the main drivers for issuing covered bonds, especially when compared to other capital markets' funding sources. Low yields and continued compressions of swap spreads have reduced the absolute funding advantage of covered bonds over unsecured debt and residential mortgage-backed securities (RMBS). However, when, for example, comparing secondary swap spread levels of 6 7 year Dutch Covered Bonds with those of an Aa-rated Dutch issuer and prime RMBS spreads, there is still an advantage of approximately 8 bp and 10 bp, respectively. It is apparent that the comparative advantage versus unsecured funding is even more attractive for lower rated issuers (see Exhibit 18.6).

Although using covered bonds as a funding alternative to MBS leads to lower funding cost on a gross basis, this has to be put in relation to the effect of the capital relief the issuer would have had if he had issued MBS instead. However, with Basel II reducing the capital requirements of a large part of residential mortgage loans held on the balance sheet to 35 per cent from 50 per cent, the incentive of funding these assets with RMBS should reduce. It is thus likely that Basel II will also lead to a more risk-sensitive behaviour when deciding between on- and off-balance sheet securitisation. Issuers will most likely use better quality assets for on-balance sheet securitisation such as covered bonds while trying to maximise the capital effect by using lower quality assets for asset-backed securities (ABS) and MBS.

Exhibit 18.6

Asset swap spreads of AAB senior unsecured bonds vs covered bonds

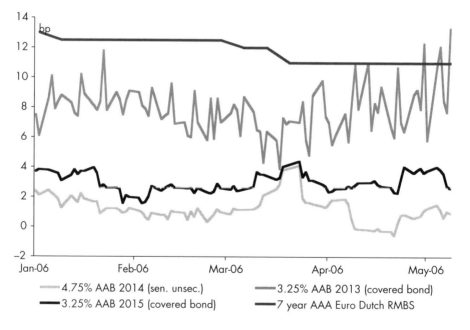

Source: BNP Paribas, Reuters.

By issuing covered bonds, especially in the liquid jumbo market, issuers can get access to more liquid funding sources by addressing institutional investors which buy jumbo covered bonds as a substitute for government and agency bonds. Although the market making theoretically provides a certain minimum liquidity for each jumbo irrespective of its size, jumbos which significantly exceed the minimum size can provide additional liquidity. In addition, a number of investors can only buy a certain maximum percentage of the total outstanding amount of a single bond. However, most investors do not require a minimum amount in excess of €1bn. In fact, the size of new jumbo issuance has been increasing noticeably since the market came into existence (see Exhibit 18.7). However, secondary trading levels do not reflect any premium for extra-large jumbos. In some cases these issues trade even wider and show higher volatility than smaller jumbos.

Targeting the liquid segment of the market does not always lead to the lowest funding cost. In many cases the non-jumbo or private placement market offers better funding levels and provides, especially for smaller issuers, more flexibility in their funding strategy. In a starting phase the jumbo covered bond is thus often used to increase market visibility and increase access to investors. As an issuer, or even a whole market, becomes more established, part of the jumbo funding gets supplemented by non-jumbo issuance. Recent examples have been in France but also in Spain, where non-jumbo issuance is starting to increase.

Exhibit 18.7

Jumbo issuance by initial size

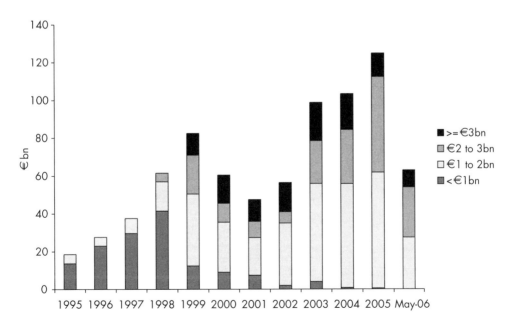

Source: BNP Paribas.

The depth of this investor base coupled with the high ratings of the covered bonds allow issuers also to raise liquidity in the capital markets in a stressed scenario, for example, a downgrading of the unsecured rating. Flexible access to liquid bond markets also appeals to banks that fund their mortgage lending mainly on a deposit basis.

In these cases covered bonds can provide issuers the ability to fund themselves in maturity buckets that would otherwise not be open to them or just at rather unattractive spread levels. In these cases covered bonds can help to improve the matching of the, usually long-dated, mortgage asset base and the liability side.

Covered bond investors

Alongside the growing issuer base, the investor base for covered bonds has expanded as well, especially on a geographical level. Even though there are no reliable statistical data on the placement of covered bonds, there has been a clear trend of rising internationalisation of the investor base, which traditionally has been largely dominated by German investors (see Exhibit 18.8). In fact, it can be observed that the introduction of covered bond frameworks within the various European countries has significantly helped that development. The creation of an own covered bond product usually raises the awareness of investors not only

Exhibit 18.8

Underwriters of all covered bonds with a minimum size of €1bn

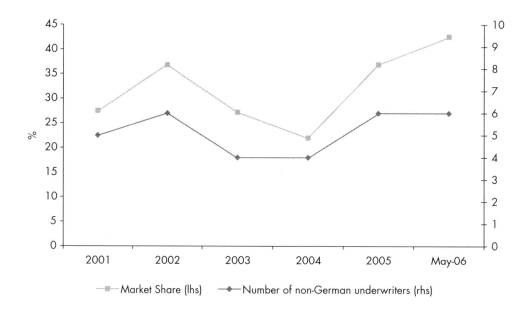

Source: Bondware.

for their own covered bonds but also for covered bonds from other countries. In many cases, the creation of a covered bond framework has also led to a preferential treatment of covered bonds in terms of risk weighting within the respective country. The lowering of the risk weighting of covered bonds to 10 per cent from 20 per cent further supports investor acceptance. The UK, with the planned implementation of a covered bond regime, is one of the latest examples for such a development. Internationalisation beyond the borders of Europe has progressed as well, though at a significantly lower rate. The main drivers of this process have been increasing buying activity of non-European central banks and, to some extent, Asian institutional investors.

Top ratings and high liquidity are the two main product features of jumbo covered bonds that appeal to its main investor groups. These investors are banks, central banks, insurance companies and funds. The share of bank investors in jumbo covered bonds has been growing significantly over the past five years. With an approximate primary placement level of 35 per cent to 55 per cent, they have one of the most important investor groups in covered bonds. Besides passing covered bonds on to their retail network, banks are using covered bonds to a large extent for their treasury. In doing so, banks take advantage of the high credit quality, the possibility to refinance their holdings with the ECB and the possibility to unwind larger parts of their positions due to the high liquidity. In addition, they are the only investor group that benefits from the lower risk weighting of covered bonds. Thus, the growing importance of bank investors is likely to increase the impact of the risk weighting of covered bonds, especially under Basel II where the risk weighting is likely to be less homogeneous (see Chapter 6 – Risk weighting). While non-EU banks do not benefit from a lower risk weighting their pricing impact should remain limited since the large majority of bank investors are still found in the EU and especially within the euro area.

Central banks have also increased in importance within the covered bond investor group. Their share in new jumbo issuance ranges approximately between 10 per cent and 25 per cent. Besides liquidity and rating, which understandably are even more important for central banks, other factors such as type of collateral, maturity and issue currency can have a significant impact on their appetite. Due to their relatively conservative investment behaviour at least some central banks have mainly concentrated on public sector covered bonds. However, the changing market structure with increased issuance of liquid mortgage covered bonds is beginning to shift the focus more towards this product group. There is still a strong preference towards the short and middle part of the curve and despite the increase of central bank investment in euro covered bonds US dollar-denominated covered bonds usually still see an even higher central bank share.

Insurance companies and funds are the remaining main investor group in covered bonds. Their share in a new issue can vary between approximately 10 per cent and 40 per cent. Due to the large variety and different investment needs within this segment it is difficult to find a certain pattern or preference when it comes to covered bonds. In general, it can be assumed that the share of this investor group has either stagnated or fallen within the last five years. Compressed spreads and limited pick-up vs government debt might be one of the reasons for this development since many of these investors put a strong preference on outright yields.

Conclusion

Within the past ten years covered bonds have become an important European asset class. Despite its diversity and heterogeneity the market is unified by its core strengths: security and liquidity. Although market expansion might take place at a somewhat lower rate than since 2002, covered bonds will continue to be an attractive funding and investment alternative. Future developments, such as the introduction of Basel II, could even increase the potential of covered bonds as it emphasises the complementary character of covered bonds compared to ABS and MBS. In that sense the occurrence of non-European covered bonds seems to be more likely than ever with the inherent potential of tapping into a truly global investor base.

Chapter 19

Convertible bond case studies

Moorad Choudhry
KBC Financial Products

Introduction

We consider here two recent convertible bond issues, which are described in the termsheets attached as Annexes 1 and 2. The termsheet is essentially a shortened version of the prospectus or offering circular and details the conditions under which the bond is issued. Investors would look for some, or indeed all, of the following terms in the offer prospectus, which are considered to be favourable from an investor viewpoint. A lack of these features – or their opposite – would be less favourable to investors:

- no call feature, or no early call;
- protection against share dilution;
- early convertibility;
- continuous convertibility;
- senior or unsubordinated in capital structure;
- redemption on maturity;
- automatic conversion if in investor interest ('sleeping investor clause');
- converted shares immediately eligible for dividend;
- dividend and extraordinary dividend protection; and
- takeover protection.

There is a wide variety of instruments in the convertible bond market; the two case studies we consider here reflect this variation.

Gujarat NRE Coke Limited

US$60m convertible senior zero-coupon bonds due 2011

Lead managers	KBC Financial Products UK Limited
	Silverdale Services Limited
Sole underwriter	KBC Financial Products UK Limited

This is a zero-coupon convertible issued in March 2006, with an option to convert to shares of the issuer. The issuer is listed on the Bombay Stock Exchange. The redemption amount is 139.36 per cent and the bond was issued at par. The zero-coupon is favourable for the issuer who has lower cash flow cost as a result, while the investor gains an exposure to the equity while still retaining a positive yield-to-maturity.

Exhibit 19.1 shows the issuer's equity and the convertible bond price performance of the bond from the issue date up to 19 May 2006, with the bond tracking the equity closely. Exhibit 19.2, which is screen YA from Bloomberg, shows the positive yield-to-maturity on the bond at the price quoted on 19 May 2006.

The termsheet for this issue is given at Annex 1.

USG People N.V.

€115m subordinated unsecured 3 per cent bonds due 2012

Lead underwriters	ING
	Rabobank
Selling agent	KBC Financial Products UK Limited

The issuer of this convertible, United Services Group N.V. (USG people), is a Dutch corporate entity. It announced the acquisition of a Belgian-domiciled entity, Solvus N.V., on 14 June 2005. The acquisition was funded initially by a €900m bridging loan, and then subsequently funded partially by a share issue and convertible issue. This deal is an example of a company taking the opportunity to raise capital with an equity premium and effectively issue cheaper equity. Exhibit 19.3 shows the share price performance of USG through 2005. The price rises steadily up to, and subsequent to, the convertible bond issue on 28 September 2005. The performance of the share price may well have influenced investors in their decision to buy the convertible, which was over-subscribed nine times over. The popularity of the issue among investors is also reflected in the final coupon of 3 per cent, which was at the tightest end of the 3–3.50 per cent range announced when the underwriters first marketed the deal.

Exhibit 19.4 shows the bond price performance from issue up to May 2006, with the equity price also noted on a separate axis.

The termsheet for this issue is given at Annex 2.

Exhibit 19.1

Gujarat NRE Coke convertible price performance, April–May 2006

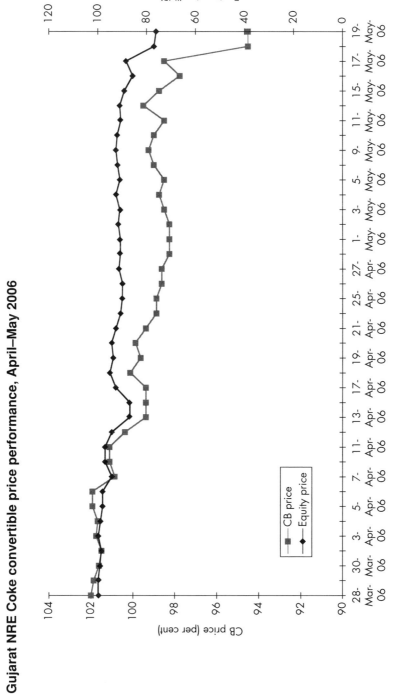

Source: KBC Financial Products.

Exhibit 19.2

Bloomberg page YA for Gujarat NRE Coke convertible bond, 19 May 2006

BOND:

PRICE	94½ (US)	STOCK: NGNC PRICE	63.5 (IR)
YIELD	8.115	ANNUAL DIVIDEND	3.
QUOTED IN	US	QUOTED IN	IR
DURATION (YEARS)	4.885	CURRENT IR/US CROSS RATE	45.715
ACCRUED INTEREST/BOND			

CONVERSION TERMS

CONVERSION RATIO	35728.000	OR	CONVERSION PRICE	2.7989 (US)
CASH REQ (US)/100,000 FACE			DILUTION PROTECTION	100%
COST OF CARRY (%)	4.96303		PROVISIONAL PRICE	162½ (IR)
SHORT REBATE (%)	3.97042		HEDGE RATIO (%)	100
HAIRCUT (%) ON STOCK	0		CASH REQUIRED FOR HEDGE	44872.35

			PREMIUM:		
CURRENT YIELD:	BOND (US)	4.72		POINTS	44.87
	STOCK (IR)	–4.724		PERCENT PREMIUM	90.42
	ADVANTAGE	–5064.248 = –11.3%		PARITY	49.63
	NET CASH FLOW (US)/YR			PROVISIONAL HEDGE	42.00
BREAK-EVENS:	YLD ADV.	–10.05 (YRS)		BREAKEVEN P & L	********
	CASH FLOW	–8.86 (YRS)			

Exhibit 19.3

USG share price performance leading up to convertible bond issue

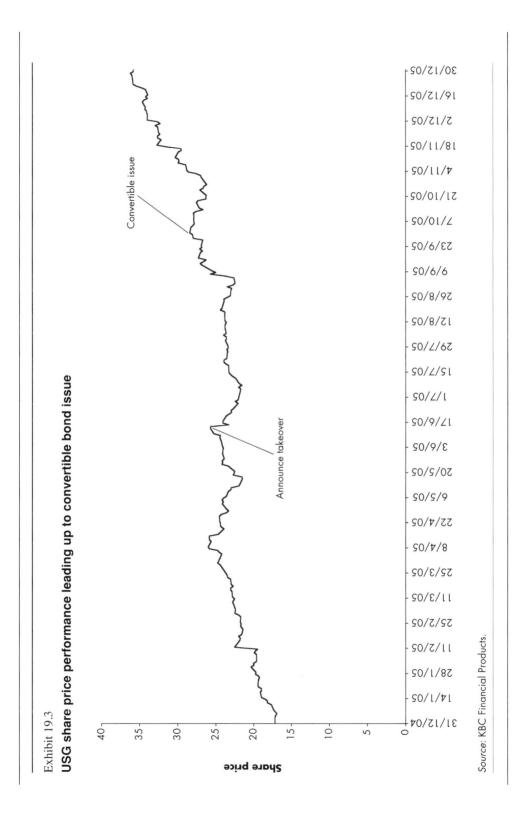

Source: KBC Financial Products.

Exhibit 19.4

USG equity and convertible bond price performance from bond issue to May 2006

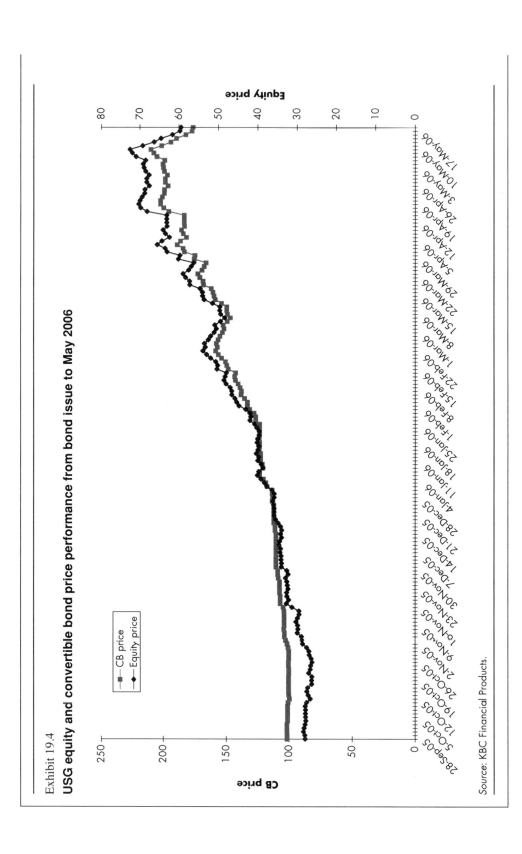

Source: KBC Financial Products.

Annex 1

Termsheet for Gujarat NRE Coke Limited convertible bond

US$ 60,000,000 Convertible Senior Zero Coupon Bonds due 2011

Term Sheet

Issuer:	Gujarat NRE Coke Limited (the 'Company').
Issue:	US$ 50,000,000 aggregate principal amount of Convertible Bonds due 2011 (the 'Bonds').
Over-allotment Option:	US$ 10,000,000 has been fully exercised, increasing issue size to US$ 60,000,000.
Status of the Bonds:	The Bonds constitute direct, unsecured and unconditional obligations of the Company and rank and will rank *pari passu* and without any preference among them. The payment obligations of the Company under the Bonds shall (subject as aforesaid and subject to any obligations preferred by mandatory provisions of law) at all times rank at least equally with all of its other present and future direct and unconditional obligations.
Rating:	The Bonds will not be rated.
Shares:	Ordinary shares of INR 10 each of the Company (the 'Shares'), listed on the Bombay Stock Exchange (BSE), the National India Stock Exchange (NSE) and the Calcutta Stock Exchange (CSE).
Closing Date:	On or around 11 April 2006.
Maturity Date:	On or around 12 April 2011 (5 years and 1 day after Closing Date).
Coupon:	Zero
Issue Price:	100% Redemption Price at 139.36% Maturity.
Gross Yield to Maturity:	6.75%, calculated on a semi-annual basis.
Conversion Premium:	24.1927% of Reference Share Price (defined below).
Conversion Price:	INR 125.00.
Reference Share Price:	INR 100.65 (the closing price of the Shares on the BSE on 27 March 2006).
Exchange rate on Conversion:	INR 44.66 / US$ 1.0 (the Reserve Bank of India's USD to INR reference exchange rate on 27 March 2006).
Conversion Right:	Shares of the Company at the prevailing Conversion Price and by reference to the Fixed Exchange Rate.
Denomination:	US$ 100,000 and integral multiples thereof.
Conversion Ratio:	35,728 Shares per Bond.
Conversion Period:	At any time on or after 12 April 2006 and up to the close of business (at the place where the Certificate is deposited for conversion of that

Bond) on the seventh Business Day (or if such day is not a Business Day, the next preceding day which is a Business Day) prior to the date fixed for redemption.

Redemption at Option of the Company:

To the extent permitted by applicable law, the Bonds may be redeemed at the option of the Company in whole, but not in part at the Early Redemption Amount:

(i) at any time on or after [27 April 2009] (3 years and 15 days after Closing Date), provided that the aggregate value at the closing price of the Shares on the BSE (translated into US$ at the initial exchange rate of the Reserve Bank of India) on each of not less than 20 Business Days in any period of 30 consecutive Business Days ending not earlier than the seventh day prior to the date on which the relevant notice of redemption is given by the Company to the Bondholders shall have exceeded 130 per cent of the Early Redemption Amount in effect on such Business Day; or

(ii) if at any time prior to the date on which the relevant notice of redemption is given by the Company, less than 10 per cent in principal amount of the Bonds remain outstanding.

In order to exercise such option, the Company should give not less than 30 nor more than 60 days notice to the Bondholders and the Trustee.

Redemption for Taxation Reasons:

To the extent permitted by applicable law, the Bonds may be redeemed at the option of the Company in whole, but not in part, at any time at the Early Redemption Amount in the event of certain changes affecting taxes in India.

Settlement upon Conversion:

Shares only.

Conversion Price Adjustment:

Standard adjustment for any dilution will be applied, including (i) bonus or special dividends paid with respect to the Shares, (ii) free distribution or issuance of Shares, (iii) sub-division, consolidation and reclassification of Shares, (iv) rights offering, (v) warrants and (vi) other issues resulting in unreasonable dilution of Shares.

Extraordinary Dividend: Protection:

To the extent permitted by applicable law, there will be adjustment to the Conversion Price for an Extraordinary Cash Dividend. An Extra ordinary Cash Dividend occurs if, at the effective date, the total amount of:

(i) any cash dividends paid or declared by the Company on the Shares, prior to deduction of any withholding tax plus any corporate tax attributable to that dividend; and

(ii) all other cash dividends paid or declared on the Shares in the 365 consecutive day period prior to the effective date (other than any dividend or portion thereof previously deemed to be an Extraordinary Cash Dividend) (the previous dividends), except that where the date of announcement for dividends for two different fiscal years has occurred in such 365 day period, such dividends relating to the earlier fiscal year will be disregarded for the purpose of determining the previous dividend ((a) and (b) together being the total current dividend) equals or exceeds on a per Share basis 3 per cent of the Average Closing Price of the Shares during the Relevant Period provided that any dividend paid or declared by the Company will not constitute an Extraordinary Cash Dividend if the amount paid or declared by the Company is equal to an amount not greater than 120 per cent of the dividends paid or declared by the Company in the previous fiscal year.

Negative Pledge: For so long as any Bond remains outstanding, the Company will not, and will procure that no other person will, create or permit to subsist any mortgage, charge, pledge, lien or other form of encumbrance or security interest to secure certain types of indebtedness and the Company will further procure that no other person will give any guarantee or indemnity in respect of such indebtedness.

Events of Default: Yes. The Bonds will contain a cross default provision with a threshold of US$ 5,000,000 along with certain events that will permit the Bonds immediately to become due and payable at their principal amount.

Change of Control Put: To the extent permitted by applicable law, unless the Bonds have been previously redeemed or repurchased and cancelled or converted, each Bondholder shall have the right, at such Bondholders option, upon the occurrence of a Change of Control (as defined in the Conditions), to require the Company to repurchase all (or any portion of the principal amount thereof which is US$100,000 or any integral multiple thereof) of such Bondholders Bonds at the Early Redemption Amount on the date set by the Company for such repurchase, which shall be not less than 30 days nor more than 60 days following the date on which the Company notifies the Bondholders of the Change of Control.

Delisting Put: To the extent permitted by applicable law, unless the Bonds have been previously redeemed or repurchased and cancelled or converted, in the event that the Shares cease to be listed or admitted to trading on the BSE or the NSE, each Bondholder shall have the right, at such Bondholder's option, to require the Company to repurchase all (or any portion of the principal amount thereof which is US$100,000 or any integral multiple thereof) of such Bondholder's Bonds at a price equal to the Early Redemption Amount. The date for such repurchase shall be set by the Company, and shall not be less than 30 days nor more than 60 days following the date the Company delivers written notice to the Trustee of the delisting.

Lock Up: 90 days lock up on further issues of equity or convertible bonds with a carve out for (i) issues of unlisted warrants and (H) shares issued in connection with the proposed merger with FCGL.

Sales Restrictions: The Bonds are being offered by the Company to institutional investors outside of India and outside of the United States, in reliance on Regulation S under the United States Securities Act of 1933.

257

Governing Law:	English law.
Listing:	Application has been made for the admission of the Bonds to the official list of the Luxembourg Stock Exchange and admission to trading on the Euro MTF Market.
Clearing/ Settlement:	Euroclear, Clearstream
Common Code:	24913589
ISIN:	XS0249135897
Trustee, Principal Paying and Conversion Agent and Transfer Agent:	The Bank of New York.
Registrar:	The Bank of New York.
Luxembourg Listing Agent:	The Bank of New York Europe Ltd
Joint Lead Managers:	KBC Financial Products UK Limited and Silverdale Services Limited.
Stabilisation:	FSA.

Annex 2

Termsheet for USG People N.V. convertible bond

usg people

Terms & Conditions

Issuer:	USG People N.V. (the 'Issuer').
Issue type:	EUR denominated convertible bonds (the Bonds) convertible into ordinary shares in the capital of USG People ('Ordinary Shares'), which are listed on Eurolist by Euronext Amsterdam N.V.
Status:	The Bonds and the interest thereon constitute unconditional, unsecured and subordinated obligations of the Issuer and will rank *pari passu* amongst themselves and at least *pari passu* with all the Issuer's existing and future unconditional, unsecured and subordinated obligations and in priority to indebtedness which by its terms ranks junior to the Bonds (including but not limited to the subordinated loan entered into between the Issuer and Stichting Start).
Underlying Shares:	(New) ordinary shares of USG People NV. (ISIN code NL0000354470, Bloomberg USG NA, Reuters USG.AS).
Rating:	The Issuer and the Bonds will not be rated.
Currency:	EUR.
Initial Issue Size:	100,000,000.
Over-allotment Option:	15,000,000 over-allotment option (15% of Initial Issue Size) has been fully exercised.
Maturity Date:	Expected to be on or before 18 October 2012 (7 years).
Issue Price:	100%.
Coupon:	3% per annum payable annually in arrears.
Redemption Price:	100%.
Yield to Maturity:	3%.
Conversion Price:	€35.83 (or 27% over the VWAP of the Issuer's Ordinary Shares over the bookbuilding period).
Conversion period:	On or after a date expected to be 28 November 2005 up to the close of business on the seventh calendar day prior to the final Maturity Date or such earlier date on which the Bonds are called for redemption by the Issuer.
Issuer Call Option:	• At any time on or after a date expected to be 18 October 2010, the Issuer may redeem all but not some only of the Bonds for the time being outstanding at their principal amount together with interest accrued to but excluding the date fixed for redemption provided that, within a period of 30 consecutive Trading Days ending not earlier

than the fifth Trading Day prior to the date on which the relevant notice of redemption is given to Bondholders, the official closing price of a Ordinary Share for 20 Trading Days shall have been at least 130% of the Conversion Price then in effect on each of such Trading Days.

- In addition, the Issuer may at any time redeem all but not some only of the Bonds for the time being outstanding at their principal amount, together with interest accrued to but excluding the date fixed for redemption, if, prior to the date of the relevant notice of redemption is given to the Bondholders, less than 10% in principal amount of Bonds originally issued remain outstanding.

Investor Put Option on Change of Control:	Upon the occurrence of a Change of Control (as defined in the terms of the Bonds); Bondholders may require the Issuer to redeem any of their Bonds at their principal amount plus interest accrued to but excluding such date of redemption.
Adjustment of Conversion Price in event of Change of Control:	In the event of a Change of Control investors will be entitled to convert the Bonds for a period of 60 days following notice of the Change of Control at a Conversion Price that may be adjusted downwards in accordance with a ratchet.
Adjustment of Conversion Price/Anti-dilution:	Typical anti-dilution provisions dealing with, *inter alia*, share consolidations, share splits, bonus issues, spin offs, distributions (including extra-ordinary dividends) and new issuance at a greater than 5% discount to the then prevailing market price.
Extra-ordinary Dividend:	A dividend will be an extraordinary dividend if, together with all other dividends in respect of the same financial year, the dividend will exceed a yield threshold of 3.5% of a Reference Price (as defined in the terms of the Bonds).
Negative Pledge:	Yes.
Events of Default:	Yes (including cross default provision subject to a 15,000,000 threshold).
Taxation:	No tax call, no gross-up.
Lock-up:	The Issuer and Hovu Beheer N.V., our major shareholder, have each agreed to a lock-up of 180 days subject to customary exceptions.
Governing Law:	Dutch.
Trustee:	NV Algemeen Nederlands Trustkantoor ANT.
Joint Global Co-ordinators and Joint Book-runners:	ING Wholesale Banking and Rabo Securities.
Selling Agent for Rabo Securities:	For the purpose of this transaction KBC Financial Products UK Ltd ('KBC FP') will act as selling agent for Rabo Securities.
Co-lead Manager:	Kempen and Co.
Selling Restrictions:	No offer or sales into the US, Australia, Canada or Japan. Standard restrictions apply elsewhere. The bond offering shall, subject to certain

exceptions including private placements in accordance with Section 4(2) of the US Securities Act of 1933, as amended (the "Securities Act"), be made outside the United States in accordance with Regulation S under the Securities Act.

Denomination:	1,000 and integral multiples thereof.
Form:	The Bonds will be issued in registered form.
Documentation:	Prospectus is expected to be available on 30 September 2005.
Listing of the Bonds:	Application will be made to list the Bonds on Eurolist by Euronext Amsterdam NV. 'As, if and when trading' on Eurolist by Euronext Amsterdam N.V. is expected to commence on Thursday 29 September 2005.
Security Codes:	ISIN: XS 0230850389. Common code: 023085038. Euronext Amsterdam fondscode: 15568.
Clearing of the Bonds:	Application will be made for the Bonds to be accepted for delivery through Euroclear, Clearstream Luxembourg and Euroclear Nederland.
Paying and Conversion Agent:	Rabo Securities.
Use of Proceeds:	The Issuer entered into a bridge loan to finance the Solvus acquisition and part of USG's and Solvus' existing debt. The aggregate net proceeds of the convertible bond offering will be used to repay part of the bridge loan.

Timetable

Pricing Date:	28 September 2005.
Allocation Date:	28 September 2005.
Closing/ Settlement Date:	Expected to be on or before 18 October 2005.